the value of children

introduction and comparative analysis

Presented to the
Michigan State University
Department of Sociology
Library
by
Professor John Useem
and
Professor Ruth Hill Useem

volume one

the value of children
a cross-national study

introduction and comparative analysis

fred arnold
rodolfo a. bulatao
chalio buripakdi
betty jamie chung
james t. fawcett
toshio iritani
sung jin lee
tsong-shien wu

with the assistance of
sonia c. albores

east-west population institute · east-west center · honolulu hawaii

iv

Library of Congress Cataloging in Publication Data (Revised)

Main entry under title:

The Value of children.

  Includes bibliographies.
  CONTENTS: v. 1. Arnold, F. et al. Introduction and
comparative analysis. —v. 2. Bulatao, R.A. Philippines.
—v. 3. Arnold, F. and Fawcett, J.T. Hawaii.
  1. Children. 2. Family. I. East-West Population
Institute.
HQ751.V34   301.42'7   75-8934
ISBN 0-8248-0383-3 (v. 1)

Published in 1975 by the East-West Population Institute, East-West Center,
Honolulu, Hawaii.
Printed in the United States of America.
Distributed by the University Press of Hawaii, Honolulu, Hawaii 96822

contents

TABLES, FIGURE, AND EXHIBIT

Figure

Exhibit

preface

The seven volumes in this series contain basic findings from the Value of Children project, a comparative study of the social, economic, and psychological determinants of childbearing behavior. This was an exploratory research effort, intended to provide guidance for a larger and more definitive study that is now under way. The exploratory study was conducted in six countries: the Republic of China (Taiwan), Japan, the Republic of Korea, the Philippines, Thailand, and the United States (Hawaii).

In this first volume, the project as a whole is described, selected results are presented in comparative form, and basic project documents, such as the questionnaire and descriptions of constructed variables, are included in appendices.[1] Volumes 2 to 7 present the results for each of the six countries, published in the order in which the manuscripts were ready for printing. Each country report is intended to stand by itself, for the purpose of presenting substantive findings for the country concerned. The reader interested in viewing those findings in comparative perspective, or in obtaining more details about the methodology of the study, should become familiar with the contents of this first volume.

The Value of Children project was conceived and organized by James Fawcett, who also served as project coordinator. It should be

---

1 See also Fawcett et al. (1974), an earlier publication summarizing the basic comparative findings. Portions of that paper are incorporated in the text and tables of this volume.

emphasized, however, that this project has been a genuinely collaborative effort. The investigators have worked as equal partners from the earliest stage of designing the study to the final write-up of results. The collaborative nature of the project is reflected, for instance, in the alphabetical listing of the authors of this first volume. Because so many of the decisions about this project were made in workshops involving the group as a whole, it would in fact be impossible to assign either credit or blame for design of the study to particular persons. It should be noted, however, that the reports for each country are individually authored and do reflect the views of individual investigators.

The title page of this volume lists the seven investigators for the project, five from Asian countries and two from Hawaii. Also listed on the title page are Betty Jamie Chung and Sonia Albores. Dr. Chung, a social psychologist from Hong Kong, joined the project while in residence as a fellow at the East-West Population Institute. She assumed special responsibility for the design of comparative analyses for the project. Sonia Albores, a doctoral candidate in psychology at the University of Hawaii, has been associated with the project since its inception and has played a key role in carrying out the project at each stage.

Those who have made major contributions in each country are acknowledged by name in the country reports; those who have been involved with the project as a whole are mentioned below. It must be added, however, that in a project as large as this we are bound to be indebted to many people to whom proper credit can never be given.

A significant factor in the success of this project has been the full support given by the former director of the East-West Population Institute, Paul Demeny, and subsequently by the acting director, Keith Adamson, and the current director, Lee-Jay Cho.

Lois Hoffman, whose theoretical writings are acknowledged in the introduction to this report, served as a consultant to the project and gave valuable advice on research design and questionnaire content.

Peter Norris contributed to the design of the questionnaire and assisted in the planning and implementation of data processing for the six countries. Robert Bloedon assumed primary responsibility for the actual processing of data. Others who participated in the centralized data processing include Ann Midkiff, Fred Kau, and Douglas Kubota, all working under the general supervision of Minja Choe.

Financial support for the project was provided by the Ford Foundation, the Canadian International Development Research Centre (IDRC), and the U.S. Agency for International Development (AID). The Ford Foundation support covered research costs in Japan, Taiwan, and Hawaii as well as international coordination costs. Support from IDRC covered research costs in Korea, the Philippines, and Thailand, plus workshop costs. The AID support, through an institutional contract with the East-West Population Institute, covered costs of organizing the project and supplementary costs for the research in Hawaii and international coordination.

Dr. Ozzie Simmons, Ford Foundation, and Drs. Walter Mertens and Alan Simmons, IDRC, have been closely involved with the study and have provided helpful advice at various stages.

The very substantial secretarial work connected with the project was handled through most of the project by Joan Choi, and later by Ruby Ogawa and Maggie Teo. Final production of the volumes was the responsibility of Lois Bender. The investigators are indebted to them for their help.

Finally, we wish to thank Donald Yoder for his editorial contribution to the first volume and to express our special gratitude to Sandra Ward, publications officer of the East-West Population Institute, for competent and sensitive editorial work in bringing the entire series to press.

1

introduction

Children are more than the object of their parents' attention and love;
they are also a biological and social necessity. The human species per-
petuates itself through children; cultural, religious, and national groups
transmit their values and traditions through children; families maintain
their lineage through children; and individuals pass on their genetic
and social heritage through children. The ultimate value of children is
the continuity of humanity. But how is this social imperative reflected
in the thoughts, feelings, and behavior of those who produce children,
the parents? And how do social influences and personal needs interact,
in the face of constraints, to result in a certain number of children being desired or born? These are the broad questions to which this study,
within the limitations of its social science methods, is addressed.

Population research has dealt with many aspects of actual, desired,
and ideal family size, and research in child development has examined
in detail parent-child relationships. But seldom in the social sciences
has there been empirical study of a fundamental question: Why do
people want children? Answers to that question should shed light on
many aspects of fertility behavior. People can want children without
having them; they can also have children without wanting them. The
interaction between motivations for childbearing and the effective
practice of contraception is an important topic for study. The strength
of motivations to have children should have an effect on the occur-
rence and timing of the first birth as well as on eventual family size.
Moreover, different types of motivation, as they come into play at

different points in the reproductive cycle, should have specific effects on both family size and family composition.

One of the main purposes of the research reported here is to describe and analyze reasons for wanting children; the research deals also with reasons for not wanting children, or costs entailed in having children. The "value" of children refers to a hypothetical net worth of children, with positive values (satisfactions) balanced against negative values (costs).[1] In this research, satisfactions and costs of children are assessed through questions asked in interviews with parents. The emphasis is therefore on *perceived* satisfactions and costs, and the value of children is directly linked to the needs, attitudes, and values of parents.[2]

It is obvious that children serve many functions for parents and fulfill many needs. Satisfactions and costs are therefore conceived broadly to encompass economic, social, and psychological dimensions. An assumption to be tested by the study is that perceived satisfactions and costs of children are a major motivational force in childbearing and that they interact with situational barriers and facilitators to affect both family-size preferences and fertility.

An important feature of this research is that it was conducted in six countries in comparative form. Motivations for childbearing are assumed to be neither entirely unique to the individual nor common to the species, but to consist of some of those elements plus a substantial component of culturally influenced desires. It is only through a comparative study that one can determine with confidence what is culturally conditioned. Beyond that, a comparative study permits at least limited insight into aspects of behavior that may be universal, which is a point of substantial interest with respect to childbearing. It is also true that a comparative study is inherently more convincing than a study conducted in only one country, at least if the results show a sensible pattern across cultures.

In this comparative report and in the country reports the implications of the findings for population policies and programs are discussed. The recommendations are necessarily tentative, in view of the exploratory nature of the project, but they do point out the usefulness

---

1 These terms and the more encompassing term *motivations* are used interchangeably in this volume.

2 For a discussion of the distinctions between needs, attitudes, and values in the social science literature, see the introduction to the Philippines volume in this series (Bulatao, 1975). For a discussion of values and related concepts in the study of fertility, see Spengler (1966).

of research in this area. Many population policies aim to provide alternatives to the satisfactions of children or to increase the actual or perceived costs of children. In that context, detailed empirical studies of how parents think and feel about the satisfactions and costs of children are obviously relevant.

The remainder of this first chapter discusses theoretical and conceptual aspects of research on the value of children, reviews policy issues, and describes the procedures involved in organizing the cross-national study. Chapter 2 deals with the methodology of the study and Chapter 3 provides basic descriptive data on the samples in the six countries, including selected data on fertility and family planning. Chapters 4 and 5 analyze comparative findings pertaining to the value of children. Chapter 6 discusses the implications of those findings, reviewing them from several perspectives; it also contains recommendations concerning policies and programs that may influence the value of children and fertility behavior.

Conceptual framework

The value of children is a topic upon which theorizing about fertility from differing academic viewpoints has begun to converge. In sociology and demography, in economics, in anthropology, and in psychology, a common emphasis on the value of children as a determinant of fertility trends and decisions may be found. Since childbearing is to a significant extent a purposive behavior,[3] in the sense that most people do something at some point in the reproductive cycle to limit childbearing, it is not surprising that the anticipated satisfactions and costs of children should be seen as a major influence on that behavior. It is surprising, however, that systematic research on the satisfactions and costs of children has been so late in coming.

The report of a conference on the satisfactions and costs of children compares the disciplinary approaches (Fawcett, 1972:5–7):

In sociology and demography, the satisfactions and costs of children have been discussed as a partial explanation for the demographic transition. The shift from a rural, agricultural society to an urban, industrialized one implies a reduction in economic benefits from children and an increase in costs. Other changes, such as higher levels of education, tend to increase awareness and desires related to alternatives to children. Changing family structures, along with alterations in economic activities of the family, tend to make large numbers of children dysfunctional.

Economists have in recent years developed more systematic approaches to

---

3 *Purposive* is used in preference to the term *rational*, which implies to some people a conscious weighing of the full range of relevant alternatives.

understanding the satisfactions (or benefits) and costs of children. These approaches include both macro-level analyses of the ways in which changing economic conditions affect the birth rate and micro-level theories that treat childbearing as a choice among alternative courses of action, with particular attention to income and price variables. Recent work has focused on refinement of the definition and measurement of income and price variables and on the role of tastes or preferences in childbearing decisions. Economic theories have been tested against available data and, to a more limited extent, have generated research designed to gather data on the specific elements contained in the theories.

In psychology, including the specialty of child psychology, little attention has been given to the satisfactions and costs of children or, more generally, to the effects of children on parents. Only within the past few years have attempts been made to apply psychological theory and knowledge to this topic. This recent work tends to emphasize the emotional relationship between parent and child, the significance of children for validation of sex roles or adulthood roles, and the social status connected with parenthood. Economic costs and benefits of children are treated mainly in terms of parents' perceptions of those dimensions. A number of research projects have been initiated recently to assess the psychological value of children.

The anthropological literature contains scattered references to the functions of children, including their economic functions, in various societies, but these data have not been systematically appraised. Of particular interest is the contribution made by children of various ages to the functioning of households in different types of agrarian setting, a topic on which investigations are now proceeding. Also of potential relevance is the study of belief systems pertaining to the values of children in furthering or maintaining particular forms of family lineage, cultural-religious traditions, and so on. Recent interest among anthropologists in studying fertility has stimulated efforts to look at the satisfactions and costs of children in a total cultural context.

At the time of that conference in 1972, it was the work of economists that was primarily associated with the value of children, particularly through the writings of Becker (1960), Easterlin (1969), Leibenstein (1957), and Robinson and Horlacher (1971). In the few years since then, economic and other approaches have been greatly extended, both theoretically and empirically.

Economic theorizing has been broadened to include systematically household-production as well as consumption functions, with the parents' allocation of time and other resources to children treated as an investment in human capital. Recent work in economics is collected in two volumes of conference proceedings edited by Schultz (1973, 1974). In addition, several important studies of the economic costs and benefits of children have been reported (for example, Cramer, 1975; Espenshade, 1972, 1973; Mueller, 1972a; O'Donnell, 1974; Reed and McIntosh, 1972; Turchi, 1973), and a lively literature on theoretical and methodological issues has emerged (including

Ben-Porath, 1974; Easterlin, 1975; Freedman, 1974; Leibenstein, 1974; Namboodiri, 1972; Turchi, 1975). In the microeconomic theories of fertility, primary attention is of course given to economic aspects of the value of children, while social and psychological aspects are labeled as "tastes" or "preferences," are often assumed to be constant, and are largely ignored. Only a few economists, such as Easterlin and Turchi, have called for systematic incorporation of these social and psychological dimensions within the context of microeconomic theories.

It may be noted, however, that a body of conceptual and empirical work that gives equal attention to social and psychological dimensions, along with economic dimensions, has also emerged recently. Berelson, in the 1972 annual report of the Population Council, has provided an essay containing a historical perspective as well as a taxonomy of value-of-children dimensions. The U.S. National Institute of Child Health and Human Development has convened two workshops to discuss research priorities for the study of the value of children; one focused on economic aspects and the other on noneconomic aspects. A review article with a psychological perspective, which is discussed further below, has been published (Hoffman and Hoffman, 1973). Empirical studies of the value of children have been conducted in the United States (see Beckman, 1974; Bourque et al., 1975; Evanson, 1974; Kirchner, n.d.; Terhune, 1973), in Latin America (Turner, 1974), in Asia (Chung, Cha, and Lee, 1974; Hull, 1975; White, 1975),[4] and in Europe.[5]

For the cross-national study reported here, the major stimulus comes from work in psychology. As noted by Fawcett (1970:110–111):

A theme that underlies much of the speculation about motivations for childbearing is that social change brings about changes in the way children are valued, in relation to alternative sources of satisfaction. That topic, the values attached to

---

4 Other work on the value of children in Asia includes a survey carried out in Hong Kong by the Social Research Centre of the Chinese University, a psychologically oriented pilot survey conducted in West Malaysia by the Malaysian Centre for Development Studies, and an ongoing project emphasizing the economic value of children being carried out jointly by the Malaysian Department of Statistics and the Rand Corporation.

5 Aspects of the value of children are included in the Third Fertility Survey in Belgium, as described in a bulletin from the Ministry of Public Health and the Family and Population Study Centre, Brussels, 30 June 1975. Pilot studies of the value of children have also been carried out at the Netherlands Interuniversity Demographic Institute.

children and functions served by children, should be a prime target for psychological research. It is a clearly defined subject that lends itself to methods of psychological assessment and it is an area where good empirical data, especially in
comparative form, are lacking. It is surely true that children serve different functions in different kinds of societies, as well as between strata within a society and
in the same strata in different eras. The needs of parents and demands on parents
vary with changes in other dimensions, such as occupational roles and normative
child-rearing styles; the ways in which children satisfy parental needs vary likewise
with parent-child relationships that differ in manner and strength. An important
sub-topic is the difference in perceived value of male and female children, with
a view toward the impact on fertility of means to predetermine sex of offspring
or of adoption of children as a method to attain desired sex composition.

Knowledge about the perceived value of children can be interpreted within
the framework of a functional approach to motivation and can also provide an
additional dimension for tests of the economic decision approach to fertility,
where values are often assumed to be uniform in a homogeneous population. . . .
It is not only the positive values attached to children that need study, but also
the perceived costs, direct and indirect. These factors, in turn, would be incorporated into a model where childbearing choices are balanced, in terms of utility,
against other kinds of choices.

At a more specific level, the work of Hoffman and Hoffman (1973)
had a major influence on the development of this project. Their article
reviews what is known about the satisfactions and costs of children,
presents a theoretical model for research in this area, and discusses
how the model may help to explain variations in fertility behavior, including cultural differences and historical trends in the motivation to
have children. Their model contains five broad sets of variables: the
value of children, alternative sources of the value, costs, barriers, and
facilitators. The first set, the value of children, is the element that is
developed in greatest detail. Nine categories are discussed, each intended to reflect particular psychological needs or functions served by
having children. The categories are:

1. Adult status and social identity
2. Expansion of the self, tie to a larger entity, "immortality"
3. Morality: religion, altruism, good of the group; norms regarding sexuality,
   impulsivity, virtue
4. Primary group ties, affection
5. Stimulation, novelty, fun
6. Achievement, competence, creativity
7. Power, influence, effectance
8. Social comparison, competition
9. Economic utility

As summarized by Lois Hoffman (1972:28—29), the elements of
the model interact to affect fertility and suggest ways in which fertility might be altered:

Alternatives pertain to other avenues, besides children, for fulfilling a value. Costs refer to what must be lost or sacrificed to obtain a value in any particular way. Barriers and facilitators refer to the factors that make it more difficult, or easier, to realize the particular value by having children.

These five concepts can be used to predict a person's desire for children, or the desires of a group. Changes elsewhere in the social structure might affect any of the five variables and thus affect fertility motivation. Furthermore, if public welfare required a change in fertility motivation—either an increase or decrease—a program could be launched by directing an attack at any or all of these five points.

The Hoffman and Hoffman model provides an ultimate goal for research on the value of children. The present study is regarded as an initial step toward that goal. Figure 1.1 shows the general conceptual framework for the study and indicates the major categories of variable that were included. In this heuristic model, the dimensions of the value of children are viewed as a set of variables intervening between sociodemographic factors and psychological and social orientations on the one hand and fertility and family planning on the other. The basic aims of the study were to obtain adequate data on the sets of variables shown in Figure 1.1 and to explore the relationships among those variables in a cross-cultural context.

It should be noted that this study was not designed for model-testing or hypothesis-testing, except in the most general sense. Eventually, however, research on the value of children should progress in that direction. In contrast to the simple conceptual model shown in Figure 1.1, a predictive model would, for example, specify the type of relationship expected between each dimension of the value of children and other components of the model. Moreover, important feedback effects would be included, such as the influence of prior fertility experience, including sex composition of the family, on current perceptions of the value of children. Interactions within the set of value-of-children dimensions would also be considered. For example, perceived economic costs of children should be assessed in relation to expected economic benefits. And, ideally, the additional components that Hoffman and Hoffman refer to as barriers, facilitators, and alternatives would be included. The exploratory analyses contained in this series of volumes are designed to lead toward the development of such an explicit predictive model.

The conceptual organization of the 15 dimensions of the value of children shown in Figure 1.1 was not developed in advance of the study; rather, it resulted from analysis of the data. In the construction of the questionnaire, an attempt was made to include multiple aspects of the value of children in the structured questions, but many open-

Figure 1.1 Conceptual model for the Value of Children Study

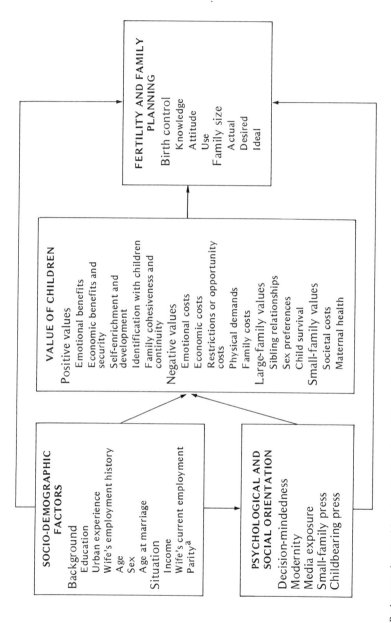

SOCIO-DEMOGRAPHIC FACTORS

Background
  Education
  Urban experience
  Wife's employment history
  Age
  Sex
  Age at marriage
Situation
  Income
  Wife's current employment
  Parity[a]

PSYCHOLOGICAL AND SOCIAL ORIENTATION

Decision-mindedness
Modernity
Media exposure
Small-family press
Childbearing press

VALUE OF CHILDREN

Positive values
  Emotional benefits
  Economic benefits and security
  Self-enrichment and development
  Identification with children
  Family cohesiveness and continuity
Negative values
  Emotional costs
  Economic costs
  Restrictions or opportunity costs
  Physical demands
  Family costs
Large-family values
  Sibling relationships
  Sex preferences
  Child survival
Small-family values
  Societal costs
  Maternal health

FERTILITY AND FAMILY PLANNING

Birth control
  Knowledge
  Attitude
  Use
Family size
  Actual
  Desired
  Ideal

a   Parity may be considered a situational variable or a family-size variable, but not both at the same time.

ended questions were also included so that dimensions not previously identified could still be assessed. The 15 categories shown in Figure 1.1 were based on an examination of responses to both structured and open-ended questions, for all six countries. The process of categorization was partly empirical, based on correlations and factor analysis, and partly judgmental. It may be noted that, in comparison with the Hoffman and Hoffman categories, the positive values in this scheme are less detailed and less closely linked to psychological concepts. The negative values, on the other hand, are more detailed, and categories of values have been added that relate specifically to large and small families. Following are brief descriptions of the value-of-children dimensions derived from this research:

POSITIVE GENERAL VALUES

1. *Emotional benefits.* Happiness, love, companionship, fun; also viewed in reverse as relief from strain and avoidance of boredom or loneliness
2. *Economic benefits and security.* Benefits from children's help in the house, business, or farm, from care of siblings, and from sharing of income; old-age security for the parents, including economic support, physical care, and psychological security
3. *Self-enrichment and development.* Learning from the experience of childrearing; becoming more responsible and mature; incentive and goals in life; being viewed as an adult, a grown woman or man; self-fulfillment; feeling of competence as a parent
4. *Identification with children.* Pleasure from watching growth and development of children; pride in children's accomplishments; reflection of self in children
5. *Family cohesiveness and continuity.* Children as a bond between husband and wife; fulfillment of marriage; completeness of family life; continuity of family name and traditions; producing heirs; having future grandchildren

NEGATIVE GENERAL VALUES

1. *Emotional costs.* General emotional strain; concern about discipline and moral behavior of children; worry over health; noise and disorder in household; children as nuisance
2. *Economic costs.* Expenses of childrearing; educational costs
3. *Restrictions or opportunity costs.* Lack of flexibility and freedom; restrictions on social life, recreation, travel; lack of privacy; restric-

tions on career or occupational mobility; no time for personal
needs and desires

4. *Physical demands.* Extra housework, caring for children; loss of
sleep; general weariness

5. *Family costs.* Less time with spouse; disagreements over rearing of
children; loss of spouse's affection

LARGE-FAMILY VALUES

1. *Sibling relationships.* Desire for another child to provide companionship for existing children; enriching the lives of children; avoiding an only child

2. *Sex preferences.* Specific desire for a son or daughter; desire for
a certain combination of sexes among children

3. *Child survival.* Concern that existing children may die; need for
more children to have enough survive to adulthood

SMALL-FAMILY VALUES

1. *Maternal health.* Concern that too many pregnancies, or pregnancy when the mother is beyond a certain age, is bad for the
mother's health

2. *Societal costs.* Concern about overpopulation, belief that another
child would be a burden to society

These 15 categories encompass most of the descriptive findings
on the value of children from this study, and they seem to represent
fairly well the way people think about the satisfactions and costs of
children in a variety of cultural settings. They do not, of course, represent all the motivations for and against childbearing. Biological drives
or maternal needs (see Bardwick, 1974) are not represented, for instance, and these empirically derived categories encompass mainly
conscious, admissible reasons for wanting or not wanting children. The
deeper, less readily verbalized motivations stressed by psychoanalysts
(see, for example, Wyatt, 1967) do not appear here, nor do some of
the socially less desirable motivations, such as proof of sexual potency
or the need to dominate others.

It is important to note that specific dimensions within the listing
of general positive and negative values have differing implications for
family size. Not all positive values require a large number of children
for fulfillment, for instance, and some negative values may have a
stronger effect on the decision to have the first child than on the decision to stop having children. The fertility implications of different

dimensions of the value of children are discussed in connection with the results reported in later chapters.[6]

Relevance for population policies

In most of the recent research and writing on the value of children, particular attention is given to the potential impact on population policy of work in this area. In brief, the value of children is seen as an important link in the chain of events through which general social and economic changes are related to fertility changes. If this link does in fact exist, then knowledge about the value of children can be useful both for analyzing social and economic policies that may have population effects and for formulating explicit population policies and programs to influence the value of children and fertility.

The debate over population policy in recent years has revealed some fundamental areas of agreement, as well as some disagreements (see Teitelbaum, 1974). The Plan of Action issued by the World Population Conference in 1974 stressed economic development and better income distribution as indirect means to affect population trends, but did not neglect social programs, such as the improvement of the status of women; it also recognized the need for explicit population activities, such as family planning programs. Within the population field, there is a broad consensus that both development programs and family planning programs are necessary, but that neither alone is sufficient to bring about long-term societal regulation of fertility trends.

A point that remains at issue is the need for selective social and economic policies, including incentive and disincentive programs, that are designed explicitly to influence childbearing motivations (or the demand for family planning services). Policies of this kind have been categorized and discussed by a number of authors (see, for example, Berelson, 1969, 1971; Stycos, 1974), and it has been argued that only by selective social changes that weaken motivations for large families can societies hope to deal with population problems (see Davis, 1967; Rich, 1973). Over the years, demographic researchers have attempted to identify those aspects of socioeconomic development that are most closely linked to fertility change. Nearly all such studies deal only with macro-level variables, however, and are not fully convincing with

---

6 Since these 15 categories were derived from a synthesis of the data, they do not appear in precisely this form in the tables showing results of the research. Rather, the tables show more specific categories, based in part on coding schemes developed earlier, which can in nearly all cases be fit within the 15 categories.

respect to inferences about childbearing motivations. Research on the value of children can help to fill that gap. As information about determinants of economic and noneconomic aspects of the value of children becomes available, recommendations may be made for specific social and economic policies that will influence indirectly the value of children and childbearing motivations. Recommendations may also be made for incentives, disincentives, and educational programs that have direct effects on the perceived satisfactions and costs of children. Such policies and programs will be useful to countries that wish to accelerate fertility declines instead of waiting for the long-term fertility effects that may accompany general economic development, better income distribution, and the expanded availability of family planning services.

The cross-national study

The Value of Children (VOC) project began in late 1971 with exploratory work carried out in Hawaii. As a first step, intensive interviews were conducted with eight men and ten women of diverse national and ethnic origin. These interviews consisted mainly of open-ended questions about satisfactions and costs of children, plus attempts to discern differences in satisfactions and costs according to age and sex of children. A set of Likert-type attitude items on the value of children, derived mainly from the theoretical literature, was also administered to the respondents.

After these exploratory interviews were analyzed, a more structured instrument, including an expanded set of attitude items, was developed for a pilot test. A number of important open-ended items pertaining to advantages and disadvantages of children and childbearing decision processes were also included in this pilot test. Interviews were conducted with 118 husbands and wives in Hawaii, mainly Japanese, Filipino, or Caucasian.

While the Hawaii pilot test was under way, initial steps were taken to organize the cross-national study. Potential research collaborators in Asia were contacted by the project coordinator and plans were made for a research conference that would launch the project.

In April 1972, a conference on assessment of the satisfactions and costs of children was held at the East-West Center in Honolulu. There were 24 participants. Nine working papers dealing with theoretical and methodological aspects of research on the value of children provided a focus for the conference. These papers, along with summaries of panel presentations, discussants' remarks, and round-table discussions, were published in the conference report (Fawcett, 1972).

Immediately after the conference, a two-day workshop was held to design and implement the cross-national Value of Children project. Participants were the coinvestigators for the six countries involved in the project. During the workshop, the investigators decided upon the goals of the study, a tentative list of variables to be assessed, a conceptual framework incorporating those variables, the sampling design, and a tentative timetable for the project. Many of the concepts and variables were selected from theoretical papers and research reports presented at the preceding conference, especially the papers by Hoffman (1972) and Mueller (1972b) and the report of the pilot project carried out in Hawaii (Fawcett, Albores, and Arnold, 1972).

After the workshop, each investigator developed questionnaire items to assess a specified set of variables. For each variable, items were developed by two or more investigators. The pool of items created in this way was then screened, and the best items were chosen for inclusion in the pretest questionnaire.

Translation of the pretest questionnaire, including back-translation, was carried out in each country. The questionnaire was then administered to a small sample of husbands and wives, both rural and urban. Each investigator prepared a pretest report with recommendations for revisions and additions to the questionnaire. Particular attention was given to items that presented translation difficulties.

The pretest reports provided the basis for constructing the basic, or core, questionnaire for the VOC project. The investigators agreed that the complete core questionnaire would be employed in each country and every effort would be made to achieve conceptual equivalence in translation of the items. To supplement the core questionnaire, items were added in each country to measure dimensions unique to the culture or of particular interest to the investigator.

On completion of the fieldwork, structured items were coded. A second workshop was then held in Hong Kong to compare preliminary results, develop common coding schemes for content analysis of open-ended questions, and determine procedures for subsequent data analysis. After this workshop, a second round of coding was conducted.

To carry out the first stage of data analysis, a research assistant from each country spent one month at the East-West Population Institute, becoming familiar with the computer programs that were used to analyze the core data from all six countries. Computer output and data tapes were then returned to each country for interpretation and further analysis.

At a later stage, the investigators for the project spent about one month working together at the East-West Population Institute, at which time partial drafts of the country reports were written and comparative analyses were initiated. Work on these analyses and reports then continued in the home countries.

Throughout all phases, the project coordinator performed a number of centralized functions, notably the synthesis of materials received from the scattered coinvestigators, the management of a communications system to facilitate the flow of ideas among all participants in the project, and administrative monitoring of the project's progress.

2

methodology

The methodology employed in this study reflects basic decisions that were made at the initial planning workshop for the project:
1. Comparable data would be collected in several cultures.
2. Contrasting groups would be studied within each culture.
3. Interviews with parents would provide the basic data.
4. Both husband and wife would be interviewed.

Comparability of data

While one of the main goals of the study was to make cross-cultural comparisons of the value of children, it was also recognized that interview data from diverse cultural-linguistic groups can never be fully comparable. Nevertheless, several steps were taken to enhance comparability. Probably the most important of these steps was the involvement of experienced local researchers at the earliest stages of the study. The participation of social scientists from all six countries in the design of the questionnaire provided reasonable assurance that the content and structure of the research would not be incompatible with the locales in which the study was to be conducted.

A critical element of this participation was the carrying out of local pretests, with the best available procedures used for translating the questionnaire into local languages. Translation of a research instrument is not a mechanical process, since conceptual equivalence rather than literal equivalence is sought. The investigators in each country fully understood the purposes of the questions and their intended analytic use, so their judgment in matters of translation could be relied on with some confidence.

The translation was not entrusted to a single individual, however, since convergence of judgments is desirable in such a subtle area. In preparing the pretest questionnaire for local use, standard procedures involved translation from English to the local language by someone other than the investigator, an independent back-translation from the local language to English by a second person, comparison of the two English versions by the investigator, then resolution of discrepancies by the investigator in consultation with the translators. Whenever possible, the initial translation to the local language was done by a social scientist experienced in field research.

The pretest itself then provided feedback on the adequacy of translation as well as on clarity of items, comprehensibility, range and appropriateness of responses, and so on. In each country, the pretest included both urban and rural respondents and persons with high and low educational levels. As a result of the pretests carried out in the six countries, the initial questionnaire was modified substantially, after which additional translations and back-translations were carried out. In the judgment of the investigators, the final core questionnaire has a high degree of conceptual equivalence across countries and the results are reasonably comparable. This judgment tends to be supported by analysis of trends and patterns in the data across countries.

Sampling

The decision to study contrasting groups in each country was dictated by several considerations. Since this was regarded as an exploratory study and the intention was to complete the study in a short time, a relatively small sample was required. At the same time, it was necessary to obtain results which could be meaningfully analyzed and which would include a wide range of responses for the variables under study. The best solution appeared to be to select several groups, each relatively homogeneous and each located at a different point on a hypothetical continuum of VOC measures. Selection of the sample groups was also consistent with the assumption that fertility differences are due in part to differences in the economic value of children in urban and rural settings and in modern and traditional sectors of the society. Respondents were selected according to the following sample criteria:

Sex and age group	Urban middle	Urban lower	Rural	All groups
Wives (ages 20–34)	60	60	60	180
Husbands (ages 20–44)	60	60	60	180
All respondents	120	120	120	360

The precise definitions of the subsamples and selection criteria were left to the investigators in each country. It was agreed, however, that within the definitions established sample households would be selected in a systematic way and that the definitions would aim to provide strong contrasts. Descriptions of the sampling criteria and profiles of actual samples chosen are presented in each country report.

To be eligible for the sample, husband and wife had to be living together and had to have at least one child. Although it would have been interesting to include couples without children in the sample, this was not felt to be practical because of the difficulties in locating a meaningful number of childless respondents and because a special questionnaire would have been required for them.

The decision to include both husbands and wives in the sample stemmed from the recognition that the data from an exploratory study would be seriously incomplete if collected from only one sex. The collection of data from both husbands and wives raises the possibility, however, that results might be contaminated by communication between spouses. Attempts were made to avoid this in two ways: by interviewing both spouses simultaneously and independently whenever possible; and, when one had been interviewed first, by strongly urging no discussion until the second spouse had been interviewed. The latter procedure was more common than the first, and its effectiveness cannot be assessed. It is somewhat reassuring, however, to note in this context the length and complexity of the questionnaire. It appears unlikely that communication between spouses could have been specific to many items, although a general discussion could certainly have heightened the sensitivity of one spouse to the issues being studied and, depending on how the purpose of the study was perceived, could have produced a certain bias.

Interviewing

The use of interviews as the basic method of data collection was in part dictated by the nature of the sample, which would include many respondents with little education and even some illiterates. Self-administered instruments were obviously not feasible. Moreover, in all countries considerable experience and expertise were available for conducting field interviews.

It was recognized, however, that the topics to be studied could not be adequately assessed through simple "opinion survey" techniques. Thus the investigators decided that the questionnaire should include a number of open-ended questions in which depth probes would be used and, for more refined analyses, should also include multi-item attitude scales. The use of several methods for assessing similar concepts could also provide internal evidence of validity, if comparable patterns of data emerged from different methods of measurement.

With the complexity of the questionnaire in mind, special emphasis was given to quality of data collection, as controlled through selection, training, and supervision of interviewers. It was decided that, for this study, interviewers with training in the social sciences would best be able to appreciate the qualitative aspects of the interview. Accordingly, interviewers in most cases were selected from among university seniors or graduate students who had social science training and, preferably, field research experience.

A basic interviewer's manual was compiled for the study and was used as part of a minimum one-week training program for interviewers that also included supervised practice interviewing. In all countries, close day-to-day supervision was also exercised in the field, with particular attention given to quality checks on the initial questionnaires from each interviewer.

As a final point related to interviewing, it should be noted that there are clear limitations to the types of data that can be collected through field interviews with a sample of persons from different cultures with varying levels of education. Depth of analysis is an important limitation; although open-ended questions with probes were used extensively, this study obviously has not assessed motivations for childbearing that operate at an unconscious level. Moreover, it tapped only partly the motivations that are difficult to verbalize for reasons of social acceptability, complexity, or emotional connotation. At a more general level, the cross-cultural design of the study forced the content toward a simple common denominator: items that did not work or were unacceptable in one country were excluded from the core questionnaire for all countries. Many interesting issues were thus abandoned for comparative purposes, although some were retained in a country-specific context.

A certain richness is inevitably lost in a comparative study, when compared to a study in a single culture. However, the gains to be made by a comparative study in disentangling the universal and the culture-specific, and in providing cross-cultural replication that enhances confidence in validity, may greatly outweigh the loss in richness.

The questionnaire

The final core questionnaire had at least three notable features:
1. It was relatively long.
2. About half the items were innovative in content; that is, they covered topics which had not been included in previous studies.
3. The format of questions was varied, ranging from open-ended items to simple yes-no items, and key concepts were measured by several items with different formats.

The complete core questionnaire is reproduced as Appendix A. Most of the core questionnaire was standardized; however, some sections (on such topics as religiosity and rural economic status) were required of all countries but not standardized in content, to allow for local variations. Also not shown in the core questionnaire are the country-specific items that were added in each locale according to the interests of the particular investigator. Both the unstandardized core items and the country-specific items are discussed in each country report.

The following list summarizes the content of the core questionnaire, with major topics listed under five general headings. The order of this list does not reflect the sequential arrangement of the questionnaire and, for ease of comprehension, the topics are simply labeled without describing the items that make up their component parts. The core questionnaire contained over 400 items in all.

VOC dimensions
1. Advantages for respondent of having children, compared with no children (open-ended with ranking of advantages)
2. Disadvantages for respondent of having children, compared with no children (open-ended with ranking of disadvantages)
3. Perception of reasons why most people have children (open-ended)
4. Importance of having at least one girl (structured)
5. Reasons why girl is important (open-ended)
6. Importance of having at least one boy (structured)

7. Reasons why boy is important (open-ended)
8. Strength of boy preference—how many daughters before stopping (structured)
9. Reasons for wanting another child (structured, 17 items)
10. Reasons for not wanting another child (structured, 9 items)
11. Beliefs about children and childbearing (Likert-type attitude scale, 45 items)
    a. Positive functions of children (parental benefits: identity, social status, security, competence, pride, altruism, love, companionship, family solidarity)
    b. Costs of children and propensity to consider alternatives (economic burden, physical work, worry, loss of freedom, opportunity costs, decisional factors)
    c. Perceived controls over childbearing (fatalism, sex-role imperative, social pressures)
12. Economic/practical help expected from daughters (open-ended)
13. Economic/practical help expected from sons (open-ended)
14. Expectations regarding living with children in the future, children as source of financial support in the future (structured)
15. Perceived costs of children: amount spent on children; whether children are seen as economic benefit or cost; number of children respondent could raise before they became heavy financial burden; effect of doubled income on wanted family size; effect of free education on wanted family size; perceived burden of educational costs (structured and open-ended)
16. Perceived changes in functions of children: whether generational changes in willingness of children to give money to parents, live with parents, support parents in old age, help with chores or business (structured)

Family-size dimensions

1. Current number of children
2. Number of additional children wanted
3. Reasons for not wanting fewer children (open-ended)
4. Reasons for not wanting more children (open-ended)
5. Ideal number of children if starting over
6. Ideal number of boys and girls
7. Ideal ordering of sex of children
8. Definition of number of children in a small family
9. Definition of number of children in a large family
10. Beliefs about effects of large or small family size on child

Moderator dimensions
1. Attitudinal modernity (OM scale)[1]
2. Mass-media exposure
3. Ownership of consumer durables
4. Communication with spouse about family size
5. Communication with spouse about birth control
6. Husband-wife influence in decision-making
7. Which spouse has stronger desire for children
8. Pressure from others regarding contraception, abortion, family size
9. Religiosity
10. Educational aspirations for children
11. Perceived adequacy of income and relative economic status

Birth control dimensions
1. Awareness of, knowledge about, and use of contraceptive methods (26 items)
2. General opinion about contraception
3. Contraception attitude scale
4. General opinion about abortion
5. Abortion attitude scale

Respondent's background and status
(Approximately 40 items covering age, marital history, education, occupation, income, religion, urban/rural experience, education and occupation of parents, birth order, number of own or adopted children)

Two points should be made about the actual sequence of items in the core questionnaire: the most important open-ended items were asked before answers could be suggested to the respondent by the structured items; and nearly all the VOC measures were covered in the first half of the interview (the latter half was devoted mainly to sociodemographic information).

The key open-ended items were questions 4 and 6 on perceived advantages and disadvantages of children (compared with having no children). Preceding items concerned only the screening, the record of children in the household, and an initial open-ended question on the comparison between what children learn at home and at school. For

---

1 The scale used was a modified version of the overall modernity (OM) scale developed by Smith and Inkeles (1966).

questions 4 and 6, the interviewers were instructed to probe deeply and to take as much time as needed. These items provided the most convincing respondent-generated data on the value of children, and accordingly the content-analyzed responses are given prominence in the country reports and in the comparative analyses.

Most of the VOC items were placed at the beginning of the interview to ensure that the respondent was alert for these key items, and also because it was thought that the respondent could see the distinctions among somewhat similar items more readily if they were close together. Moreover, with this arrangement the interview questions would not seem redundant. (In the pretest, where VOC items were scattered throughout the questionnaire, respondents often complained about answering the same question two or more times.)

The time required for the interview averaged 77 minutes, ranging from 64 minutes (Japan) to 84 minutes (Hawaii). Interview time was approximately the same for men and women. On the average, urban middle-class interviews were shortest and rural interviews longest, but the pattern varied across countries.

A section of the questionnaire that deserves special comment is question 42, a Likert-type attitude scale composed of 45 items. A six-point response dimension was used, ranging from strongly agree to strongly disagree, with no neutral category. (In the coding, nonresponse was coded as a midpoint 4, with 7 representing strongly agree and 1 strongly disagree.) In the attitude scale (shown in Appendix A), the response format was not the standard continuum with extreme responses at each pole; instead, a two-stage procedure was used. Respondents were asked first to decide whether they agreed or disagreed with the statement, then to decide on the strength of their response. (In some countries, the strength of response was illustrated in a diagram with steps labeled strongly, moderately, and slightly in descending order.) This two-stage procedure was used because experience indicated that the opposite-pole continuum format was not meaningful in a number of cultures, particularly to respondents with little education.

The 45 items were designed to tap a wide variety of beliefs about the functions of children and childbearing. They were selected from a review of the literature and extensive pretesting. In the first intensive interviews in Hawaii, 75 items were tried out. Based on the results of these interviews, an expanded set of 110 items was developed for the subsequent exploratory study with 118 respondents in Hawaii. The conceptual organization of those items and data from the scales are presented in Fawcett, Albores, and Arnold (1972). As a result of the exploratory study, a set consisting of 65 items was constructed for the cross-national pretest. On the basis of the pretest in six countries and with a view to the necessity of reducing the length of the total questionnaire, the final set was reduced to 45 items.

The 45 items were grouped according to a conceptual scheme to ensure that important concepts were measured by more than one item. It was not expected that the items grouped conceptually would necessarily produce psychometrically valid scales in cross-cultural use, although statistical criteria such as item-total correlations were employed to aid in the refinement of the item set at various stages. Other criteria—such as theoretical relevance, applicability in six cultures, and subjective judgments of worth—were also given substantial weight. The intention was to develop a set of diverse items that could be applied in varied settings, then to derive scales empirically both within countries and across countries. The nine scales used for comparative analysis are described in Chapter 4 of this volume.

While most questions in the core questionnaire were asked of both husbands and wives, a few questions were designed explicitly for one sex. Only husbands were asked about ownership of consumer durables, for instance, and only wives were asked for a complete pregnancy history and about arrangements for child care if they worked.

Data analysis

The major aim of the analysis in this study was to identify important dimensions of the value of children. Toward that end, a variety of analytic techniques was applied. In presentation of results, emphasis is given to descriptive findings about the value of children, particularly those based on content analysis of open-ended questions.

The style of presentation for the descriptive data in the country reports is derived from the sampling design of the study. As noted earlier, the samples were drawn to provide contrasting groups: urban middle class, urban lower class, and rural. In each group, both husbands and wives were interviewed. The basic format for data presentation in the country reports follows this sample design whenever possible, displaying, for instance, mean values for the three socioeconomic groups, the two sex groups, and the total sample. Through this procedure the reader is able to examine, across sample groups and across countries, the major trends in the VOC dimensions. As background for understanding those trends, each country report contains demographic profiles for the three socioeconomic groups and the two sex groups, including such variables as age, education, income, and parity.

In the comparative analysis, results are presented to show comparisons across countries within socioeconomic groups. Data for the total sample in each country are usually omitted because the sampling procedures do not allow combining the results for the three subgroups to obtain results for a larger population—that is, general statements cannot legitimately be made about the value of children in Korea as compared with Taiwan. However, the middle class in one country can be compared with the middle class in other countries, and the cross-cultural differences and similarities among SES groups can be discussed. The tables in this comparative volume are designed to highlight such SES comparisons and are organized also to facilitate regional and subcultural comparisons. In all tables the East Asian countries are listed first (Korea, Taiwan, Japan), then ethnic groups in Hawaii (first Japanese for comparisons with Japan, then Caucasians, then Filipinos for comparisons with the Philippines), and finally the Southeast Asian countries (Philippines, Thailand).

Husbands and wives are treated as independent groups in these volumes, rather than as couples within which a reciprocal influence exists. These presentations are regarded as appropriate to the initial stage of analysis and as logically prior to couple comparisons. The data given in the country reports indicate the similarities and differences between husbands and wives treated in the aggregate. Husband-wife analyses are not presented in this comparative volume, however, in part because of the complexities involved in adding this breakdown to analysis of six countries and three socioeconomic groups. More importantly, the differences between aggregate responses for husbands and wives are shown in the country reports to be relatively small in most cases; the exceptions are noted in a separate section on husband-wife differences in this volume. The special analyses necessary to treat the couple as a unit and to compare responses of spouses within the couple unit will provide the substance for later reports.

Beyond the descriptive level, the structure of the data was analyzed by using such techniques as correlations and factor analysis. At a theoretical or conceptual level, such analyses show how the VOC dimensions fit within a broader framework of antecedent and consequent variables. This leads toward the development of explicit, testable hypotheses for future studies. At a practical level, these analyses permit reduction of the data set to manageable proportions. Attitude measures were combined into multi-item scales through factor analysis, for instance, and some questionnaire items were simply omitted from the analysis either because they were statistically redundant or because they showed no interesting relationships.

As another method of data reduction, considerable effort was devoted in this study to the development of a priori constructed variables and indices. This was motivated both by a desire to make the results more manageable and by the conviction that indices based on multiple measures have greater stability and can be more confidently interpreted, especially in cross-cultural comparisons. Appendix B lists the constructed variables and indices, describes their derivation, and indicates the range of numerical values and the meaning of those values for each variable or index.

The analyses described above provide a basic picture of the content and structure of the data set and show trends across major groups in the sample. Regression analyses were also employed to examine the predictive relationships among the variables. The main emphasis in this analysis is on the explanation of fertility and family planning variables, using as predictors VOC variables alone and in combination with sociodemographic variables. This analysis provides also a comparison of relative explanatory power among different VOC dimensions, through analysis of the regression coefficients.

Multiple regression techniques were employed also to predict VOC dimensions by using sociodemographic variables as predictors. The results of those analyses are not included in this volume, but are presented in some country reports.

In general, it should be noted that the country reports contain many variables and many types of analysis that do not appear in this volume. The selected results in the chapters that follow are intended to highlight major findings, while the country reports provide more detailed analyses as well as interpretations of results in the light of particular cultural and social settings.[2]

---

2 For several reasons, statistics presented in this volume may differ slightly from those in the country reports. For instance, the distinction between urban middle class and urban lower class was made on the basis of initial sampling classifications for the comparative tabulations, while a more precise distinction was used in some country reports. Also, certain statistical procedures, such as factor analyses and regression analyses, were carried out in some countries by using somewhat different sets of variables and techniques. In general, however, the findings and conclusions do not differ substantially as a result of such analytic variations.

3

sample characteristics and fertility indices

This chapter presents demographic profiles for the samples in each of the six countries. Emphasis is given to similarities and differences across subgroups (urban middle class, urban lower class, and rural) as background for presentations of data on the value of children by subgroup. Results are presented for indices of fertility and family planning, as well as background and situational characteristics of the respondents. Most of the data in these descriptive profiles are also analyzed by correlations and multiple regressions in Chapter 5.

Demographic characteristics

As shown in Table 3.1, the subgroups in each country do differ in the expected manner on indices of socioeconomic status. On education, for instance, the middle class is always highest, the lower class is intermediate, and the rural group is lowest. The size of the difference varies by country, of course, and in Japan the differences between groups are quite small. In Asian countries other than Japan, the rural respondents' education is mainly at the primary school level, the urban lower-class respondents generally have one to three years' more education than the rural, and the middle-class respondents typically are secondary school graduates, some of whom have gone to college.

The mean age of respondents tends to be similar across subgroups, as it should be with age as a sampling criterion. (Wives had to be in the age range 20–34 with husbands 20–44, and the aim in each country was to obtain approximately equal numbers of wives in the 20–24, 25–29, and 30–34 age ranges.) The overall mean age for husbands and wives in all six countries is about 31 years.

A younger age at marriage among the lower socioeconomic groups is indicated by a longer duration of marriage for the rural respondents and, to a lesser degree, for the urban lower-class respondents in most countries. (Japan and Hawaii show some exceptions to the trend, owing partly to a younger sample in the urban lower class.)

The number of living children is generally smallest among the middle class, who are better educated and more recently married. (Again, Japan and Hawaii are exceptions.) Comparing the urban lower class and the rural group, the mean number of children for these two groups is about the same in Taiwan and the Philippines, while it is higher for the rural in Korea, Thailand, and among Filipinos in Hawaii. (The rural figure is higher than the urban lower in Japan, but still only equal to the urban middle–2.0 children.)

Urban experience of respondents was measured by a question about the number of years lived in a "large town or city" and the number of years lived "on a farm or in the country." The data shown in Table 3.1 are the means, across respondents in each SES group, of the percentage of the respondent's life that was spent in an urban area.

Except in Korea, the data show that the middle-class and lower-class groups have had approximately equal amounts of urban experience, with mean percentages ranging from 62 to 89. The figure for lower-class Koreans is only 46, reflecting a higher proportion of rural-urban migrants in that group. In all countries, there is very little urban experience among the rural respondents, indicating a minimal amount of urban to rural migration.

Family-size indices

Data on desires and perceptions regarding family size were collected from a number of questions. Table 3.2 summarizes the results, for each SES group, for the following indices:

1. Number of living children (repeated here for comparison)
2. Number of children wanted (based on asking whether the respondent wanted any more children and, if so, how many more, which is then added to parity)
3. Ideal number of children (based on asking how many children would be wanted "in your ideal family, if you were starting all over")

Table 3.1 Characteristics of samples
(Education, age, years of marriage, number of living chil-
socioeconomic group)

Country and SES group	Education[a]		Age	
	Mean number	Standard deviation	Mean number	Standard deviation
Korea				
Urban middle	15.4	1.4	33.3	3.8
Urban lower	8.0	3.4	31.8	4.6
Rural	6.2	3.4	31.9	4.6
All groups	9.8	4.9	32.2	4.4
Taiwan				
Urban middle	12.2	3.4	30.2	5.4
Urban lower	6.0	2.0	30.3	5.0
Rural	4.7	3.1	28.8	4.2
All groups	7.6	4.4	29.8	4.9
Japan				
Urban middle	12.3	2.4	32.6	4.5
Urban lower	11.4	2.3	30.4	4.4
Rural	10.6	1.6	31.8	3.4
All groups	11.4	2.2	31.6	4.2
U.S. (Hawaii)				
Japanese				
Urban middle	13.6	1.8	30.8	4.5
Urban lower	12.3	1.2	29.3	4.9
Caucasian				
Urban middle	13.9	1.8	29.4	3.6
Urban lower	11.7	1.5	27.8	4.7
Filipino				
Urban lower	10.7	3.1	30.6	4.6
Rural	7.0	2.8	33.6	5.7
All groups	11.7	3.1	30.0	5.0
Philippines				
Urban middle	12.6	3.5	30.2	5.1
Urban lower	9.8	3.6	30.5	5.5
Rural	7.0	3.6	31.4	5.7
All groups	9.9	4.2	30.7	5.4
Thailand				
Urban middle	13.8	3.2	34.0	4.7
Urban lower	5.6	3.6	28.6	5.2
Rural	4.2	2.0	31.8	6.1
All groups	7.8	5.2	31.6	5.8

a   Years of formal education.

dren, urban experience, and number in sample, by country and

Years of marriage		Living children		Urban experience	
Mean number	Standard deviation	Mean number	Standard deviation	(mean percentage of life lived in urban area)	(Number in sample)
6.6	2.5	2.5	0.8	79	(120)
7.3	3.9	2.7	1.1	46	(132)
9.2	4.2	3.4	1.4	8	(126)
7.7	3.8	2.8	1.2	44	(378)
5.2	3.0	2.2	1.1	68	(144)
6.9	3.7	2.9	1.1	68	(144)
7.8	4.5	2.8	1.2	1	(144)
6.7	3.9	2.6	1.2	46	(432)
7.2	3.1	2.0	0.7	66	(136)
5.7	3.7	1.6	0.7	62	(134)
8.2	3.8	2.0	0.6	2	(142)
7.0	3.7	1.9	0.7	43	(412)
6.6	3.6	2.0	1.4	84	(98)
7.4	4.2	2.0	1.0	89	(76)
7.6	2.9	2.0	1.0	87	(95)
7.1	4.5	2.5	1.7	84	(87)
6.9	4.8	2.4	1.5	78	(126)
11.1	5.2	3.2	2.0	3	(84)
7.5	4.4	2.3	1.5	71	(557)
6.6	4.8	3.0	1.9	87	(136)
7.9	4.3	3.4	1.9	79	(126)
8.3	4.9	3.3	1.9	6	(127)
7.6	4.7	3.2	1.9	57	(389)
6.8	3.8	2.2	1.1	75	(120)
7.6	4.2	2.8	1.6	62	(120)
9.4	4.8	3.3	1.5	7	(120)
7.8	4.4	2.8	1.5	48	(360)

Table 3.2 Selected indices related to family size
(Means and standard deviations, by country and socio-

Country and SES group	Living children		Children wanted[a]	
	Mean number	Standard deviation	Mean number	Standard deviation
Korea				
Urban middle	2.5	0.8	2.8	0.8
Urban lower	2.6	1.1	3.0	1.0
Rural	3.4	1.4	4.1	1.2
Taiwan				
Urban middle	2.2	1.1	2.7	1.0
Urban lower	2.9	1.1	3.2	1.1
Rural	2.8	1.2	3.4	1.2
Japan				
Urban middle	2.0	0.7	3.0	1.4
Urban lower	1.6	0.7	2.7	1.1
Rural	2.0	0.6	2.6	0.9
U.S. (Hawaii)				
Japanese				
Urban middle	2.0	1.4	3.0	1.2
Urban lower	2.0	1.0	2.7	1.0
Caucasian				
Urban middle	1.9	1.0	2.7	1.2
Urban lower	2.5	1.7	3.3	1.5
Filipino				
Urban lower	2.4	1.5	3.6	1.6
Rural	3.2	2.0	3.7	1.5
Philippines				
Urban middle	3.0	1.9	3.8	1.6
Urban lower	3.4	1.9	3.9	1.7
Rural	3.3	1.9	4.4	1.7
Thailand				
Urban middle	2.2	1.1	3.0	1.2
Urban lower	2.8	1.6	3.4	1.5
Rural	3.3	1.5	3.8	1.5

a Number of living children plus number of additional children wanted.

b Number of children respondents would want to have if they were starting their families again.

c Estimated number of children in typical family in community.

d Small or large family as perceived by respondents.

economic group)

Children ideal[b]		Children of "typical couple"[c]		Children in a "small" family[d]		Children in a "large" family[d]	
Mean number	Standard deviation	Mean number	Standard deviation	Mean number	Standard deviation	Mean number	Standard deviation
2.7	0.7	2.9	0.5	2.4	0.9	4.4	1.1
2.9	0.9	3.5	3.3	2.7	0.9	4.6	1.2
3.4	1.1	4.2	1.2	2.8	1.0	5.6	1.8
2.4	0.8	3.2	0.7	2.5	0.6	4.9	1.6
3.1	1.1	3.3	0.8	2.7	0.8	5.4	1.7
3.2	0.9	3.6	0.6	2.5	0.9	5.5	2.2
3.1	1.0	2.6	0.5	1.4	0.6	4.3	0.9
3.2	1.4	2.6	0.5	1.4	0.5	4.3	0.9
2.9	0.8	2.7	0.5	1.6	0.6	3.9	0.7
3.1	1.2	3.1	1.1	2.1	0.7	5.3	1.5
3.1	1.2	3.3	0.8	2.0	0.7	5.6	1.9
2.7	1.2	3.2	0.9	1.8	0.7	5.1	1.6
3.0	1.2	4.0	1.3	2.2	0.8	5.9	2.7
3.4	1.4	3.5	1.0	2.6	0.9	6.3	2.0
3.8	1.4	3.8	0.6	2.9	0.6	4.8	1.1
3.7	1.4	5.5	1.7	3.1	1.2	7.2	2.6
3.7	1.6	5.9	2.2	3.1	1.1	7.2	2.7
4.3	1.4	6.0	1.7	3.7	1.5	8.4	3.1
2.9	1.1	3.2	0.6	2.5	0.7	5.1	1.6
3.1	1.6	3.8	1.4	3.0	1.1	6.0	2.5
3.4	1.6	3.8	1.7	3.0	1.0	6.0	1.9

4. Number of children for a typical couple in the community (based on asking how many children "a typical couple in this community has by the time they stop having children")
5. Number of children in a "large" and "small" family (based on respondent's definition; for example, "When you think of a small family, how many children would be in it?")

Table 3.2 shows that, on the average, the couples in these samples (who are relatively young) were motivated to have more children: wanted family size is larger than parity, for all SES groups in all countries. For these respondents, then, questions about the value of children should have been personally meaningful. They already had at least one child, so they had some experience with childrearing, and many of them wanted, and expected, to have more children.

In general, wanted and ideal family size are quite similar, with a tendency for the ideal size to be slightly smaller. The principal exceptions are in Japan and among Japanese in Hawaii, where ideal family size is consistently larger than wanted, the difference being substantial especially in the lower class. This may indicate a motivation for larger families that has been suppressed by socioeconomic circumstances.

The response on number of children for a "typical" couple is difficult to interpret, since it involves an undefined reference group and presumably an older cohort. Perhaps most notable here is the extremely high response for all groups in the Philippines. Apparently the current generation of childbearers in the Philippines do see themselves as participants in a demographic transition. That is, their own fertility desires and ideals are strikingly lower than what they perceive to have been typical in their community in recent times. Nevertheless, it should be noted that wanted and ideal family size are still consistently higher for Filipinos than for other groups included in this study.

Perceptions of a "large" and "small" family vary considerably across countries and across SES groups. The Filipinos are distinctive here also, in this case by the larger numbers they give in defining both large and small families. (For the rural Filipinos in our sample, a "small" family has 3.7 children on the average.) For all countries and nearly all subgroups, the means for wanted and ideal family size fall between what is defined as large and small families, with a tendency to be closer to the number defined as small.

Contraceptive use and timing

Practice of contraception is relatively common among the groups sampled in this study, as shown in Table 3.3. For the urban middle class, about three-fourths of the respondents were practicing some form of birth control at the time of the interview in all countries except the Philippines, where slightly over half were practicing. Among the urban lower class the percentage of respondents practicing is generally lower and more variable, ranging from 44 percent in Korea to 80 percent among Japanese and Caucasians in Hawaii. Among rural respondents, roughly one-fourth were practicing in Korea, one-half in Taiwan, the Philippines, Thailand, and among Filipinos in Hawaii, and three-fourths in Japan.

The proportion of respondents who had ever used a contraceptive method is higher than that of current users and is generally highest for the urban middle class and lowest for the rural groups. Among urban middle-class respondents, the proportion of ever-users ranges from 97 percent in Thailand to 71 percent in the Philippines. For the urban lower group, the proportion who had ever practiced contraception is highest among Caucasians and Japanese in Hawaii (95 and 93 percent respectively) and lowest among Koreans (52 percent). Among rural respondents, only the Japanese reported a high incidence of contraceptive use (88 percent). Knowledge of contraception, like practice, declines across SES groups.

Preference for the modern contraceptive methods (pill, IUD, and sterilization) was strongest among middle- and lower-class Caucasians and Japanese in Hawaii, and among middle- and lower-class respondents in Taiwan and Thailand. In general, fewer rural than urban contraceptors had used the modern methods. The low level of use of modern methods in Japan is attributable to the limited availability of the pill and the popularity of condoms in that country.

The significance of these figures for the present study should be viewed in the light of what it means to practice contraception. A majority of respondents were engaging in behavior that was intended to limit birth or regulate pregnancy. That is, they were able to view childbearing as an act that is at least partially under voluntary control. These respondents were not fatalistic about childbearing and they were not ignorant about birth control. Rather, they were capable of using relevant information, such as the perceived value of children, to guide their own reproductive behavior.

The use of contraception prior to the first birth shows substantial variation across countries and subgroups. Only for the middle class in Japan and Hawaii is there substantial use of birth control to delay the first birth (47 percent in Japan, 38 percent among Japanese in Hawaii, and 53 percent among Caucasians in Hawaii). The next highest figure

Table 3.3 Contraceptive knowledge, contraceptive use, and first birth
(By country and socioeconomic group)

Country and SES groups	Methods know how to use (mean number)	Currently using a method (percentage)
Korea		
Urban middle	4.6	70
Urban lower	3.0	44
Rural	2.8	22
Taiwan		
Urban middle	5.5	74
Urban lower	3.8	59
Rural	2.4	54
Japan		
Urban middle	5.8	80
Urban lower	5.1	60
Rural	4.2	77
U.S. (Hawaii)		
Japanese		
Urban middle	6.9	83
Urban lower	6.3	80
Caucasian		
Urban middle	7.0	71
Urban lower	6.5	80
Filipino		
Urban lower	4.2	53
Rural	4.4	47
Philippines		
Urban middle	4.4	57
Urban lower	3.5	56
Rural	2.3	46
Thailand		
Urban middle	6.1	76
Urban lower	3.5	55
Rural	2.5	50

a   Includes respondents currently using a method. Percentages include couples expecting a child at the time of the interview who had ever used a contraceptive method.

interval

Ever used a method (percentage)[a]	Ever used pill, IUD, or sterilization (percentage)	Used a method before first birth (percentage)	First birth interval in months
84	45	12	13.6
52	42	0	10.9
44	34	7	20.3
85	67	8	14.3
71	62	2	9.7
58	53	0	13.7
93	16	47	19.7
86	11	34	18.6
88	21	15	18.5
94	76	38	16.6
93	76	29	11.6
95	88	53	22.5
95	91	35	10.6
69	46	3	12.3
50	38	3	18.8
71	35	1	11.9
76	50	7	17.8
54	34	4	13.1
97	80	12	21.5
77	68	6	18.9
52	49	1	13.6

Table 3.4 Attitudes toward birth control and abortion
(Percentage approving, by country and socioeconomic

Country and SES group	Use of birth control by married couples	Birth control to delay first birth	Abortion by married woman to prevent unwanted birth
Korea			
Urban middle	91	25	74
Urban lower	93	8	84
Rural	93	10	69
Taiwan			
Urban middle	94	60	33
Urban lower	91	64	24
Rural	84	52	29
Japan			
Urban middle	82	47	20
Urban lower	77	36	22
Rural	75	38	28
U.S. (Hawaii)			
Japanese			
Urban middle	91	86	43
Urban lower	87	83	49
Caucasian			
Urban middle	87	89	38
Urban lower	89	71	26
Filipino			
Urban lower	62	38	10
Rural	73	14	0
Philippines			
Urban middle	85	23	9
Urban lower	91	27	10
Rural	78	25	5
Thailand			
Urban middle	89	63	7
Urban lower	66	48	4
Rural	58	31	0

NOTE: Respondents who said they had not heard of birth control or abortion were not asked whether they approved, either generally or conditionally, of contraception or abortion. More rural respondents in Asian countries than other groups claimed ignorance about

group)

Abortion if dangerous to give birth	Abortion if pregnant from rape	Abortion if cannot afford another child	Abortion if pregnancy interferes with wife's work
88	81	73	26
77	88	69	33
69	80	80	54
86	75	59	22
89	73	60	34
85	71	58	38
99	90	54	26
94	91	65	20
89	92	70	36
97	93	69	25
92	88	59	17
91	72	43	25
87	66	38	14
84	58	36	10
96	67	2	4
88	29	35	14
81	32	36	14
86	25	30	9
87	63	34	15
53	42	27	19
60	43	29	15

abortion; the percentage of approval for these groups, using as a denominator only those who admitted knowledge, may be artificially elevated.

is 12 percent for middle-class Koreans and Thais. The lower class shows a similar picture, but with somewhat lower levels in Japan and Hawaii. Among rural respondents practice of contraception before the first birth is very rare, the highest figure being 16 percent in Japan. Although our sample is biased by the exclusion of couples without children, it does appear that regulation of births typically is not considered until after the first child is born. By this time couples are "locked into" the parental role, so that certain values which might affect whether or not to have children become less salient or even irrelevant (such as the opportunity costs for the mother).

It should be noted, however, that the data on first birth intervals bear little relationship to the reported timing of first use of contraception (including rhythm and withdrawal). For example, the longest birth interval among Asian respondents is shown for middle-class Thais, of whom only 12 percent reported use of contraception prior to that birth. And in Japan there are substantial differences across SES groups in early use of contraception, but very small differences in birth intervals. These discrepancies could of course be accounted for by other factors, such as frequency of intercourse, but it is likely also that there was some misreporting of contraceptive use and birth intervals.

Attitudes toward contraception and abortion

As might be expected in this sample, attitudes toward contraception are generally favorable. However, approval is tempered by the situation in which use of birth control takes place.

As shown in Table 3.4, a majority of respondents in all countries and all SES groups approved of married couples using birth control. The lowest level of approval was 58 percent, in rural Thailand. When the question was asked with respect to use of birth control to delay the birth of the first child, however, striking declines in approval are shown for Korea and the Philippines, and, to a somewhat lesser extent, for all other groups except the middle-class Caucasians and the Japanese in Hawaii. Less than one-fourth of all respondents in Korea and the Philippines approved of the practice of birth control before the birth of the first child.

Approval of abortion varies greatly from country to country. With respect to the general question of a married woman getting an abortion to prevent an unwanted birth, approval by a majority is shown only in Korea, and very low levels of approval (below 10 percent) are shown in the Philippines and Thailand. The pattern changes drastically, however, when situational considerations are introduced. In general, approval ratings run from high to low when the situations are ordered as in Table 3.4: if a doctor says it will be dangerous to give birth, if the pregnancy resulted from rape, if the couple cannot afford another baby, and if pregnancy interferes with the wife's career. This trend generally holds within countries and SES groups, but the absolute level of approval varies substantially across countries and subgroups. In comparisons across countries, the Philippines and Thailand, with their strong Catholic and Buddhist orientations, are consistently low in approval of abortion. Even in some places where abortion is legalized and accessible, however, such as Japan and Hawaii, approval of abortion is surprisingly low.

It is apparent that decisions about having children are affected by many factors in addition to the perceived satisfactions and costs of the children themselves. One of those factors is the "psychological cost" of preventing a pregnancy or birth, which is determined in part by attitudes toward contraception and abortion.

4

major dimensions
of the value of children

The main purpose of this study was to assess comprehensively the perceived satisfactions and costs of children. A comparative summary of those unique data is presented in this chapter.

Because the study was exploratory, many different types of questions were employed to measure the value of children. As discussed earlier, open-ended questions were relied on heavily to minimize instrument influences and to allow respondents to describe the satisfactions and costs of children in their own words, rather than in predetermined categories imposed by the investigators. At the same time, however, many structured questions were used, all of them based on pretest experiences in the six countries. Comparison of responses from open-ended and structured questions permits a check on measurement influences, and the structured items also provide data more suitable for certain types of statistical analysis.

It must be noted, however, that the open-ended and structured questions are not strictly comparable in meaning. The content as well as the format of the questions was varied, both to avoid redundancy in the interview and to explore a wider domain of responses. For example, an open-ended question asked about the advantages and disadvantages of having children compared with not having children; a set of structured items asked about reasons for wanting or not wanting another child; a set of attitude items asked about the degree of importance of various values associated with children. Each of these types of items gives a somewhat different perspective on the value of children, and the responses obviously cannot be directly compared. However, similarities in the *patterns* of responses to various questions can reasonably be expected, and the existence of such similarities across individuals, subgroups, and countries should enhance confidence in the validity of the overall results.

The sections that follow are organized according to the type of questions from which the responses were derived. The commentary describing the tables provides a brief summary of these extensive data on the value of children. In Chapter 6, the data from different types of questions are integrated and further interpreted.

Economic values

Much of the discussion of the value of children in the population literature focuses on economic benefits and costs. Data on economic values will therefore be shown first separately, then again in the broader context of their relationship to social and psychological dimensions of the value of children.

Economic theories of fertility suggest that, in many societies, people want children because they expect that children will contribute to the family economically. To what extent are such expectations actually held by people in different societies and different socioeconomic strata? Table 4.1 shows the scores by country on a composite index of expected economic help. The index combines several elements: expectations of practical help from sons and from daughters, degree of reliance on children for old-age support, and the importance of economic motives in wanting another child.

Table 4.1 Index of expected economic help from children
(By country and socioeconomic group)

Country	Urban middle	Urban lower	Rural
Korea	4.3	8.5	10.3
Taiwan	6.5	10.3	12.8
Japan	3.1	4.3	7.8
U.S. (Hawaii)			
Japanese	6.5	7.2	na
Caucasian	5.1	6.3	na
Filipino	na	12.5	15.6
Philippines	11.8	12.7	15.0
Thailand	7.3	13.5	14.3

NOTE: Index was constructed by combining five structured items on economic help expected from children both in the parents' old age and before parents grow old. The range of possible scores is from 0 (no help expected) to 17 (a great deal of help expected).

na—not applicable because subsample did not include persons in this socioeconomic group.

Expectations of economic help from children are shown to be highest for rural respondents in all countries, and the scores for urban lower-class respondents are consistently between rural and urban middle-class scores. Comparing across countries, economic expectations are highest among Filipino respondents, both in the Philippines and in Hawaii. The next highest scores are shown for Thailand and Taiwan. Economic expectations are lowest in Japan. Urban middle-class respondents generally do not have high expectations of economic help from children, but the Philippines is an exception: economic values appear to be important for all Filipino respondents.

Table 4.2 has a narrower focus—reliance on children for old-age support—and the data shown are percentages of respondents who express such an expectation. The pattern is similar to the more general index of Table 4.1. In all countries, more than 70 percent of rural respondents expect to rely on their children when they are old. Among urban lower-class respondents, more than half expect old-age support, except in Japan and among Japanese and Caucasians in Hawaii. Expectations are again distinctly high for the middle class in the Philippines, and old-age support emerges as important also for the middle class in Taiwan.

These data demonstrate clearly that children are viewed as having

Table 4.2 Percentage of respondents who expected to rely on children for financial support in old age
(By country and socioeconomic group)

Country	Urban middle	Urban lower	Rural
Korea	25	62	72
Taiwan	47	80	92
Japan	29	31	73
U.S. (Hawaii)			
Japanese	19	25	na
Caucasian	2	23	na
Filipino	na	62	80
Philippines	73	82	89
Thailand	26	83	90

NOTE: Table is based on the percentage of respondents who answered either "a little" or "a good deal" to a structured question about how much they expected to rely on their children in old age, or who mentioned children in response to an open-ended question about sources of old-age support.

na—not applicable because subsample did not include persons in this socioeconomic group.

economic value by large numbers of parents in different societies, and the results show also the expected inverse relationship between socioeconomic status and expected economic help, with particularly strong expectations of help expressed by parents in rural settings.

Theoretically, it would be useful to have an index of the perceived net economic value of a child—the algebraic sum of expected benefits minus expected costs over time. In this study, no such formulation is attempted. Benefits and costs are measured and analyzed separately, and perhaps rather crudely. In all countries, it was found in pretests that respondents were either unable or unwilling to discuss in detailed terms the financial aspects of childrearing. Most parents appeared to have little notion of what it actually costs to raise a child, and many were reluctant to discuss children as if they were consumer goods. In this study economic measures, particularly for costs of children, are couched in rather general terms; that is, components of costs and benefits are not fully specified and relationships to aspects such as age and "quality" of the child are not explored.

Table 4.3 shows results for a global measure of the costs of children that appears to be meaningful. The question attempts to relate the resources of the family to the costs of different numbers of children by asking whether one child (two, three, etc.) would be fairly easy to raise economically, somewhat of a financial burden, or a heavy financial burden. Table 4.3 indicates the percentage of respondents who believed that three or fewer children would be a heavy financial burden.

Table 4.3 Percentage of respondents who believed that three or fewer children would be a heavy financial burden
(By country and socioeconomic group)

Country	Urban middle	Urban lower	Rural
Korea	53	72	55
Taiwan	26	33	41
Japan	24	39	24
U.S. (Hawaii)			
Japanese	18	18	na
Caucasian	17	15	na
Filipino	na	19	25
Philippines	10	17	7
Thailand	41	43	38

na—not applicable because subsample did not include persons in this socioeconomic group.

Only in Korea did a majority of parents consider as many as three children a heavy burden financially. Perceived economic pressures are relatively high in Thailand, but even there only about 40 percent of parents, regardless of socioeconomic group, said that three (or fewer) children would cause a heavy financial burden for the family. Filipinos generally showed the lowest perceived costs of children (as well as the highest perceived benefits, as discussed earlier).

The data suggest a curvilinear relationship between perceived costs and socioeconomic status: in Korea, Japan, the Philippines, and Thailand, the urban lower class showed a higher sensitivity to costs than either the middle-class or the rural respondents. Lower-class respondents are exposed to many of the same high urban cost factors as the middle class while having less income, and compared to the rural group they presumably face higher costs and also receive fewer benefits. The last factor—expected economic benefits—may of course have entered into respondents' calculations of economic burden, which would affect particularly the rural group. This source of influence would not change the meaning of the results, but caution in interpreting Table 4.3 is indicated for other reasons.

Correlational analyses using an index based on these data, which are presented later, show that the perceived financial ease of raising a larger family correlates positively with both income and parity. This finding suggests that responses do reflect an assessment of the costs of children in relation to financial resources, but may reflect also a rationalization of an existing family size—parents with a large number of children may be reluctant to say that their children cause a heavy financial burden. Of course, it may also be true that those who choose to have a large family, for whatever reasons, really do not feel that children are a financial burden. In any event, the complex interactions of this variable with others demonstrate that it cannot be considered simply as an antecedent factor influencing family-size decisions. As with other dimensions of the value of children, the perceived economic burden must be regarded as both a cause and an effect of fertility: values are one of the factors influencing childbearing decisions, but prior fertility experience also has an effect on values. These interactions should be borne in mind when interpreting the descriptive findings below. Causal relationships are discussed further in Chapters 5 and 6.

Salient general values

Under this heading are included the full range of satisfactions and costs of children that are derived from questions not linked specifically to number of children or sex of child—that is, responses concerning the general reasons or motivations for having and not having children. Data of this type were obtained from open-ended questions and from structured attitude scales. Both economic and noneconomic dimensions of the value of children are included.

To handle the responses to open-ended questions, a coding scheme for content analysis was developed cooperatively by the investigators. This coding scheme is shown in Exhibit 4.1; examples of the type of responses included in each code category are shown in Appendix C. The coding scheme contains 49 specific advantages or satisfactions, organized under nine major headings, and 25 specific disadvantages or costs, organized under eight major headings. Content analyses were conducted independently by two coders in each country and discrepancies were resolved with the assistance of a third person, usually the investigator. Responses were always coded into the specific categories, but in the analyses these categories were sometimes collapsed and the simpler set of major code headings was used.

At the beginning of the interview respondents were asked to describe in their own words the advantages and disadvantages of having children, compared to not having any children, and to rank the advantages and disadvantages that were most important to them. Tables 4.4 and 4.5 show the major code headings under which the first-ranked advantages and disadvantages were coded, for respondents in each socioeconomic group in each country.

Table 4.4 reveals that the emotional satisfactions of having children—happiness, love, companionship—were ranked first in importance by a substantial percentage of respondents in all countries, particularly the urban respondents. By contrast, economic benefits and security were more often given first ranking by rural respondents.

In general, the psychologically oriented satisfactions, including personal development of the parent and childrearing satisfactions as well as the emotional gratifications such as happiness, were viewed as more important by the better-educated middle class. It is of interest to note also that benefits to the family unit, which pertain mainly to cohesion of the nuclear family, were of greater importance to respondents living in the impersonal social context of urban areas.

Consistent with data from other questions discussed earlier, middle-class respondents in the Philippines gave greater importance to economic benefits and security than did middle-class respondents in other countries. Concern with economic benefits was highest in Thailand and among Filipinos, for all socioeconomic groups.

Kin group benefits (notably continuity of family name and ancestor

Exhibit 4.1 Major code categories and specific code categories used in the content analysis of responses: advantages and disadvantages of having children

---

ADVANTAGES

Happiness, love, companionship

Companionship, avoidance of loneliness
Love, affection
Play, fun with children; avoidance of boredom
Relief from strain, distraction from problems
Happiness for individual parent (general)
Happiness for family
Uniqueness, specialness in parent-child relationship

Personal development of parent

Character development, responsibility, maturity, morality
Incentives to succeed, striving to provide for children
Fulfillment of self, completeness as person
Extension of self
Learning from experience of childrearing
Motherhood, fatherhood; adulthood
Proof of fertility, masculinity, femininity

Childrearing satisfactions

Pride in children's accomplishments
Pleasure from growth, development of children
Children to carry out parent's hopes, aspirations
Opportunity to teach, guide, instill values
Satisfaction in one's childrearing ability, accomplishment
Satisfaction in providing for children

Economic benefits, security

Economic help in old age
Companionship, comfort, care in old age
Unspecified help in old age
Economic help (old age not mentioned)
Comfort, care (old age not mentioned)
Help in housework, family chores; practical help
Sharing financial responsibility; insurance, security
Help in family business, farm
Help in taking care of other children
Unspecified help (old age not mentioned)

Exhibit 4.1 *(continued)*

Benefits to family unit

Children as bond between spouses
Children as reason for, fulfillment of marriage
Children as family life, complete or close-knit family

Kin group benefits

Continuity of family name
Continuity of family traditions
Enhancement of reputation of family
Having future grandchildren
Children as heirs, someone to inherit family wealth
Religious rituals, ancestor worship
To increase strength, power of kin group
To satisfy desires of spouse
To satisfy desires of other kin

Social, religious influences

Conformity to social norms
Conformity to religious norms
Children as benefits to society

General, intrinsic value of children

Children as treasure, wealth, assets
Instinctive, natural to have children
General wanting, liking children

Other advantages

DISADVANTAGES

Financial costs

Educational costs
General financial costs

Emotional costs

Responsibility of parenthood
Discipline, moral behavior
Health problems of children
Concern over children's future success, happiness
Concern about satisfying children's present wants
Noise, disorder, nuisance
General rearing problems
General emotional strain

Exhibit 4.1 *(continued)*

Physical demands on parents

Health hazard of pregnancy; maternal health
Physical work, tiredness caused by children

Restrictions on alternative activities

Restrictions on time
Restrictions on travel
Restrictions on social life, recreation
Restrictions on job, career
Restrictions on personal wants
Restrictions on privacy
General lack of flexibility, freedom

Marital problems

Less time, interaction between spouses
Disagreements over children
General marital problems

Kin group costs, problems of inheritance

Disadvantages relating to, affecting kin group

Societal costs, overpopulation

Disadvantages relating to, affecting society; concern about overpopulation

Other disadvantages

---

worship) were especially important in Taiwan and, to lesser degrees, in Korea and Thailand. In none of the countries did respondents rank social or religious influences as important reasons for having children.

With respect to disadvantages of having children (Table 4.5), three types stand out in importance: financial costs, emotional costs, and opportunity costs (restrictions on alternative activities). Rural respondents tended to rate either financial costs or emotional costs as most important, except in Japan (where rural respondents rated opportunity costs as more important than financial costs) and Thailand (where rural respondents rated physical demands as more important than emotional costs). Urban lower-class respondents showed a pattern similar to the rural, except that they consistently elevated opportunity costs to somewhat higher levels of importance. Among the middle class, emotional costs or opportunity costs were of greatest importance to respondents in most countries; in the Philippines and Thailand, however, opportunity costs were not important and financial costs were relatively more important.

Only in rural Thailand were physical demands on parents of great importance, and only in urban Korea did a substantial number of respondents cite marital problems as an important disadvantage of having children. Societal costs, such as overpopulation, were hardly ever cited as a general disadvantage, possibly because this open-ended question was posed with a personal frame of reference.

Results for the specific code categories, from which the data cited above were derived, are presented in Appendix Tables D1 to D4. These detailed results are not discussed here, but they are incorporated in the discussion of findings in Chapter 6 and are examined fully in each country report.

Table 4.6 shows responses for a different type of open-ended question: "In your opinion, what are the main reasons why people around here want children?" This question was designed to elicit perceived norms rather than personal motivations, but it probably functioned also as a projective technique and the responses may reflect in part personal motivations that people are reluctant to attribute to themselves. In this table the specific code categories are used rather than the major code headings. In comparison with the question on personal advantages, three aspects of the results in Table 4.6 are noteworthy: the motivation "continuity of family name" was attributed to others more than to self, particularly in Korea and Taiwan; the idea that it is "instinctive or natural" to have children emerges; and security and old-age support were perceived to be particularly important by the rural respondents and, to a lesser degree, by the urban lower class, consistent with data presented earlier from both structured and open-ended questions.

Attitude scales were used as another approach to measurement of the general satisfactions and costs of children. The conceptual scheme that was originally used to organize the 45 attitude items was subsequently modified on an empirical basis by relying heavily on a factor analysis of the aggregate sample of 2,591 cases as well as separate factor analyses by country and by socioeconomic group. By these means, nine VOC attitude scales were constructed for use in the comparative analysis. The scales include 31 of the 45 items in the questionnaire.

The items constituting each scale are shown in Table 4.7, along with the mean score for each item in each country. In Table 4.8, the mean scores for each of the nine scales are shown by socioeconomic group.

Table 4.4 Advantages of having children
(Percentage of respondents who assigned first ranking to country)

SES group and country	Major code category			
	Happiness, love, companionship	Personal development of parent	Childrearing satisfactions	Economic benefits, security
URBAN MIDDLE				
Korea	34	10	29	3
Taiwan	62	4	5	3
Japan	37	19	24	2
U.S. (Hawaii)				
Japanese	26	18	18	1
Caucasian	37	21	16	2
Philippines	38	11	4	30
Thailand	34	17	3	6
URBAN LOWER				
Korea	42	8	18	11
Taiwan	39	1	4	9
Japan	54	10	14	3
U.S. (Hawaii)				
Japanese	29	16	21	3
Caucasian	33	17	18	2
Filipino	62	3	3	15
Philippines	24	9	7	46
Thailand	15	4	1	66
RURAL				
Korea	27	9	19	21
Taiwan	19	1	11	36
Japan	44	9	20	11
U.S. (Hawaii)				
Filipino	25	4	1	63
Philippines	23	6	7	60
Thailand	14	2	*	60

* Less than 1 percent.

each of specific major code categories, by socioeconomic group and

Benefits to family unit	Kin group benefits	Social, religious influences	General, intrinsic value of children	Other advantages
9	10	1	3	*
13	10	2	2	*
14	3	1	*	*
20	1	1	9	2
14	1	1	3	*
12	1	1	2	*
28	9	2	1	1
8	12	0	1	1
3	40	1	2	1
17	1	2	*	*
20	1	*	4	*
16	2	1	1	*
11	2	*	2	*
7	4	1	2	*
3	8	2	*	1
2	17	3	2	*
4	25	2	1	*
5	7	1	2	*
4	1	*	1	*
2	*	2	*	*
3	17	3	*	*

Table 4.5 Disadvantages of having children
(Percentage of respondents who assigned first ranking to country)

SES group and country	Major code category		
	Financial costs	Emotional costs	Physical demands on parents
URBAN MIDDLE			
Korea	20	35	4
Taiwan	17	53	5
Japan	10	30	2
U.S. (Hawaii)			
Japanese	8	26	1
Caucasian	16	25	2
Philippines	29	54	3
Thailand	32	51	8
URBAN LOWER			
Korea	41	41	3
Taiwan	35	47	5
Japan	8	41	3
U.S. (Hawaii)			
Japanese	22	18	3
Caucasian	20	30	*
Filipino	30	32	7
Philippines	34	50	1
Thailand	50	32	5
RURAL			
Korea	42	44	4
Taiwan	49	34	9
Japan	14	53	2
U.S. (Hawaii)			
Filipino	81	11	2
Philippines	39	51	4
Thailand	42	21	28

* Less than 1 percent.

each of specified major code categories, by socioeconomic group and

Restrictions on alternative activities	Marital problems	Kin group costs, problems of inheritance	Societal costs, over-population	Other disadvantages
28	12	*	*	1
25	*	*	*	*
50	8	*	*	*
35	2	*	*	*
39	5	*	*	2
12	1	*	*	1
7	*	1	*	1
13	1	*	*	1
14	*	*	*	*
48	*	*	*	*
38	4	*	*	*
21	5	1	*	2
20	*	*	*	*
13	1	*	*	1
12	*	*	*	2
8	1	*	*	1
9	*	*	*	*
28	1	1	1	*
1	*	*	*	1
6	*	*	*	*
9	*	*	*	*

Table 4.6 Why people want children
(Five most frequently mentioned reasons ranked according to percentage of respondents mentioning them, by socioeconomic group and country)

SES group and country	1 Reason	%	2 Reason	%	3 Reason	%	4 Reason	%	5 Reason	%
URBAN MIDDLE										
Korea	Continuity of family name	33	Happiness for family	32	Instinctive, natural to have children	18	Satisfaction in one's childrearing ability, accomplishment	18	Having future grandchildren	14
Taiwan	Continuity of family name	49	Don't know	40	Companionship, avoidance of loneliness	16	Unspecified help in old age	13	Instinctive, natural to have children	8
Japan	Happiness for family	16	Prime value in life	15	Instinctive, natural to have children	14	Children as family life, complete or close-knit family	14	Children as heirs, someone to inherit family wealth	14
U.S. (Hawaii) Japanese	General wanting, liking children	31	Children as family life, complete or close-knit family	21	Companionship, avoidance of loneliness	20	Don't know	13	Children as reason for, fulfillment of marriage	13
Caucasian	Don't know	18	General wanting, liking children	18	Instinctive, natural to have children	17	Continuity of family name	16	Other people's reasons same as respondent's	15
Philippines	Happiness for family	35	Companionship, comfort, care in old age	28	Play, fun with children; avoidance of boredom	25	Help in housework, family chores; practical help	22	Happiness for individual parent, general responses	16
Thailand	Don't know	30	Continuity of family name	20	No reason given	17	Happiness for family	13	Companionship, avoidance of loneliness	12

	1		2		3		4		5	
URBAN LOWER										
Korea	Continuity of family name	53	Happiness for family	26	Instinctive, natural to have children	17	Pleasure from growth, development of children	14	Companionship, comfort, care in old age	12
Taiwan	Continuity of family name	75	Unspecified help in old age	26	Instinctive, natural to have children	10	Companionship, avoidance of loneliness	9	Don't know	9
Japan	Happiness for family	21	General wanting, liking children	15	Don't know	15	Instinctive, natural to have children	13	Children as heirs, someone to inherit family wealth	10
									Prime value in life[a]	10
U.S. (Hawaii)										
Japanese	General wanting, liking children	32	Continuity of family name	25	Companionship, avoidance of loneliness	24	Instinctive, natural to have children	17	Children as family life, complete or close-knit family	15
Caucasian	General wanting, liking children	26	Love, affection	19	Children as family life, complete or close-knit family	16	Don't know	15	Instinctive, natural to have children	13
Filipino	Happiness for individual parent (general)	49	Companionship, avoidance of loneliness	29	Children as reason for, fulfillment of marriage	17	Unspecified help in old age	16	Continuity of family name	10
Philippines	Happiness for family	40	Companionship, comfort, care in old age	36	Help in housework, family chores; practical help	24	Play, fun with children; avoidance of boredom	17	Unspecified help (old age not mentioned)	13
Thailand	Don't know	26	Continuity of family name	18	Unspecified help in old age	17	No reason given	14	Companionship, avoidance of loneliness	11
RURAL										
Korea	Continuity of family name	59	Companionship, comfort, care in old age	17	Conformity to social norms	13	Proof of fertility, masculinity, femininity	12	Pride in children's accomplishments	10
									Economic help in old age	10

Table 4.6 (continued)

SES group and country	1 Reason	%	2 Reason	%	3 Reason	%	4 Reason	%	5 Reason	%
RURAL (continued)										
Taiwan	Continuity of family name	56	Unspecified help in old age	32	Don't know	9	Companionship, avoidance of loneliness	6	Conformity to social norms	6
									Instinctive natural to have children	6
Japan	Children as heirs, someone to inherit family wealth	32	Prime value in life	22	Happiness for family	22	Companionship, avoidance of loneliness	11	Happiness for individual parent	9
U.S. (Hawaii) Filipino	Companionship, avoidance of loneliness	67	Unspecified help in old age	44	Happiness for individual parent (general)	43	Love, affection	11	Continuity of family name	6
Philippines	Companionship, comfort, care in old age	32	Happiness for family	27	Help in housework, family chores; practical help	20	Economic help (old age not mentioned)	20	Play, fun with children; avoidance of boredom	17
Thailand	Continuity of family name	38	Companionship, comfort, care in old age	19	Help in housework, family chores; practical help	18	Don't know	18	No reason given	14

NOTE: Responses have been coded by category (see Exhibit 4.1). In cases where two or more reasons were mentioned by the same percentage of respondents, identical ranking is indicated by the omission of vertical rules.

a Translated from the Japanese expression *ikï-gai*–literally, "one's life worthwhile." The response is similar to the English expression "goals and incentives from children," but because it implies an emphasis on present satisfactions from raising children it has been coded as a country-specific response category.

SOURCE: Derived from a content analysis of responses to question 73 of the VOC questionnaire.

Table 4.7 Mean scores on 45 VOC attitude items
(By subscale and country)

Scale and items	Korea	Taiwan	Japan	U.S. (Hawaii)	Philippines	Thailand	Grand mean
Continuity, tradition, security (VOC Scale 1)							
A good reason for having children is that they can help when parents are too old to work	4.6	5.1	2.7	4.1	6.3	6.0	4.8
It is important to have children so that the family traditions will live on	6.2	6.3	4.7	5.0	6.3	6.0	5.8
One of the best things about having children is the true loyalty they show to their parents	3.9	5.8	4.1	5.3	6.4	6.6	5.4
A man has a duty to have children to continue the family name	5.9	6.3	4.0	4.4	6.1	6.6	5.6
A person can feel that part of him lives on after death if he has children	5.5	5.7	4.8	5.5	6.4	6.6	5.8
Parenthood satisfactions (VOC Scale 2)							
Just the feeling a parent gets of being needed is enough to make having children worthwhile	6.0	5.8	5.6	5.6	6.4	6.0	5.9
A person who has been a good parent can feel completely satisfied with his achievements in life	5.9	6.1	5.5	6.1	6.5	6.3	6.1
One of the best things about being a parent is the chance to teach children what they should do and what they should not do	6.3	6.3	5.4	5.8	6.6	6.4	6.1
Role motivations (VOC Scale 3)							
It is only natural that a man should want children	6.3	6.2	5.9	5.3	6.6	5.9	6.0
A girl becomes a woman only after she is a mother	5.8	5.8	5.4	3.7	6.2	6.5	5.6

Table 4.7 (continued)

Scale and items	Country and mean score						Grand mean
	Korea	Taiwan	Japan	U.S. (Hawaii)	Philippines	Thailand	
After becoming a parent, a person is less likely to behave immorally	5.9	5.4	6.1	3.7	5.0	5.4	5.2
It is only natural that a woman should want children	6.1	6.2	6.0	5.6	6.5	6.2	6.0
A boy becomes a man only after he is a father	5.5	5.5	4.4	3.2	5.8	6.2	5.1
Happiness and affection (VOC Scale 4)							
It is only with a child that a person can feel completely free to express his love and affection	5.5	5.6	5.8	3.7	5.8	6.4	5.5
The family with children is the only place in the modern world where a person can feel comfortable and happy	5.7	6.1	2.9	3.9	6.0	6.1	5.1
A person who has no children can never really be happy	5.1	4.6	3.6	2.6	4.5	6.0	4.4
Goals and incentives (VOC Scale 5)							
Having children gives a person a special incentive to succeed in life	6.6	6.3	6.7	6.0	6.4	6.5	6.4
Having children around makes a stronger bond between husband and wife	5.8	6.0	6.2	5.9	6.8	6.7	6.2
One of the highest purposes of life is to have children	6.3	5.0	5.8	5.4	6.6	6.4	5.9
Social status (VOC Scale 6)							
A young couple is not fully accepted in the community until they have children	5.0	4.4	2.5	2.2	3.1	4.1	3.6
A person with children is looked up to in the community more than a person without children	5.1	4.7	3.0	2.8	4.5	5.0	4.2

External control (VOC Scale 7)

Considering the pressures from family and friends, a person really doesn't have much choice whether or not to have children	2.9	3.1	2.8	1.9	3.5	3.1	2.9
It isn't right for a couple to interfere with nature by deciding to limit the number of children they will have	2.6	2.5	5.1	2.3	3.9	3.8	3.4

Costs of children (VOC Scale 8)

Children limit you in what you want to do and where you want to go	5.0	4.7	4.5	5.0	4.3	5.2	4.8
Having children causes many disagreements and problems between husband and wife	4.8	3.2	3.0	3.8	3.5	4.3	3.8
Raising children is a heavy financial burden for most people	5.9	5.7	4.8	4.8	5.4	6.3	5.5
When you have children, you have to give up a lot of other things that you enjoy	4.7	4.9	4.3	4.8	5.5	6.1	5.0

Decision-mindedness (VOC Scale 9)

A couple ought to think seriously about the inconveniences caused by children before they have any	5.0	4.8	5.8	4.6	5.8	5.5	5.2
The first thing a couple should think about when deciding to have children is whether or not they can afford it	5.5	5.9	5.1	5.0	6.3	5.6	5.6
Before having a child, a couple should consider whether they would rather use their money for something else	3.5	3.6	2.5	3.0	5.4	3.7	3.6
Before having a child, a couple should consider whether it would interfere with the wife's work or not	4.0	4.6	4.2	3.2	4.3	4.7	4.2

NOTE: Possible scores range from 1 (strongly disagree) to 7 (strongly agree).

Table 4.8 Mean scores on VOC attitude scales
(By socioeconomic group and country)

SES group and country	Attitude scales[a]		
	1 Continuity, tradition, security	2 Parenthood satisfactions	3 Role motivations
URBAN MIDDLE			
Korea	4.2	6.2	5.8
Taiwan	5.1	5.7	5.4
Japan	3.6	5.2	5.4
U.S. (Hawaii)			
Japanese	4.0	5.4	3.6
Caucasian	3.4	4.9	3.2
Philippines	6.0	6.6	5.9
Thailand	5.9	6.1	5.6
URBAN LOWER			
Korea	5.5	6.0	5.9
Taiwan	6.1	6.2	5.8
Japan	3.6	5.4	5.6
U.S. (Hawaii)			
Japanese	4.6	5.8	3.8
Caucasian	4.2	5.8	3.8
Filipino	6.0	6.3	4.9
Philippines	6.2	6.4	5.9
Thailand	6.6	6.3	6.2
RURAL			
Korea	5.9	6.0	6.0
Taiwan	6.4	6.2	6.2
Japan	4.9	5.7	5.7
U.S. (Hawaii)			
Filipino	6.9	6.9	6.3
Philippines	6.6	6.6	6.3
Thailand	6.7	6.4	6.4

NOTE: Possible scores range from 1 (strongly disagree) to 7 (strongly agree).

a   See Table 4.7 for the items contained in each scale.

4 Happiness and affection	5 Goals and incentives	6 Social status	7 External control	8 Costs of children	9 Decision- mindedness
5.2	6.4	4.1	2.0	5.0	4.3
4.9	5.4	3.8	2.4	4.6	5.0
3.9	6.0	2.7	3.9	4.2	4.3
3.1	5.3	2.4	1.7	4.4	4.4
2.4	4.8	2.4	1.9	4.5	4.5
5.4	6.6	3.3	3.5	4.5	5.2
6.0	6.6	3.3	2.1	5.5	4.4
5.7	6.2	5.4	2.9	5.2	4.5
5.6	6.0	4.8	3.1	4.6	4.4
3.8	6.2	2.7	4.2	4.4	4.4
3.6	5.6	2.1	2.1	4.6	4.6
3.5	5.5	2.5	2.0	4.5	4.3
5.1	6.5	3.4	3.0	4.6	3.8
5.2	6.5	3.7	3.8	4.8	5.2
6.2	6.4	4.9	4.0	5.4	5.1
5.3	6.1	5.6	3.3	5.2	4.7
5.7	5.9	5.2	2.8	4.8	4.8
4.6	6.4	2.9	3.9	3.8	4.4
1.8	6.8	1.3	1.4	5.2	1.7
5.7	6.6	4.4	3.8	4.7	5.9
6.2	6.5	5.4	4.2	5.6	5.2

and country. Appendix Tables D5 and D6 indicate the interscale correlations and the item-total correlations for each scale by country.

Most of the items and scales represent positive values or satisfactions and, partly for that reason, the mean scores shown in Tables 4.7 and 4.8 tend to be high. (The possible scores range from 7 for strongly agree to 1 for strongly disagree.) It is likely also that the scores are influenced by elements of social desirability and acquiescence, the extent of which would presumably vary across groups. Since reliability of the scales was not assessed, the results for these attitude scales must be interpreted with caution, particularly with respect to differences in level of responses across countries. In this section the content and structure of the scales are examined and the pattern of results is discussed in relation to results from other measures of similar dimensions of the value of children. In Chapter 5 the VOC scales are correlated with other variables and are used in regression analyses that compare the predictive power of different types of measures.

The first six scales deal with various benefits to the parent from having children; the scales are positively intercorrelated in all countries, although at widely differing levels. In the first scale—*continuity, tradition, security*—children are seen as a means for transmitting the family name and traditions, as being loyal to the parents and providing a sense of immortality, and as a source of help in old age. The scale on *parenthood satisfactions* includes the sense of achievement from being a good parent, the satisfaction of providing guidance to children, and the feeling of being needed. *Role motivations* encompass the "naturalness" of wanting children, the connection between parenthood and adulthood (becoming a man or a woman), and the responsibility and maturity that come with being a parent. The *happiness and affection* items include the parent's expression of love for the child and the general sense of happiness associated with children and family life. *Goals and incentives* from children refer to the ideal of serving a higher purpose in life by having children and to the more concrete notions of children binding the spouses together and providing an incentive for accomplishment in life. The *social status* items refer to the acceptance and respect that couples obtain from the community by having children.

The remaining three scales deal with dimensions other than satisfactions and generally are not highly correlated with the first six scales, although there are notable exceptions. *External controls* consist of two dimensions: pressure from others for childbearing and a moralistic or fatalistic view against birth limitation. This scale, it should be noted, is positively correlated with the social status scale in all countries. The *costs of children* are broadly defined to include opportunity costs, financial costs, and emotional costs to the marital relationship. *Decision-mindedness* refers to the propensity to consider costs of various kinds in making decisions about having children, and this scale is positively correlated with the scale on costs.

As noted above, the scores for the attitude items tend to be positive (above the midpoint of 4), reflecting agreement with the preponderance of statements describing the benefits of children. Substantial variation is shown across countries, however. In Hawaii, 39 percent of the items show a mean score indicating disagreement; Japan and Korea have the next highest levels of disagreement (23 percent and 16 percent), with the remaining countries even lower. Thus, the degree to which the scales are "balanced" with positive and negative items varies, and these differences may be due in part to the differential influence of response sets.

The correlational structure of the scales, on the other hand, is rather similar across countries, as shown by the item-total correlations in Appendix Table D6. The range across nine scales of mean item-total correlations is as follows: Korea, .62–.86; Taiwan, .62–.86; Japan, .61–.82; Hawaii, .67–.88; Philippines, .63–.83; Thailand, .60–.87. There is then a reasonably strong clustering of items for each scale, although exceptions for particular items in particular countries may be noted in Appendix Table D6.

The data from the nine attitude scales, shown in Table 4.8, are generally consistent with the data from open-ended questions presented earlier. For middle-class parents, the highest scores are shown for the psychologically oriented dimensions, such as "parenthood satisfactions" and "goals and incentives." Rural parents, by contrast, have very high scores on the scale labeled "continuity, tradition, security" (except in Japan), as well as on the scales for psychological satisfactions. The scores on "continuity, tradition, security" are generally lowest in Japan and highest in the Philippines. The pattern for the urban lower class generally falls between the middle class and the rural. It is of interest to note that relatively little variation across groups is shown for the scales on "costs of children" and "decision-mindedness" (the latter of which contains a strong component of financial costs), although there is a tendency for higher scores going from middle class to lower class to rural, which again is consistent with the open-ended responses.[1] The influence of external forces–"social status" and

---

1 Scores on some scales for rural Filipinos in Hawaii seem inconsistent with other data for this group and may reflect errors in the translation into Ilocano (see Arnold and Fawcett, 1975).

"external controls"—is rejected by most respondents, although social status shows somewhat greater strength among lower-class and rural respondents (compared to the middle class) and appears to be more important in Japan, Taiwan, and Thailand than in other countries. External influences were seldom mentioned in the open-ended questions. "Role motivations"—traditional sex roles and parental roles— were accepted by most respondents (except Japanese and Caucasians in Hawaii), and scores tend to be slightly higher among low SES and rural respondents, as would be expected.

Son and daughter preference

All the results discussed above pertain to the satisfactions and costs of children in general. While parents obviously do think about children and value them in such broad terms, they also value sons and daughters differently. This section explores both the extent of such sex preferences and the motives behind them.

Respondents were asked, "How important is it for you to have at least one (boy/girl) among your children?" Table 4.9 shows the percentage replying "very important" for sons and for daughters, in each socioeconomic group in the six countries. Probably the best indicator of son preference in these data is the difference between the percentage for son and daughter. In all cases, the percentage saying "very im-

Table 4.9 Importance of sons and daughters
(Percentage of respondents who said it is "very important" to have a son or daughter among their children, by country and socioeconomic group)

Country	Urban middle		Urban lower		Rural	
	Son	Daughter	Son	Daughter	Son	Daughter
Korea	78	61	94	55	96	69
Taiwan	74	41	91	51	93	57
Japan	72	67	70	64	79	65
U.S. (Hawaii)						
Japanese	55	49	58	53	na	na
Caucasian	39	38	65	55	na	na
Filipino	na	na	96	90	100	67
Philippines	96	89	86	80	96	94
Thailand	86	72	80	61	83	67

na—not applicable because subsample did not include persons in this socioeconomic group.

portant" is higher for sons. The greatest differences are shown for Korea and Taiwan; substantial differences are shown also for Thailand. In the Philippines, the absolute level of this response is very high, but almost equally so for sons and for daughters. Rural Filipinos in Hawaii, however, had a preference for sons. Caucasians and Japanese in Hawaii showed both a low absolute level of response and little difference between sons and daughters. Responses for Japan were somewhat higher than those for Hawaii in level but with a substantial difference favoring sons only among rural respondents.

Respondents were also asked what they would do if they did not have any sons and kept having daughters: would they continue having babies until they had a boy or would they stop after a certain number of girls? Table 4.10 shows the percentage in each group who would continue until they had a boy and, for the remaining respondents, the mean number of girls they would have before stopping.

Generally, very few middle-class respondents said they would continue having daughters indefinitely, but in all countries they indicated that they would persist in efforts to have a son up to about three daughters (3.7 in the Philippines). For lower-class and rural respondents in Asian countries, except Japan, from about one-fourth to one-half of respondents said they would persist indefinitely in efforts to have a son. From these data, son preference is lowest overall in Japan and Hawaii, and it is about equally low for urban respondents in Korea, Taiwan, and Thailand. The responses in the Philippines presumably are elevated by the generally high level of desired family size in that country.

Another index of son preference was constructed by combining information about whether the respondent would want the first child to be a boy or a girl and the proportion of boys and girls in the respondent's ideal family. Scores on that index, where 7 represents a strong preference for boys and 1 represents a strong preference for girls, are shown in Table 4.11. While the differences shown by this index are not large, the scores based on family composition do indicate some preference for sons in every group and do confirm the stronger preference for sons among lower-class and rural respondents in Korea and Taiwan.

To explore the motivations related to sex preference, respondents were asked a simple open-ended question: "Why is it important to you to have a (boy/girl)?" The content-analyzed responses are presented in Tables 4.12 and 4.13.

Continuity of family name was overwhelmingly the most frequently

Table 4.10 Persistence to have sons

(Percentage who would continue having daughters until a son came and, for those who would stop, mean number of daughters before stopping, by country and socio-economic group)

Country and SES group	Percentage who would continue having daughters	Mean number of daughters before stopping
Korea		
Urban middle	2	2.9
Urban lower	26	3.0
Rural	41	3.5
Taiwan		
Urban middle	7	2.8
Urban lower	28	3.1
Rural	24	3.3
Japan		
Urban middle	11	2.9
Urban lower	11	2.7
Rural	4	2.8
U.S. (Hawaii)		
Japanese		
Urban middle	2	3.1
Urban lower	0	3.1
Caucasian		
Urban middle	4	2.9
Urban lower	9	3.0
Filipino		
Urban lower	18	3.3
Rural	51	3.4
Philippines		
Urban middle	19	3.7
Urban lower	27	3.6
Rural	33	3.9
Thailand		
Urban middle	11	3.0
Urban lower	33	3.2
Rural	47	3.3

cited reason for wanting a boy, except in Japan and among rural respondents in the Philippines (Table 4.12). Old-age support and various types of economic and practical help were also cited often. In Thailand, conformity to religious norms ("making merit") was important for lower-class and rural respondents. Except in Japan and Hawaii, sons were wanted mainly to serve long-term economic, social, or religious functions. Emphasis on the psychological satisfactions of sons while they are children—companionship for the father, behavioral and personality traits—appeared mainly in Japan and among Japanese and Caucasians in Hawaii.

Daughters, on the other hand, were wanted everywhere mainly for the psychological satisfactions and practical help they provide while they are still children and remain with the family (Table 4.13). Companionship for the mother, behavioral and personality traits, help with housework—these were by far the most frequently cited reasons for wanting daughters, presumably reflecting universal aspects of female sex-role prescriptions. It is also noteworthy that the sex ratio in the family was often mentioned with respect to daughters—that is, they were wanted not so much for intrinsic qualities but to provide a "proper" ratio of boys and girls. Economic support and old-age security were rarely mentioned in connection with daughters, although

Table 4.11 Index of son preference
(Based on desire for first child to be a son and proportion of boys in ideal family composition, by socioeconomic group and country)

Country	Urban middle	Urban lower	Rural
Korea	4.5	4.7	4.7
Taiwan	4.4	4.6	4.6
Japan	4.2	4.3	4.3
U.S. (Hawaii)			
Japanese	4.1	4.1	na
Caucasian	4.1	4.4	na
Filipino	na	4.2	4.2
Philippines	4.2	4.2	4.1
Thailand	4.4	4.3	4.3

NOTE: Index ranges from 1 (strong preference for daughters) to 7 (strong preference for sons).

na—not applicable because subsample did not include persons in this socioeconomic group.

Table 4.12 Reasons for wanting boys

(Five most frequently mentioned reasons ranked according to percentage of respondents mentioning them, by socioeconomic group and country)

SES group and country	1 Reason	%	2 Reason	%	3 Reason	%	4 Reason	%	5 Reason	%
URBAN MIDDLE										
Korea	Continuity of family name	49	Comfort, care (old age not mentioned)	33	Continuity of family traditions	16	Conformity to social norms	10	Having future grandchildren	9
Taiwan	Continuity of family name	69	Unspecified help in old age	8	Unspecified help (old age not mentioned)	7	Conformity to social norms	7	Satisfy desires of other kin	7
									Only son belongs to us	7
Japan	Behavior, personality of boys (positive)	29	Companionship, closeness with father	23	Continuity of family name	12	Parents' preferred sex ratio	9	Extension of self	7
U.S. (Hawaii)										
Japanese	Continuity of family name	43	Companionship, closeness with father	30	Behavior, personality of boys (positive)	10	Parents' preferred sex ratio	8	Mixture of sexes for benefit of children	7
Caucasian	Continuity of family name	40	Companionship, closeness with father	36	Parents' preferred sex ratio	13	To satisfy desires of the spouse	10	Mixture of sexes for benefit of children	9
Philippines	Continuity of family name	34	Help in taking care of other children	24	Economic help (old age not mentioned)	22	Help in housework, family chores; practical help	17	Behavior, personality of boys (positive)	7
Thailand	Continuity of family name	71	Help in taking care of other children	19	Behavior, personality of boys (positive)	13	Extension of self	6	Help in housework, family chores; practical help	5

URBAN LOWER					
Korea	Continuity of family name 68	Comfort, care (old age not mentioned) 35	Companionship, comfort, care in old age 17	Sharing financial responsibility; insurance, security 9	Conformity to social norms 6
Taiwan	Continuity of family name 80	Unspecified help in old age 21	To satisfy desires of other kin 7	Conformity to social norms 7	Help in family business or farm 6
Japan	Behavior, personality of boys (positive) 53	Companionship, closeness with father 32	Children as heirs, someone to inherit family wealth 19	Unspecified help (old age not mentioned) 15	Children to carry out parents' hopes, aspirations 8
U.S. (Hawaii)					
Japanese	Continuity of family name 45	Companionship, closeness with father 19	Behavior, personality of boys (positive) 10	To satisfy desires of spouse 10	Parents' preferred sex ratio 6
Caucasian	Continuity of family name 50	Companionship, closeness with father 30	Behavior, personality of boys (positive) 15	Help in taking care of other children 12	To satisfy desires of spouse 8
Filipino	Continuity of family name 46	Help in housework, family chores; practical help 17	Companionship, closeness with father 9	Help in taking care of other children 6	Behavior, personality of boys (positive) 4
Philippines	Continuity of family name 29	Economic help (old age not mentioned) 24	Help in taking care of other children 16	Help in housework, family chores; practical help 12	Companionship, closeness with father 4
Thailand	Continuity of family name 55	Conformity to religious norms 13	Unspecified help in old age 10	Help in housework, family chores; practical help 10	Economic help in old age 9 / Benefits to society 9

Table 4.12 *(continued)*

SES group and country	1 Reason	%	2 Reason	%	3 Reason	%	4 Reason	%	5 Reason	%
RURAL										
Korea	Continuity of family name	51	Companionship, comfort, care in old age	25	Comfort, care (old age not mentioned)	20	Economic help in old age	13	Religious rituals, ancestor worship	13
Taiwan	Continuity of family name	65	Unspecified help in old age	41	Unspecified help (old age not mentioned)	9	Sharing financial responsibility; insurance, security	7	Help in family business, farm	6
Japan	Children as heirs, someone to inherit family wealth	64	Behavior, personality of boys (positive)	18	Companionship, closeness with father	18	Unspecified help in old age	8	Unspecified help (old age not mentioned)	7
U.S. (Hawaii)										
Filipino	Continuity of family name	90	Help in housework, family chores; practical help	31	Companionship, closeness with father	4	To satisfy desires of spouse	1	Mixture of sexes for benefit of children	1
Philippines	Economic help (old age not mentioned)	50	Help in housework, family chores; practical help	18	Continuity of family name	14	Help in family business, farm	12	Help in taking care of other children	10
Thailand	Continuity of family name	58	Conformity to religious norms	26	Children as benefits to society	26	Economic help (old age not mentioned)	15	Religious rituals, ancestor worship	12

NOTE: Responses have been coded by category. In cases where two or more reasons were mentioned by the same percentage of respondents, the identical ranking is indicated by the omission of vertical rules.

SOURCE: Derived from a content analysis of responses to question 30 of the VOC questionnaire.

Table 4.13 Reasons for wanting girls
(Five most frequently mentioned reasons ranked according to percentage of respondents mentioning them, by socioeconomic group and country)

SES group and country	1 Reason	%	2 Reason	%	3 Reason	%	4 Reason	%	5 Reason	%
URBAN MIDDLE										
Korea	Behavior, personality of girls (positive)	56	Companionship, closeness with mother	34	Happiness for family	22	Mixture of sexes for benefit of children	11	Parents' preferred sex	10
Taiwan	Behavior, personality of girls (positive)	35	Companionship, closeness with mother	33	Parents' preferred sex ratio	23	Help in housework, family chores; practical help	12	Mixture of sexes for benefit of children	6
Japan	Behavior, personality of girls (positive)	48	Companionship, closeness with mother	42	Help in housework, family chores; practical help	14	Mixture of sexes for benefit of children	14	Parents' preferred sex ratio	11
U.S. (Hawaii) Japanese	Companionship, closeness with mother	30	Behavior, personality of girls (positive)	30	Mixture of sexes for benefit of children	20	Parents' preferred sex ratio	11	Help in housework, family chores; practical help	11
Caucasian	Companionship, closeness with mother	31	Behavior, personality of girls (positive)	28	Parents' preferred sex ratio	16	Opportunity to teach, guide, instill values	16	Play, fun with children; avoidance of boredom	9
Philippines	Help in housework, family chores; practical help	76	Behavior, personality of girls (positive)	15	Companionship, closeness with mother	8	Comfort, care (old age not mentioned)	5	Play, fun with children; avoidance of boredom	5
Thailand	Behavior, personality of girls (positive)	53	Companionship, closeness with mother	29	Help in housework, family chores; practical help	15	Parents' preferred sex ratio	8	Love, affection	6
									Companionship, comfort, care in old age	6
									Help in taking care of other children	6

Table 4.13 (continued)

SES group and country	1 Reason	%	2 Reason	%	3 Reason	%	4 Reason	%	5 Reason	%
URBAN LOWER										
Korea	Companionship, closeness with mother	32	Behavior, personality of girls (positive)	31	Happiness for family	23	Love, affection	18	Help in housework, family chores; practical help	15
Taiwan	Companionship, closeness with mother	41	Help in housework, family chores; practical help	35	Parents' preferred sex ratio	24	Behavior, personality of girls (positive)	19	Help in taking care of other children	6
Japan	Companionship, closeness with mother	54	Behavior, personality of girls (positive)	40	Help in housework, family chores; practical help	18	Companionship, comfort, care in old age	7	Parents' preferred sex ratio	6
U.S. (Hawaii)										
Japanese	Behavior, personality of girls (positive)	29	Help in housework, family chores; practical help	27	Companionship, closeness with mother	21	Unspecified help (old age not mentioned)	11	Parents' preferred sex ratio	11
Caucasian	Companionship, closeness with mother	29	Behavior, personality of girls (positive)	29	Mixture of sexes for benefit of children	19	Parents' preferred sex ratio	11	Help in housework, family chores; practical help	14
Filipino	Help in housework, family chores;	66	Companionship, closeness with mother	14	Behavior, personality of girls (positive)	11	Unspecified help (old age not mentioned)	9	Extension of the self / Help in taking care of other children	4 / 4
Philippines	Help in housework, family chores; practical help	73	Companionship, closeness with mother	8	Behavior, personality of girls (positive)	8	Play, fun with children; avoidance of boredom	6	Companionship, comfort, care in old age	4

Thailand	Help in housework, family chores; practical help 79	Behavior, personality of girls (positive) 7	Unspecified help (old age not mentioned) 5	Help in taking care of other children 5	Other reasons 5
RURAL Korea	Behavior, personality of girls (positive) 35	Help in housework, family chores; practical help 31	Companionship, closeness with mother 31	Conformity to social norms 10	Parents' preferred sex ratio 10
Taiwan	Help in housework, family chores; practical help 47	Parents' preferred sex ratio 30	Companionship, closeness with mother 18	Religious rituals, ancestor worship 9	Behavior, personality of girls (positive) 8
Japan	Companionship, closeness with mother 41	Behavior, personality of girls (positive) 34	Help in housework, family chores; practical help 30	Satisfaction in providing for children 8	Companionship, comfort, care in old age 7
U.S. (Hawaii) Filipino	Help in housework, family chores; practical help 90	Companionship, closeness with mother 18	Behavior, personality of girls (positive) 2	Unspecified help (old age not mentioned) 2	a
Philippines	Help in housework, family chores; practical help 89	Comfort, care (old age not mentioned) 6	Help in taking care of other children 4	Unspecified help (old age not mentioned) 4	Companionship, closeness with mother 3
Thailand	Help in housework, family chores; practical help 82	Companionship, comfort, care in old age 11	Comfort, care (old age not mentioned) 9	Behavior, personality of girls (positive) 8	Unspecified help (old age not mentioned) 7

NOTE: Responses have been coded by category. In cases where two or more reasons were mentioned by the same percentage of respondents, identical ranking is indicated by the omission of vertical rules.

a   No other reasons mentioned.

SOURCE: Derived from a content analysis of responses to question 28 of the VOC questionnaire.

practical help in the household was frequently mentioned, particularly by rural respondents.

It is clear that sons and daughters have differential importance in the eyes of parents. The effects of these sex preferences on decisions related to family size are explored in the section that follows.

Family-size values

The impetus for the VOC project stemmed from a concern about population growth and therefore, at the family level, concern about number of children. Yet, it should be noted, the data discussed previously do not deal with family size directly but with general motivations for having children and reasons for wanting sons and daughters. These motivations were studied because they are important for policy purposes—to explain why people have children at all, in relation to alternative sources of satisfaction—and also because they were assumed to influence family-size decisions. Presumably the higher the level of perceived satisfactions and the lower the level of perceived costs, the more children a person is likely to have. Also, and perhaps more important, the various dimensions of satisfactions and costs should be differentially related to family size. For instance, a parent who emphasizes "fulfillment of self" by having children does not necessarily need many children to obtain that satisfaction, but a parent concerned about economic benefits and security from children is likely to want a large family. These assumptions about general satisfactions and costs are of course subject to empirical test, and such analyses are incorporated in this study. In addition to the items on general motivations, however, the interview contained questions that directly relate satisfactions and costs of children to family size. Those items are discussed in this section.

After a series of questions regarding desired family size, respondents were asked two open-ended questions: why would they not want fewer than that number, and why would they not want more?[2] The content-analyzed responses are shown in Tables 4.14 and 4.15.

It appears that ideas about the "social network" within the family have a strong influence on family-size preferences. A frequent reason for not wanting fewer children was the perceived need for companionship among children—that is, sibling relationships. The response "to

---

2 Only respondents who wanted more children were asked why they would not want fewer than the desired number. All respondents were asked why they would not want more children, with reference to desired family size for those who wanted more children and current family size for those who did not.

Table 4.14 Reasons for not wanting fewer than desired number of children
(Five most frequently mentioned reasons ranked according to percentage of respondents mentioning them, by socioeconomic group and country)

SES group and country	1 Reason	%	2 Reason	%	3 Reason	%	4 Reason	%	5 Reason	%
URBAN MIDDLE										
Korea	Want more boys	38	Want particular combination of boys and girls, balance	21	To avoid an only child	21	Can afford that number, able to raise that many	17	Good number to have, want that number	17
Taiwan	Companionship for other children	28	To avoid an only child	25	Want particular combination of boys and girls, balance	15	Good number to have, want that number	15	Want more boys	13
Japan	Companionship for other children	30	To foster character development of children	30	Good number to have, want that number	23	To avoid an only child	12	Companionship, avoidance of loneliness	11
U.S. (Hawaii) Japanese	Good number to have, want that number	55	Companionship for other children	45	Want particular combination of boys and girls, balance	18	Companionship, avoidance of loneliness	10	Want more girls	8
Caucasian	Companionship for other children	49	To avoid an only child	28	Other reasons	21	Good number to have, want that number	15	Want more boys	10
									Can afford that number, able to raise that many	10
Philippines	Companionship for other children	35	Can afford that number, able to raise that many	23	Anxiety over infant mortality	19	Happiness for individual parent	16	Happiness for family	14
Thailand	Can afford that number, able to raise that many	30	Companionship for other children	26	Want more girls	15	Anxiety over infant mortality	11	Happiness for family	6
									Good number to have, want that number	6

Table 4.14 *(continued)*

SES group and country	1 Reason	%	2 Reason	%	3 Reason	%	4 Reason	%	5 Reason	%
URBAN LOWER Korea	Good number to have, want that number	27	Want more boys	26	Companionship for other children	18	Want particular combination of boys and girls, balance	15	To avoid an only child Anxiety over infant mortality	12 12
Taiwan	Companionship for other children	22	Want more boys	17	Want particular combination of boys and girls, balance	17	Good number to have, want that number	17	Play, fun with children; avoidance of boredom Continuity of family name To increase strength, power of kin	9 9 9
Japan	To foster character development of children	51	Companionship for other children	36	To avoid an only child	15	Good number to have, want that number	15	Companionship, avoidance of loneliness Anxiety over infant mortality	5 5
U.S. (Hawaii) Japanese	Companionship for other children	59	To avoid an only child	32	Good number to have, want that number	21	Other reasons	18	General wanting, liking children Anxiety over infant mortality	9 9
Caucasian	Companionship for other children	38	To avoid an only child	24	Good number to have, want that number	22	Want particular combination of boys and girls, balance	14	General wanting, liking children	8
Filipino	Good number to have, want that number	41	Want particular combination of boys and girls, balance	30	Companionship for other children	22	Want more girls	15	Want more boys	13
Philippines	Companionship for other children	42	Can afford that number, able to raise that many	27	Want more boys	18	Want particular combination of boys and girls, balance	18	Good number to have, want that number	15

Thailand	Want more boys 24	Can afford that number, able to raise that many 21	Companionship for other children 17	Unspecified help 12	Want more girls 12
RURAL Korea	Want more boys 29	Want particular combination of boys and girls, balance 20	Good number to have, want that number 20	Anxiety over infant mortality 15	Can afford that number, able to raise that many 12
Taiwan	Want more boys 31	Companionship for other children 20	Parents will have more alternative places to live when they are old 17	Want particular combination of boys and girls, balance 14	Anxiety over infant mortality 11
Japan	Companionship for other children 36	Anxiety over infant mortality 28	Good number to have, want that number 12	To foster character development of children 10	Want more boys 9
U.S. (Hawaii) Filipino	Good number to have, want that number 50	Want particular combination of boys and girls, balance 36	Want more girls 25	Companionship for other children 25	Want more boys 11
Philippines	Can afford that number, able to raise that many 20	Anxiety over infant mortality 18	Want more boys 17	Happiness for family 15	Good number to have, want that number 15
Thailand	Anxiety over infant mortality 25	Want more boys 14	Want more girls 14	Companionship for other children 14	Unspecified help 11 / To avoid an only child 11 / Good number to have, want that number 11

NOTE: Responses have been coded by category. In cases where two or more reasons were mentioned by the same percentage of respondents, identical ranking is indicated by the omission of vertical rules.

SOURCE: Derived from a content analysis of responses to question 14 of the VOC questionnaire.

Table 4.15 Reasons for not wanting more than desired number of children or any more children
(Five most frequently mentioned reasons ranked according to percentage of respondents mentioning them, by socioeconomic group and country)

SES group and country	1 Reason	%	2 Reason	%	3 Reason	%	4 Reason	%	5 Reason	%
URBAN MIDDLE										
Korea	Financial costs (general, other)	49	To have correct number of children for rearing; ease of handling, happiness	46	Already have/will have number of children wanted; enough boys, girls	24	Financial costs (education)	17	Health hazard of pregnancy; maternal health	15
Taiwan	Financial costs (general, other)	38	To have correct number of children for rearing; ease of handling, happiness	29	Already have/will have number of children wanted; enough boys, girls	28	Financial costs (education)	21	Disadvantages to society; concern about overpopulation	7
Japan	Financial costs (general, other)	41	Housing problems	18	Health hazard of pregnancy; maternal health	15	Already have/will have number of children wanted; enough boys, girls	13	General rearing problems	9
U.S. (Hawaii) Japanese	Financial costs (general, other)	72	To have correct number of children for rearing; ease of handling, happiness	32	Already have/will have number of children wanted; enough boys, girls	23	Disadvantages to society; concern about overpopulation	11	Other disadvantages	10
Caucasian	Financial costs (general, other)	52	Disadvantages to society; concern about overpopulation	36	To have correct number of children for rearing; ease of handling, happiness	29	Already have/will have number of children wanted; enough boys, girls	24	Infecund, too old	10

Philippines	Financial costs (general, other)	88	General rearing problems	28	Financial costs (education)	25	Concern over children's future success, happiness	10	Health hazard of pregnancy; maternal health	10
Thailand	Financial costs (general, other)	45	Financial costs (education)	25	General rearing problems	20	Already have/will have number of children wanted; enough boys, girls	18	Health hazard of pregnancy; maternal health	8
URBAN LOWER									
Korea	Financial costs (general, other)	59	To have correct number of children for rearing; ease of handling, happiness	38	Financial costs (education)	22	Already have/will have number of children wanted; enough boys, girls	16	Disadvantages to society; concern about overpopulation	7
Taiwan	Financial costs (general, other)	65	Already have/will have number of children wanted; enough boys, girls	44	Noise, disorder, nuisance	9	Financial costs (education)	7	Physical work, tiredness caused by children 7; To have correct number of children for rearing; ease of handling, happiness	7
Japan	Financial costs (general, other)	55	Housing problems	18	General rearing problems	10	Already have/will have number of children wanted; enough boys, girls	10	Health hazard of pregnancy; maternal health	6
U.S. (Hawaii) Japanese	Financial costs (general, other)	72	To have correct number of children for rearing; ease of handling, happiness	26	Already have/will have number of children wanted; enough boys, girls	19	Disadvantages to society; concern about overpopulation	13	Other reasons	8

Table 4.15 *(continued)*

SES group and country	1 Reason	%	2 Reason	%	3 Reason	%	4 Reason	%	5 Reason	%
URBAN LOWER *(continued)*										
Caucasian	Financial costs (general, other)	59	To have correct number of children for rearing; ease of handling, happiness	31	Already have/will have number of children wanted; enough boys, girls	23	Disadvantages to society; concern about overpopulation	13	Infecund, too old	8
Filipino	Financial costs (general, other)	66	To have correct number of children for rearing; ease of handling, happiness	36	Already have/will have number of children wanted; enough boys, girls	22	General rearing problems	16	Health hazard of pregnancy; maternal health	5
Philippines	Financial costs (general, other)	97	Financial costs (education)	28	General rearing problems	21	Already have/will have number of children wanted; enough boys, girls	12	Concern over children's future success, happiness	10
Thailand	Financial costs (general, other)	93	Financial costs (education)	18	General rearing problems	10	Other reasons	7	Restrictions on job, career	4
RURAL										
Korea	Financial costs (general, other)	64	Financial costs (education)	48	To have correct number of children for rearing; ease of handling, happiness	22	Already have/will have number of children wanted; enough boys, girls	13	General emotional strain	9
Taiwan	Financial costs (general, other)	66	Already have/will have number of children wanted; enough boys, girls	24	Financial costs (education)	15	Physical work, tiredness caused by children	14	Disadvantages to society; concern about overpopulation	9

Japan	Financial costs (general, other)	40	General rearing problems	23	Already have/will have number of children wanted; enough boys, girls	21	Health hazard of pregnancy; maternal health	12	Restrictions on job, career	8
U.S. (Hawaii) Filipino	Financial costs (general, other)	78	To have correct number of children for rearing, ease of handling, happiness	52	Already have/will have number of children wanted; enough boys, girls	33	Discipline, moral behavior	13	Health hazard of pregnancy; maternal health	9
Philippines	Financial costs (general, other)	90	Financial costs (education)	23	General rearing problems	15	Concern over children's future success, happiness	14	Already have/will have number of children wanted; enough boys, girls	9
Thailand	Financial costs (general, other)	67	Financial costs (education)	24	Physical work, tiredness caused by children	20	General rearing problems	12	Already have/will have number of children wanted; enough boys, girls	10

NOTE: Responses have been coded by category. In cases where two or more reasons were mentioned by the same percentage of respondents, the identical ranking is indicated by the omission of vertical rules.

SOURCE: Derived from a content analysis of responses to questions 15 and 18 of the VOC questionnaire.

avoid an only child" also falls within this category, as does the idea of fostering character development of the children. Specific responses about sex preference often had this flavor also: a boy should have a sister, a girl should have a brother, a family needs a "balance" of boys and girls.

Many responses were noninformative—for example, good number to have, able to raise that many—suggesting perhaps that parents who gave them had not really thought about the reasons for wanting a certain number of children; that is, they were merely conforming (or at least responding) to normative influences.

Of greater interest are the responses coded as "anxiety over infant mortality"; a larger number of children was wanted to assure that enough would survive to adulthood. The response was fairly strong among rural respondents in all five Asian countries. This finding is consistent both with the higher mortality rates in rural areas and with the greater emphasis among rural respondents on old-age security from children. The high response in rural Japan is surprising, however.

It should be noted also that specific sex preferences are related to family-size preferences mainly among lower-class and rural respondents, with an emphasis on boys that may be connected to the greater perceived economic value of sons for these socioeconomic groups. (In Korea, however, the responses for the middle class also reflect strong sex preferences.)

With respect to reasons for not wanting more than the desired number, Table 4.15 indicates that decisions to stop having children are primarily economic decisions. In every country and in every socioeconomic group, financial costs were cited as the main reason for not wanting a larger number of children.

When pressed to provide additional reasons, many respondents again gave noninformative answers that seem to reflect normative ideas: to have the correct number, this is the number wanted, and so forth. A unique response appears for Japan: for both urban groups, housing problems were cited as the second most important reason for restricting family size. Other responses that appear with moderate frequency are health hazards of pregnancy; concern about overpopulation; and rearing problems, including specific elements of discipline, tiredness, and emotional strain.

In addition to these open-ended questions related to desired family size, 26 structured questions were asked concerning the importance of various reasons for wanting or not wanting another child. These questions were asked of all respondents, regardless of whether they were actually planning to have another child.

The 17 reasons for wanting another child and the 9 reasons for not wanting another are shown in Tables 4.16 and 4.17, along with the percentage of respondents in each socioeconomic group and each country who rated the reasons as "very important" on a three-point scale (very important, somewhat important, not important). Since the context of this question was personal—reasons why *you* may (want/ not want) another child—the items are analyzed more meaningfully with controls for current family size and composition. That is done in some country reports, but the data are too complex to present here for all six countries and all three socioeconomic groups. Rather, over-all patterns are discussed and differences are shown for two additional subgroups: those who were actually planning to have another child and those who were not. (In Chapter 5, partial correlations between these items and the number of additional children wanted are reported, controlling for parity.)

Items pertaining to the interaction between parent and child—fun to have children around, special feeling between parent and child, sharing with children, helps me to learn—were rated as very important reasons for wanting another child by a high percentage of respondents in all countries and most subgroups. These are socially desirable responses, so a high rating might be expected on those grounds, but there is after all no doubt that people do like children and this is one reason for having them. However, responses that differentiate across groups may be of greater practical value.

It was shown earlier that old-age support was an important reason for having children, especially among lower SES and rural respondents. Table 4.16 shows that this is also an important element in decisions about family size, and moreover that the response is stronger among those groups that already have a larger number of children (see Table 3.1). These data also confirm the distinctively high rating given to eco-nomic dimensions by middle-class respondents in the Philippines, and the relatively low ratings for all groups in Japan and among Japanese and Caucasians in Hawaii. Also consistent with earlier data, and indica-tive of effects on family size, are the stronger responses for family name and traditions and boy preference among rural and lower-class respondents.

Table 4.16 also reveals a tendency for Filipino respondents to give unusually high ratings to most reasons for wanting another child. This does not seem to be simply a response set, as indicated by the low rating given to influence from relatives, similar to the response to this item in other countries. It appears that many motivations for child-bearing are truly stronger among Filipinos, which is consistent with

Table 4.16 Reasons for wanting another child
(Percentage of respondents rating specified reasons as very

SES group and country	Enjoy having a small baby	Carry family name, traditions	Want a boy/ another boy	Want a girl/ another girl	Relatives feel I should have more children
URBAN MIDDLE					
Korea	13	28	24	13	2
Taiwan	10	27	28	16	6
Japan	16	10	38	29	6
U.S. (Hawaii)					
Japanese	16	12	9	12	*
Caucasian	21	13	17	4	*
Philippines	49	43	38	43	6
Thailand	37	41	28	30	6
URBAN LOWER					
Korea	23	54	37	15	7
Taiwan	11	48	29	14	3
Japan	28	6	37	27	3
U.S. (Hawaii)					
Japanese	16	18	9	17	1
Caucasian	33	25	23	15	1
Filipino	43	64	44	37	5
Philippines	43	50	33	33	8
Thailand	22	52	44	18	8
RURAL					
Korea	15	69	40	15	7
Taiwan	14	49	40	19	9
Japan	18	24	31	21	4
U.S. (Hawaii)					
Filipino	37	92	67	44	2
Philippines	62	61	51	50	16
Thailand	22	59	35	23	10

important, by socioeconomic group and country)

In my old age, have child to help me	Religious duty to have children	One more person to help family economically	Make my marriage stronger	A companion for my child/ children	Enjoy caring for raising children	Spouse wants more children
3	3	2	15	21	14	13
9	10	4	4	24	14	5
2	*	2	7	44	15	23
6	2	1	5	41	35	25
*	3	1	3	26	34	18
49	27	36	43	50	36	23
12	*	2	10	29	18	22
26	7	14	20	14	24	18
21	18	14	9	23	16	11
7	*	3	10	55	18	26
4	1	1	5	41	43	18
10	3	4	4	24	42	25
54	16	36	42	55	32	35
53	34	43	49	36	32	19
55	19	31	39	25	20	21
43	13	18	15	22	32	18
35	21	22	13	19	12	13
21	5	6	11	36	20	19
77	11	76	5	52	75	31
80	57	68	69	58	55	42
58	19	35	34	24	21	17

Table 4.16 *(continued)*

SES group and country	Fun to have children around house	Helps me to learn about life, myself	Special feeling between parent and child	Share what I have, know with children	Have enough children to survive to adulthood
URBAN MIDDLE					
Korea	29	39	29	12	5
Taiwan	40	31	42	37	12
Japan	47	47	32	12	22
U.S. (Hawaii)					
Japanese	42	47	59	56	18
Caucasian	34	45	57	60	12
Philippines	57	61	70	66	57
Thailand	42	44	51	38	36
URBAN LOWER					
Korea	40	44	28	18	11
Taiwan	32	24	35	26	30
Japan	56	46	28	10	14
U.S. (Hawaii)					
Japanese	50	56	67	63	22
Caucasian	42	59	71	63	25
Filipino	53	52	68	69	36
Philippines	49	52	63	65	56
Thailand	30	53	49	39	54
RURAL					
Korea	32	42	20	35	27
Taiwan	28	23	34	27	27
Japan	53	48	38	12	35
U.S. (Hawaii)					
Filipino	87	92	98	93	43
Philippines	71	75	79	76	80
Thailand	23	47	49	44	53

* Less than 1 percent.

Table 4.17 Reasons for not wanting another child
(Percentage of respondents rating specified reasons as very important, by socioeconomic group and country)

SES group and country	Would be financial burden to family	Spouse does not want more	Restrict my freedom to do other things I enjoy	A lot of work, bother for me
URBAN MIDDLE				
Korea	41	23	18	13
Taiwan	32	18	22	33
Japan	11	20	13	6
U.S. (Hawaii)				
Japanese	16	15	11	8
Caucasian	21	22	12	5
Philippines	39	16	18	24
Thailand	42	20	16	28
URBAN LOWER				
Korea	73	30	17	18
Taiwan	56	23	27	37
Japan	23	16	17	11
U.S. (Hawaii)				
Japanese	32	20	6	5
Caucasian	31	15	7	6
Filipino	40	21	14	15
Philippines	62	30	21	32
Thailand	77	25	39	50
RURAL				
Korea	63	22	13	31
Taiwan	69	28	46	54
Japan	20	17	10	14
U.S. (Hawaii)				
Filipino	57	32	4	6
Philippines	54	25	20	28
Thailand	67	30	43	47

Table 4.17 *(continued)*

SES group and country	Not able to spend as much time with spouse	Concerned about over-population	Emotional strain for me	Not enough attention, care to other children	Cause problems, strains between me and spouse
URBAN MIDDLE					
Korea	17	16	29	44	24
Taiwan	15	36	29	50	16
Japan	4	6	15	9	4
U.S. (Hawaii)					
Japanese	8	13	9	22	11
Caucasian	16	27	7	15	10
Philippines	10	49	25	37	26
Thailand	4	16	18	43	13
URBAN LOWER					
Korea	7	23	34	63	35
Taiwan	9	22	28	35	16
Japan	7	4	21	16	6
U.S. (Hawaii)					
Japanese	11	20	9	20	10
Caucasian	8	17	17	10	14
Filipino	15	22	15	27	11
Philippines	18	56	29	45	33
Thailand	10	20	28	52	23
RURAL					
Korea	6	24	48	62	45
Taiwan	13	30	52	49	12
Japan	2	1	18	17	10
U.S. (Hawaii)					
Filipino	2	1	2	63	4
Philippines	24	48	35	40	35
Thailand	16	30	30	48	21

the known higher levels of fertility and family-size preferences in the Philippines. Table 4.16 shows also that religious influences appear to be stronger in the Philippines, which is the only predominantly Catholic country in the study.

Concern about infant mortality as a motivation for having another child was greatest in the Philippines and Thailand, which are also the countries showing the highest level of importance for old-age support and economic help from children. Actual rates of infant mortality are also highest in the Philippines and Thailand, among the countries in this study, but are also quite high in Korea, where this factor did not emerge as an important motivation.

Table 4.17 shows that financial concerns are again dominant reasons for limiting family size. Also prominent is a specific dimension that may have been obscured in the broader coding categories for open-ended responses—that another child would mean that not enough care and attention could be given to existing children. (This would have been coded from the open-ended questions as "to have the correct number of children for rearing, ease of handling, happiness.")

Of particular importance in Table 4.17 are the relatively low ratings given to opportunity costs ("restrict my freedom to do other things I enjoy") as a reason for not wanting another child. Since opportunity costs were frequently mentioned by urban parents in the open-ended questions about disadvantages of having children (compared to not having children), and since all respondents in this study had at least one child, the obvious inference is that opportunity costs were not perceived to be great for additional children after the first. This inference is of course compatible with the observation that the first child makes the major difference in life-style, particularly for the mother.

The high rating given to opportunity costs by rural respondents in Taiwan and Thailand is perhaps linked to the similar high ratings on "work and bother" by those respondents. According to other data not shown here, these responses are strongest for women and may be related to the occupational roles of rural women in Taiwan and Thailand.

"Concerned about overpopulation" was given as a reason for not having another child by about half the respondents in each of the SES groups in the Philippines, which is higher than any other country. It should be noted, however, that Filipinos did not cite overpopulation as an important reason for limiting family size in a preceding open-ended question.

Table 4.18 Mean scores on reasons for wanting another child
(By those who want more/don't want more children and

Reason for wanting	Korea		Taiwan	
	Want more (*N*=114)	Do not want more (*N*=231)	Want more (*N*=105)	Do not want more (*N*=293)
Enjoy having a small baby	1.7	1.8	1.9**	1.4**
To carry on family name, traditions	2.4*	2.2*	2.4**	1.9**
Want a boy/another boy	2.2**	1.8**	2.3**	1.6**
Want a girl/another girl	1.6	1.6	1.8**	1.4**
Relatives feel I should have more children	1.4†	1.2†	1.4**	1.2**
To have a child to help me in my old age	1.8	1.7	1.9*	1.6*
My religious duty to have children	1.5**	1.2**	1.6†	1.4†
To have one more person to help the family economically	1.5	1.5	1.6†	1.4†
To make my marriage stronger	1.6	1.6	1.7**	1.3**
To provide a companion for my child/children	1.9†	1.7†	2.3**	1.6**
Enjoy caring for, raising children	1.9	1.9	1.9**	1.4**
My spouse wants more children	1.7	1.6	1.6**	1.2**
Fun to have children around the house	2.0	2.1	2.4**	2.0**
Raising children helps me to learn about life and myself	2.2	2.2	2.2**	1.8**
To have special feeling of love between parent and child	1.9	2.0	2.3**	1.9**
To share what I have and know with children	1.8	1.8	2.2**	1.8**
To have enough children survive to adulthood	1.7*	1.5*	2.1**	1.6**
Uncertain	(*N*=29)		(*N*=32)	

NOTE: Possible scores range from 1 (not important) to 3 (very important).

† Differences between those wanting and those not wanting another child are significant at .05.

* Differences between those wanting and those not wanting another child are significant at .01.

by country)

Japan		U.S. (Hawaii)		Philippines		Thailand	
Want more (N=199)	Do not want more (N=189)	Want more (N=289)	Do not want more (N=263)	Want more (N=154)	Do not want more (N=209)	Want more (N=119)	Do not want more (N=213)
1.7	1.8	2.1*	1.9*	2.6**	2.2**	2.2**	1.8**
1.5	1.5	2.1**	1.8**	2.4*	2.2*	2.5**	2.1**
2.2**	1.7**	1.8**	1.5**	2.4**	1.7**	2.2**	1.6**
1.8**	1.6**	1.9**	1.5**	2.5**	1.8**	2.1**	1.4**
1.2	1.1	1.1†	1.0†	1.5**	1.3**	1.4*	1.2*
1.4	1.4	1.7	1.6	2.6**	2.3**	2.2†	2.0†
1.1	1.1	1.4	1.3	2.2*	1.9*	1.3†	1.5†
1.2	1.2	1.5	1.4	2.3†	2.1†	1.7	1.6
1.6**	1.4**	1.6**	1.2**	2.5**	2.1**	1.9*	1.7*
2.6**	1.9**	2.6**	1.6**	2.7**	1.9**	2.3**	1.6**
1.9**	1.6**	2.4**	2.0**	2.5**	2.0**	2.0**	1.6**
1.9**	1.5**	2.2**	1.5**	2.2**	1.6**	2.0**	1.4**
2.6**	2.2**	2.5**	2.2**	2.7**	2.2**	2.4**	1.9**
2.4**	2.2**	2.6**	2.3**	2.8**	2.3**	2.5**	2.2**
2.2*	2.0*	2.8**	2.4**	2.9**	2.4**	2.5**	2.2**
1.6	1.5	2.7**	2.4**	2.8**	2.4**	2.4**	2.0**
1.8	1.7	1.9*	1.6*	2.7**	2.3**	2.4**	2.1**
(N=21)		(N=64)		(N=25)		(N=25)	

** Differences between those wanting and those not wanting another child are significant at .001.

As mentioned earlier, the two sets of questions on reasons for wanting or not wanting another child were asked of all respondents, regardless of whether they were actually planning to have another child. Tables 4.16 and 4.17 give the percentage of respondents who rated each reason as very important, tabulated by socioeconomic group within countries. Tables 4.18 and 4.19 present results from the same questions, but this time tabulated according to those who wanted another child and those who did not (within countries). Rather than percentages, the data in these tables are mean scores, derived from coding as follows: very important = 3, somewhat important = 2, not important = 1. The differences in mean scores for the "want" and "not want" groups were evaluated by *t*-tests, within countries; the results are shown in the tables.

Table 4.19 Mean scores on reasons for not wanting another child
(By those who want more/don't want more children and

	Korea		Taiwan	
Reason for not wanting	Want more (*N*=114)	Do not want more (*N*=231)	Want more (*N*=105)	Do not want more (*N*=293)
Would be financial burden to family	2.3**	2.6**	2.0**	2.4**
Spouse does not want more	1.6**	1.9**	1.5**	1.9**
Would restrict my freedom to do other things I enjoy	1.5†	1.7†	1.7**	2.1**
Would be a lot of work, bother for me	1.8	1.9	1.8**	2.3**
Could not spend as much time with spouse	1.4†	1.6†	1.4*	1.6*
Concern about overpopulation	1.8	1.8	1.8**	2.0**
Would be emotional strain for me	2.1	2.2	1.8**	2.2**
Would not be able to give enough attention, care to other children	2.2**	2.5**	1.9**	2.3**
Would cause problems, strains between spouse and me	2.0	2.2	1.5	1.7
Uncertain	(*N*=29)		(*N*=32)	

NOTE: Possible scores range from 1 (not important) to 3 (very important).

† Differences between those wanting and those not wanting another child are significant at .05.

* Differences between those wanting and those not wanting another child are significant at .01.

As would be expected, the data show that respondents wanting another child tended to give higher ratings to all positive motivations than did the "not want" group, and the respondents not wanting another child tended to give higher ratings to the negative motivations than did the "want" group. Examination of the larger differences between the groups, indicated by annotations for significance levels, is helpful in revealing the most important motivations related to actually planning to have or not to have another child.

Highly significant differences (.001) are shown in most countries for three related positive motivations: want a boy/another boy, want a girl/another girl, and to provide companionship for my child/children. These significantly higher scores for respondents planning to have another child thus reinforce the earlier discussion of sex prefer-

by country)

Japan		U.S. (Hawaii)		Philippines		Thailand	
Want more (N=199)	Do not want more (N=189)	Want more (N=289)	Do not want more (N=263)	Want more (N=154)	Do not want more (N=209)	Want more (N=119)	Do not want more (N=213)
1.7†	1.8†	1.8**	2.2**	2.0**	2.6**	2.2**	2.6**
1.7	1.6	1.4**	1.7**	1.6**	1.9**	1.4**	1.9**
1.6	1.5	1.4†	1.5†	1.5	1.7	1.8*	2.0*
1.4	1.5	1.3**	1.4**	1.6**	2.0**	1.8**	2.3**
1.4	1.2	1.4	1.4	1.6	1.6	1.3†	1.4†
1.2	1.2	1.6*	1.8*	2.2	2.3	1.6*	1.8*
1.6**	1.8**	1.3**	1.5**	1.6**	2.0**	1.7**	2.0**
1.5†	1.7†	1.5**	2.0**	1.9*	2.1*	2.0**	2.4**
1.2†	1.4†	1.3†	1.4†	1.7**	2.1**	1.6*	1.8*
(N=21)		(N=64)		(N=25)		(N=25)	

** Differences between those wanting and those not wanting another child are significant at .001.

ence and sibling relationships as significant determinants of family size.

Emotional benefits to the parents are reflected in several items that significantly differentiate the want/not want groups. Also important in most countries are the desires of the spouse and strengthening of the marriage through children. Carrying the family name and tradition and survival of enough children to adulthood distinguish the want/not want groups at the .01 level or higher in every country except Japan.

It is of interest that two items on expected economic benefits do not differentiate sharply between those who were planning another child and those who were not, although differences at the .01 level of significance are shown for the item on help in old age in the Philippines and Taiwan. Overall, substantially fewer items differentiate the want/not want groups in Japan and Korea than in other countries. Economic costs are shown once more to be a major factor in limiting family size, with a particularly large difference in mean scores shown for the Philippines. Only in Japan is there a very small difference between groups for the item on financial burden of another child.

Other items on which the "not want" group scores substantially higher (.001) than the "want" group in four or more countries include the perception that the spouse does not want more children, the work and emotional strain connected with childrearing, and the belief that not enough attention could be given to other children. Again, fewer differentiating items are shown for Japan and Korea than for other countries.

A few separate questions were asked to relate family size to economic benefits and costs of children. For example, the following open-ended item was included: "Some couples feel that the more children they have, the better off the family will be economically. Others feel that having a lot of children will make their family less well off. How do you personally feel about this?"

From a content analysis of responses, Table 4.20 indicates the percentage of respondents who said that a family with more children would be better off economically. The percentages generally are highest among rural respondents. In Korea, Taiwan, and the Philippines, about one out of five rural respondents thought that a larger family would be economically beneficial. Also, surprisingly high percentages (12–15 percent) may be noted for some groups of urban respondents.

Two rather straightforward questions were included in an attempt to assess the elasticity of desired family size in relation to income and

Table 4.20 Percentage of respondents who said a family with more children would be better off economically
(By country and socioeconomic group)

Country	Urban middle	Urban lower	Rural
Korea	14	15	23
Taiwan	3	6	17
Japan	5	6	6
U.S. (Hawaii)			
Japanese	12	12	na
Caucasian	3	14	na
Filipino	na	3	6
Philippines	12	12	20
Thailand	3	8	9

na—not applicable because subsample did not include persons in this socioeconomic group.

cost factors: "Suppose your family income increased, to double what it is now. Would that affect the number of children you want?" and "Suppose the government decided to provide free education for all children, up to and including college. Would that affect the number of children you want?"

Table 4.21 indicates the percentage of respondents who said they would want more children under these conditions. Conclusions from such hypothetical questions must be drawn with caution. Nonetheless, it is of interest to note that relatively few respondents, except in Thailand, said that these income and cost factors would affect their desired family size. In the East Asian countries it appears that a reduction in educational costs is more important for middle-class respondents and an increase in income is more important for lower-class respondents. In Hawaii and the Southeast Asian countries, income is the more important factor for nearly all groups, but the differences are small throughout.

Beliefs about the effects of family size on children might be expected to have some influence on fertility behavior. To explore this area, seven statements about characteristics of children were presented to respondents and, for each statement, respondents were asked whether it applied to a child from a small family or a large family. For instance, the first statement was "A child who is very open and loving toward other people." Other statements pertained to intellectual ability, popularity, closeness to parents, the child always wanting his own way, self-confidence, and happiness.

Table 4.21 Effect of the perceived costs on wanted number of children

(Percentage of respondents who said they would want more children if their family income were doubled or if free education were provided through the college level, by country and socioeconomic group)

Country	Urban middle		Urban lower		Rural	
	Dou-bled income	Free edu-cation	Dou-bled income	Free edu-cation	Dou-bled income	Free edu-cation
Korea	8	12	14	10	7	7
Taiwan	6	8	11	5	6	6
Japan	8	11	15	9	9	13
U.S. (Hawaii)						
Japanese	15	6	18	10	na	na
Caucasian	12	4	23	13	na	na
Filipino	na	na	6	5	2	0
Philippines	19	12	17	13	21	13
Thailand	23	21	34	39	40	36

na—not applicable because subsample did not include persons in this socioeconomic group.

Many of these items produced a substantial percentage of "don't know" responses, suggesting the absence of strong beliefs relating the characteristic to family size. However, certain items showed clear-cut results in each country and three items showed fairly consistent results across countries:

1. A child who is very popular with other children (associated with a *large* family by half or more of the respondents in each country except the Philippines)
2. A child who has a very close relationship with his parents (associated with a *small* family by more than half the respondents in all six countries)
3. A child who always wants his own way (associated with a *small* family by more than half the respondents in each country except Thailand)

These findings are of interest because they relate certain aspects of the quality of a child to family size. However, the results cannot in all cases be readily interpreted. Is it perceived to be good or bad, for instance, for a child to have a "very close relationship with his parents"? And do all parents prefer children with "high intellectual ability"?

Additional information about parents' preferences for characteristics of children is needed to interpret meaningfully the linkages between such characteristics and family size.[3]

Husband-wife differences

The tables in this volume do not distinguish between male and female respondents. As noted in Chapter 1, the main reason for this omission is to avoid the complexity of adding another dimension to the breakdown of data by six countries and three socioeconomic groups. Another reason is that relatively few differences between male and female respondents were found, as compared with the differences between countries and socioeconomic groups. Husbands and wives appear to share a broadly similar orientation toward children.

Similarities and differences between male and female respondents are reported and discussed in each of the country reports in this series, and in some countries additional studies using techniques for couple analysis are under way. For this comparative volume, only brief comments will be made about the differences found between male and female respondents. In general, the differences can be readily interpreted with respect to sex-role prescriptions and the division of functions within the family.

Companionship from children and the emotional relationship between parent and child tended to be more salient to women, who spend more time with the children and whose range of social relationships may be narrower than the husbands' because of being tied to the home. These factors generally were more important for women in urban areas, where households tend to be isolated socially. In a similar vein, women, who bear the major burden of child care responsibilities, were more concerned than men about the emotional strains and physical demands related to the rearing of children. The physical demands were especially important to rural women in some countries, perhaps because of the burden of other kinds of work these women are required to do.

Concerning economic aspects of children, women were more likely than men to stress expectations for economic help from children, perhaps reflecting the greater degree of economic dependence of females

---

3 In Chapter 5 an index constructed by summing six of the items that might be regarded as favorable traits is used in the prediction of number of additional children desired, where it is found to have no significant effect. However, the index is significantly correlated with ideal and desired family size in some countries.

and their longer life expectancy. Men, on the other hand, were more concerned about the economic costs of children, which is consistent with the traditional male role of family breadwinner.

Men also gave greater stress to continuity of family name. In the cultures where this stress was found to occur, it is of course the husband's family name that is continued. It is perhaps in relation to this sense of family identity that men, more than women, emphasized their feeling of pride in their children's accomplishments. This concern with the success of children may also reflect the husband's dissatisfaction or frustration with his own occupational role. Husbands also tended to place greater stress on the atmosphere of family happiness, which again may be in contrast to the atmosphere of their daily work situation.

5

the social context,
the value of children,
and family size

In the preceding chapter, attention was focused on description of value-of-children dimensions and on the relationships between those dimensions and broadly defined background characteristics—culture, as reflected by nationality, and socioeconomic status, as reflected by membership in the sample groups defined as middle class, lower class, or rural. The relationships were expressed in simple quantitative terms, mainly by differences in frequency of responses across groups.

In this chapter the background characteristics of respondents are examined at a more specific level and the pattern of relationships is extended to include fertility-related indices. Correlational analyses are used to show the strength of relationships among pairs of variables, and multiple regression analyses are used to show the interrelationships among a wider set of variables when they are used as predictors of fertility and family planning measures. Particular attention is given in regression analyses to the relative predictive power of value-of-children dimensions when background characteristics are controlled.

The data from open-ended questions about the advantages and disadvantages of children, which have proved very valuable for descriptive purposes, are not used in these analyses because of scaling problems and because the absence of a response is difficult to interpret. The structured measures provide broad coverage of the value of children, but certain important dimensions, such as opportunity costs, are not separately identified.

The analyses reported here are based on the total sample in each country, but it must be stressed that these are not representative samples. Thus, for example, urban respondents have greater weight than they should for countries such as the Philippines, Thailand, and Korea. It should also be noted that only linear methods of analyses are used, although the descriptive data indicate that some important relationships are nonlinear. Furthermore, the feedback effects of fertility and family planning are not taken into account; for example, the impact on current motivations of such significant factors as current sex composition among children is not evaluated.

It is essential to recognize these limitations, some of which are inherent in the study and some of which result from decisions regarding the extent of analysis appropriate for a small study with exploratory measurements. It is also important, however, to note that even these imperfect analyses can be very useful in determining whether future studies of this nature would be fruitful, and, if so, in identifying the dimensions and types of measurement likely to be most productive.

The data chosen for presentation fall into four blocks: sociodemographic variables, VOC economic dimensions, VOC social-psychological dimensions, and fertility and family planning indices. The variables within each block are described below.

Sociodemographic variables

1. Age
2. Income (total family income in past year)
3. Education (highest grade of formal schooling completed)
4. Urban experience (percentage of life lived in urban area)
5. Media exposure (frequency of exposure to newspapers, radio, television)
6. Marriage duration
7. Parity (number of living children plus current pregnancy)[1]

VOC economic dimensions

1. Economic burden of education (whether providing education for children would be a very heavy financial burden, somewhat heavy, or fairly easy)

---

1 Parity was included in regressions only where necessary for control purposes, namely for prediction of additional children desired.

2. Financial ease/large family (from a series of questions on financial burden of different family sizes, the smallest number of children that respondent said would be a "heavy financial burden"—the larger the number, the less the perceived financial burden)
3. Expected economic help from children (index constructed from six items on expected economic help and old-age support from sons and daughters)
4. Decreased utility of children (extent of perception that current generation is less willing than the previous one to have parents live with them, give part of wages to parents in old age, and help in house, farm, or business)
5. Economic benefits/large family (whether respondent said families with more children would be better off economically)

VOC social-psychological dimensions[2]

1. Continuity, tradition, security (VOC Scale 1)[3]
2. Parenthood satisfactions (VOC Scale 2)
3. Role motivations (VOC Scale 3)
4. Happiness and affection (VOC Scale 4)
5. Goals and incentives (VOC Scale 5)
6. Social status (VOC Scale 6)
7. External controls (VOC Scale 7)
8. Costs of children (VOC Scale 8)
9. Decision-mindedness (VOC Scale 9)
10. Reasons for wanting another child (summed scores on importance of 17 reasons for wanting another child)[4]
11. Reasons for not wanting another child (summed scores on 9 reasons for not wanting another child)[5]
12. Benefits to children of large family (summed scores on beliefs that children from large families are more open and loving, more intellectual, more popular, have closer relationship with parents, have greater self-confidence, are happier)

---

2 Although they are called "social-psychological" dimensions for convenience, these indices also contain significant elements of economic benefits and costs (see items 1, 8, 9, 10, and 11).

3 See Table 4.7 for items contained in VOC Scales 1 to 9.

4 See Table 4.16 for list of 17 reasons.

5 See Table 4.17 for list of 9 reasons.

Fertility and family planning indices

1. Number of contraceptive methods known (summed scores on whether respondent claimed knowledge of IUD, pill, condom, diaphragm, rhythm, withdrawal, vasectomy, tubal ligation)
2. General birth control attitude (strength of approval or disapproval of married couples' practicing birth control)
3. Situational birth control attitude (summed score on approval of use of birth control to delay first birth, to space subsequent births, to stop having children)
4. Current use of birth control (whether or not respondent was currently using any method)
5. Number of living children (own children and other children living as part of family)
6. Number of additional children desired ("If you could have just what you want, how many *more* children would you like to have?")
7. Number of children wanted (number of living children plus additional children desired)
8. Ideal number of children ("In your ideal family, if you were starting all over, how many children would you want to have altogether?")

The conceptual model for this study, illustrated earlier in Figure 1.1, assumes a mediating role for the VOC dimensions. That is, these essentially attitudinal measures are viewed as representing personal dispositions that result from past experience and influence behavior. More specifically, the perceived satisfactions and costs of children are regarded as significant elements in determining birth control behavior and decisions about number of children. Two essential questions about this model can be answered by the analyses reported here: (1) Is there a statistical association between VOC measures and fertility or family planning indices? and (2) To what extent is this association independent of the background and situation of the respondents? In addition, knowledge about the statistical structure of the data set permits a better understanding of the meaning of the many variables that were measured.

The correlations among variables will be reviewed first. Following that, a summary of regression results for eight dependent variables will be presented. Then the components of prediction for two of those dependent variables will be discussed.

Correlations among variables

To indicate distinctiveness or overlap among various measures and to shed light on the interpretation of VOC dimensions and their fertility implications, this section presents selected correlations among sociodemographic variables, VOC measures, and family size and family planning indices.

Sociodemographic variables. Table 5.1 shows the intercorrelations among the six sociodemographic variables that were chosen for inclusion in the regressions: age, income, education, urban experience, media exposure, and marriage duration. Also shown are the correlations of these variables with parity, which is sometimes used as a control variable among the predictors, but which is also an important dependent variable. Most of the correlations among these background and situational variables are statistically significant, but the strength of the significant relationships varies substantially.

Certain patterns are consistent across countries. For example, the variables that would represent socioeconomic status—income, education, urban experience, and media exposure—tend to be positively intercorrelated. There are some exceptions, however, and the correlations among these and other variables in Japan are quite low. Another positive cluster is shown for age, marriage duration, and parity, as would be expected. Education is negatively related to parity in all countries, although the relationship is relatively weak in the Philippines and quite weak and insignificant in Japan.

The variables showing least consistency across countries are age and income. The differences related to age are partially attributable to sampling variations within countries. For instance, in Thailand the middle-class sample was substantially older than the other two groups sampled, resulting in a stronger positive correlation between age and some SES measures in that country. In Hawaii the rural Filipino group was older than the other groups, and this fact is reflected in the strong negative correlations of age with education and urban experience.

The varying relationships with income are probably attributable to several factors, including inadequacy of measurement (see MacDonald and Mueller, 1975). No doubt sampling procedures had some effect, and social-structural factors, such as income distribution, may be important too. Income is most strongly associated with education and urban experience in the countries where income is less evenly distributed: Korea, the Philippines, and Thailand. The relationships between

Table 5.1   Intercorrelations of sociodemographic variables
       (By country)

Variable	Age	In-come	Edu-cation	Urban experi-ence	Media ex-posure	Marriage dura-tion	Parity
Age							
Korea		.15*	.13*	.13*	.12*	.58*	.44*
Taiwan		.11†	.14*	.17*	.04	.54*	.33*
Japan		.11†	.03	.03	.08†	.56*	.34*
U.S. (Hawaii)		.15*	-.22*	-.29*	.05	.63*	.39*
Philippines		.11†	-.08	-.07	.09†	.63*	.46*
Thailand		.30*	.25*	.08	.18*	.47*	.38*
Income							
Korea	.15*		.73*	.60*	.45*	-.16*	-.13*
Taiwan	.11†		.30*	.21*	.17*	-.02	-.09†
Japan	.11†		.12*	.05	-.01	.14*	.18*
U.S. (Hawaii)	.15*		.32*	.19*	.18*	.06	-.11*
Philippines	.11†		.52*	.38*	.33*	.05	.08†
Thailand	.30*		.68*	.40*	.40*	-.20*	-.19*
Education							
Korea	.13*	.73*		.64*	.62*	-.36*	-.35*
Taiwan	.14*	.30*		.40*	.58*	-.32*	-.32*
Japan	.03	.12*		.30*	.10†	-.17*	-.05
U.S. (Hawaii)	-.22*	.32*		.45*	.22*	-.37*	-.35*
Philippines	-.08	.52*		.48*	.44*	-.25*	-.19*
Thailand	.25*	.68*		.49*	.50*	-.35*	-.34*
Urban experience							
Korea	.13*	.60*	.64*		.38*	-.23*	-.24*
Taiwan	.17*	.21*	.40*		.40*	-.12*	-.06
Japan	.03	.05	.30*		.19*	-.19*	-.10†
U.S. (Hawaii)	-.29*	.19*	.45*		.09†	-.24*	-.16*
Philippines	-.07	.38*	.48*		.40*	-.10†	-.01
Thailand	.08	.40*	.49*		.32*	-.23*	-.17*
Media exposure							
Korea	.12*	.45*	.62*	.38*		-.22*	-.20*
Taiwan	.04	.17*	.58*	.40*		-.22*	-.16*
Japan	.08†	-.01	.10†	.19*		-.08†	-.06
U.S. (Hawaii)	.05	.18*	.22*	.09†		-.01	-.08†
Philippines	.09†	.33*	.44*	.40*		.01	.00
Thailand	.18*	.40*	.50*	.32*		-.16*	-.21*
Marriage duration							
Korea	.58*	-.16*	-.36*	-.23*	-.22*		.75*
Taiwan	.54*	-.02	-.32*	-.12*	-.22*		.68*
Japan	.56*	.14*	-.17*	-.19*	-.08†		.35*
U.S. (Hawaii)	.63*	.06	-.37*	-.24*	-.01		.62*
Philippines	.63*	.05	-.25*	-.10†	.01		.73*
Thailand	.47*	-.20*	-.35*	-.23*	-.16*		.67*

Table 5.1 *(continued)*

Variable	Age	In-come	Edu-cation	Urban experi-ence	Media ex-posure	Marriage dura-tion	Parity
Parity[a]							
Korea	.44*	-.13*	-.35*	-.24*	-.20*	.75*	
Taiwan	.33*	-.09†	-.32*	-.06	-.16*	.68*	
Japan	.34*	.18*	-.05	-.10†	-.06	.35*	
U.S. (Hawaii)	.39*	-.11*	-.35*	-.16*	-.08†	.62*	
Philippines	.46*	.08†	-.19*	-.01	.00	.73*	
Thailand	.38*	-.19*	-.34*	-.17*	-.21*	.67*	

a Including current pregnancy.

† $p < .05$.

* $p < .01$.

income and family size appear to be attributable in part to marriage duration, except in Hawaii.

It should be noted that these variations in sociodemographic structure may be expected to produce different interactive effects when multivariate techniques are applied to relate sociodemographic variables to VOC and fertility indices.

VOC economic indices. Interpretation of correlational data is useful in understanding the methodological and conceptual difficulties encountered in assessing the economic value of children. As noted earlier, the measurement of economic costs is especially problematic, because parents do not know the actual costs and because they resent the idea of "pricing" children in this way. Also, adequate measurement would require taking into account differences in costs related to age and sex of children, changes over time in parents' aspirations for quality of children, and expected benefits in relation to costs.

Difficulties arise also in trying to specify precisely how economic cost and benefit factors should relate to fertility indices, with cross-sectional data. For example, awareness of costs early in the family-building cycle might tend to reduce family-size desires and actual fertility, but not necessarily in cases where long-term economic benefits are expected and are important. As another example, having a large family might be expected to produce greater awareness of the actual costs involved, but might also be associated with a tendency to justify a large family by minimizing the importance of economic costs.

To provide some insight into the measures of economic costs and benefits used in this study, Table 5.2 shows the correlations among five of the six economic indices chosen for inclusion in the regressions. Two indices pertain to economic costs of children and two pertain to economic benefits, while the scale labeled "costs of children" contains a mixture of economic and noneconomic costs.

Correlations among the three indices of costs are all in the expected direction and nearly all are significant, but many of the correlations are relatively weak. The perceived burden of educating children is positively related to the measure of general costs, and both these indices are inversely related to the perceived financial ease of raising a large family. Likewise, the two indices of benefits are positively related; expectations of economic help from children are correlated, at generally low levels, to the perception that a family is better off economically with more children. The correlations are significant in four of the six countries.

Relationships between costs and benefits are more complex, presumably because of the influence of other factors. For example, the positive correlation between perceived burden of education and expected economic help is mediated in part by socioeconomic status: poor rural parents tended to rate both dimensions high, and wealthy parents tended to rate both low.

To clarify the meaning of the economic indices, Tables 5.3 and 5.4 show the correlations of one cost index (financial ease/large family) and one benefit index (expected economic help) with five other variables: income, education, parity, additional children desired, and ideal family size.

The index of financial ease/large family tends to be positively correlated with all other variables in Table 5.3, although many correlations are quite weak. Those with more income were inclined to say they could afford a large family (except in Thailand). At the same time, those who had more children and a larger ideal family size also said they could afford a large family. The correlations of the index with education and with additional children desired vary across countries, but the significant correlations are all positive. This pattern of weak positive correlations across variables that are not all themselves positively correlated suggests multiple influences on the economic index: the responses may reflect partly an economic calculation and partly the justification of a preferred or actual family size. The index cannot be considered a pure measure of the perceived economic costs of family size, although it clearly does assess some aspects of the economic value of children.

Table 5.2 Intercorrelations of VOC economic indices
(By country)

Index	Burden of edu-cation	Costs of children	Financial ease/large family	Expected economic help	Economic benefits/large family
Burden of education					
Korea		.24*	-.13*	.36*	-.05
Taiwan		.18*	-.38*	.41*	-.05
Japan		.29*	-.27*	.05	-.14*
U.S. (Hawaii)		.21*	-.10*	.23*	-.02
Philippines		.18*	-.05	.18*	.03
Thailand		.26*	-.19*	.31*	.00
Costs of children					
Korea	.24*		-.13*	.24*	-.05
Taiwan	.18*		-.22*	.20*	-.03
Japan	.29*		-.18*	.01	-.10†
U.S. (Hawaii)	.21*		-.23*	.17*	-.05
Philippines	.18*		-.05	.12*	-.04
Thailand	.26*		-.13*	.10†	-.12†
Financial ease/large family					
Korea	-.13*	-.13*		-.02	.07
Taiwan	-.38*	-.22*		-.20*	.14*
Japan	-.27*	-.18*		.02	.09†
U.S. (Hawaii)	-.10*	-.23*		-.08†	.20*
Philippines	-.05	-.05		.10†	.16*
Thailand	-.19*	-.13*		.00	.19*
Expected economic help					
Korea	.36*	.24*	-.02		.09†
Taiwan	.41*	.20*	-.20*		.24*
Japan	.05	.01	.02		.06
U.S. (Hawaii)	.23*	.17*	-.08†		.05
Philippines	.18*	.12*	.10†		.14*
Thailand	.31*	.10†	.00		.21*
Economic benefits/large family					
Korea	-.05	-.05	.07	.09†	
Taiwan	-.05	-.03	.14*	.24*	
Japan	-.14*	-.10†	.09†	.06	
U.S. (Hawaii)	-.02	-.05	.20*	.05	
Philippines	.03	-.04	.16*	.14*	
Thailand	.00	-.12†	.19*	.21*	

† *p* < .05.

* *p* < .01.

**Table 5.3 Correlations between financial ease/large family and
selected background and fertility variables**

Country	Income	Education	Parity	Additional children desired	Ideal family size
Korea	.09†	.02	.20*	−.02	.12*
Taiwan	.24*	.16*	.13*	−.04	.08†
Japan	.21*	.15*	.13*	.15*	.22*
U.S. (Hawaii)	.14*	.03	.29*	.17*	.36*
Philippines	.18*	−.02	.34*	.02	.32*
Thailand	−.02	−.04	.20*	.18*	.39*

† $p < .05$.
* $p < .01$.

The measure of expected economic help from children, on the other
hand, presents a fairly straightforward picture (Table 5.4). A consistent and generally strong inverse relationship is shown for income and
education; that is, the wealthier and better-educated parents tended
not to expect economic help from their children. The relationships
with fertility variables are weaker and generally positive: expected economic help is related to higher parity, the desire for more children, and
a larger ideal family size.

Some of these relationships will become clearer in the context of
multivariate analyses. However, further studies with improved measurement and research design are needed for a satisfactory understanding of economic dimensions of the value of children.

Sociodemographic and VOC dimensions. Table 5.5 provides additional
information about the relationships among social status, social setting,
and the perceived value of children by showing the correlations of education and urban experience with 17 measures of the value of children.
About two-thirds of the correlations are significant in all countries except Japan, where half are significant. The level of correlations ranges
widely, from essentially zero to .71. Most of the correlations are negative—that is, those with more education and urban experience rated
these values as less important. Education and urban experience tend to
have similar relationships with the value of children, with education
being generally the stronger measure.

As a screening device, it is useful to examine only those VOC dimensions that show a correlation of .30 or higher for two or more

countries. Two economic indices meet this criterion: the burden of educating children and expected economic help. Both are negative, indicating that more educated, urbanized parents were relatively unconcerned about the costs of educating their children and did not have high expectations of economic help from them. These findings confirm the subgroup differences on various economic measures discussed earlier.

From among the VOC attitude scales, the strongest findings are shown for those scales that most clearly reflect a traditional view of parenthood and parent-child relationships: continuity, tradition, security; role motivations; social status; and external controls. The more educated parents and those with urban experience showed less agreement with the items in these scales. In addition, they were less prone to rate as important the set of 17 reasons for wanting another child.

As will be shown below, many of these same dimensions are also related meaningfully to fertility and family planning variables, suggesting that perceptions of the value of children do play a mediating role. Moreover, some VOC dimensions not emphasized here still have a connection with fertility and family planning, while others show only weak relationships in either direction.

VOC, family planning, and family-size measures. Because the patterns of correlations between VOC measures and dependent variables vary substantially across countries, it is difficult to single out those VOC dimensions that have the strongest relationships overall. Nevertheless, Tables 5.6 and 5.7 attempt such an identification, based on a rough

Table 5.4 Correlations between expected economic help and selected background and fertility variables

Country	Income	Education	Parity	Additional children desired	Ideal family size
Korea	−.52*	−.65*	.31*	.14*	.34*
Taiwan	−.21*	−.59*	.17*	.12*	.30*
Japan	−.10†	−.22*	.14*	−.05	.02
U.S. (Hawaii)	−.26*	−.53*	.21*	.12*	.25*
Philippines	−.29*	−.34*	.02	.07	.20*
Thailand	−.58*	−.71*	.25*	−.12*	.06

† $p < .05$.

* $p < .01$.

Table 5.5 Correlations of education and urban experience with eco-

Measure	Korea Education	Korea Urban experience	Taiwan Education	Taiwan Urban experience
VOC economic indices				
Economic burden/education	−.44*	−.31*	−.42*	−.26*
Financial ease/large family	.02	.01	.16*	.14*
Expected economic help	−.65*	−.51*	−.59*	−.42*
Decreased utility of children	.08†	.02	.20*	.13*
Economic benefits/large family	−.07	−.10†	−.17*	−.18*
VOC social-psychological indices				
Continuity, tradition, security (VOC 1)	−.58*	−.52*	−.50*	−.32*
Parenthood satisfactions (VOC 2)	.01	.06	−.26*	−.15*
Role motivations (VOC 3)	−.21*	−.15*	−.32*	−.14*
Happiness, affection (VOC 4)	−.21*	−.12*	−.30*	−.10*
Goals, incentives (VOC 5)	.12*	.09†	−.23*	−.10†
Social status (VOC 6)	−.41*	−.36*	−.34*	−.20*
External controls (VOC 7)	−.30*	−.31*	−.15*	.04*
Costs of children (VOC 8)	−.15*	−.08	−.15*	−.06
Decision-mindedness in childbearing (VOC 9)	−.08	−.11*	.06	−.11*
Reasons wanting another child	−.32*	−.27*	−.07	−.02
Reasons not wanting another child	−.09†	−.04	−.16*	−.16*
Benefit children/large family	.04	.05	.06	.05

† $p < .05$.
* $p < .01$.

index of consistency. Table 5.6 shows correlations for those VOC economic measures and VOC attitude scales where the correlations are of the same sign in five or more countries for each of three family planning indices (number of contraceptive methods known, situational attitudes toward birth control, and current use of birth control). In Table 5.7 the same standard is applied for three measures of family size (ideal number of children, actual number of children, and number of children wanted). These tables thus identify the VOC measures for which correlations with a set of conceptually related dependent variables are fairly consistent across countries, but they omit cases where strong correlations may have been shown in a few countries. (Significance levels are shown in the tables, but sign, rather than significance, is used as the criterion in this consistency analysis. For additional cor-

nomic and social-psychological measures of the value of children

Japan		U.S. (Hawaii)		Philippines		Thailand	
Education	Urban experience	Education	Urban experience	Education	Urban experience	Education	Urban experience
-.05	-.02	-.15*	-.14*	-.32*	-.18*	-.36*	-.20*
.15*	-.02	.03	.08†	-.02	-.09†	-.04	-.01
-.22*	-.38*	-.52*	-.44*	-.34*	-.33*	-.71*	-.46*
-.06	.01	.04	-.08†	.26*	.26*	.16*	.17*
.10	.03	.05	.09†	-.22*	-.16*	-.17*	-.11†
-.15*	-.24*	-.53*	-.43*	-.28*	-.23*	-.46*	-.25*
-.15*	-.12*	-.42*	-.32*	.03	-.01	-.22*	-.08
-.15*	-.02	-.51*	-.44*	-.22*	-.13*	-.33*	-.20*
-.09†	-.14*	-.02	.20*	-.19*	-.11*	-.20*	.02
-.12*	-.12*	-.34*	-.29*	.02	-.02	.06	.03
-.07	.00	.16*	.11*	-.28*	-.23*	-.49*	-.29*
.00	.04	-.01	.10*	-.16*	-.04	-.55*	-.29*
.02	.13*	-.13*	-.14*	-.10†	-.08†	-.07	-.06
-.07	-.01	.45*	.44*	-.22*	-.25*	-.24*	-.17*
-.10†	-.10†	-.37*	-.38*	-.19*	-.26*	-.24*	-.16*
-.12*	-.04	-.05	-.07†	-.22*	-.09†	-.39*	-.26*
-.02	.01	-.05	-.03	-.06	-.01	-.16*	-.10†

relational data, see Appendix Table D7 and the regression analyses presented later in this chapter.)

With respect to family planning (Table 5.6), all the consistent correlations are negative, indicating that those who scored higher on these VOC dimensions had less knowledge of contraception, less favorable attitudes toward the use of contraception in specified situations, and a lower level of current use of contraception. Only one economic index shows such consistent findings: the expectation of economic help from children. Four of the VOC attitude scales emerge as consistent in their relationships to family planning measures: continuity, tradition, security (VOC 1); role motivations (VOC 3); happiness and affection (VOC 4); and external controls (VOC 7).

Among the three family planning indices, in nearly all cases the

Table 5.6 Value-of-children dimensions showing consistent correlations across five or more countries with family planning indices

Dimension	Family planning		
	Knowledge	Attitude	Use
Expected economic help			
Korea	-.49*	-.13*	-.24*
Taiwan	-.42*	-.18*	-.24*
Japan	-.21*	-.07	-.15*
U.S. (Hawaii)	-.49*	-.46*	-.30*
Philippines	-.28*	-.05	-.04
Thailand	-.46*	-.26*	-.30*
Continuity, tradition, security (VOC 1)			
Korea	-.46*	-.15*	-.22*
Taiwan	-.33*	-.05	-.20*
Japan	-.23*	-.08	-.18*
U.S. (Hawaii)	-.47*	-.43*	-.24*
Philippines	-.21*	-.05	-.01
Thailand	-.23*	-.18*	-.13*
Role motivations (VOC 3)			
Korea	-.20*	-.12*	.03
Taiwan	-.18*	-.07	-.03
Japan	-.18*	-.08	-.14*
U.S. (Hawaii)	-.41*	-.40*	-.24*
Philippines	-.12*	.11†	-.03
Thailand	-.13*	-.02	-.11†
Happiness, affection (VOC 4)			
Korea	-.23*	-.06	-.02
Taiwan	-.14*	-.04	-.13*
Japan	-.26*	-.08†	-.08
U.S. (Hawaii)	-.27*	-.07†	-.11*
Philippines	-.10†	.09†	.00
Thailand	-.10†	-.10†	-.05
External controls (VOC 7)			
Korea	-.34*	-.09†	-.19*
Taiwan	-.07	-.13*	-.04
Japan	-.02	-.07	-.08
U.S. (Hawaii)	-.28*	-.24*	-.12*
Philippines	-.07	.00	-.09†
Thailand	-.37*	-.18*	-.20*

NOTE: Consistency is defined by the inclusion of all VOC economic indices and attitude scales for which correlations are of the same sign in five or more countries for each of the three family planning measures.

† $p < .05$.

* $p < .01$.

Table 5.7 Value-of-children dimensions showing consistent correlations across five or more countries with family-size indices

Dimension	Family size		
	Ideal	Actual	Wanted
Economic burden/education			
Korea	.19*	.16*	.25*
Taiwan	.17*	.24*	.22*
Japan	-.03	.05	-.01
U.S. (Hawaii)	.12*	.34*	.17*
Philippines	.09†	.21*	.16*
Thailand	.01	.23*	.17*
Financial ease/large family			
Korea	.12*	.19*	.20*
Taiwan	.08†	.15*	.13*
Japan	.22*	.09†	.20*
U.S. (Hawaii)	.36*	.27*	.35*
Philippines	.32*	.34*	.36*
Thailand	.39*	.20*	.28*
Expected economic help			
Korea	.34*	.29*	.40*
Taiwan	.30*	.17*	.27*
Japan	.02	.15*	.01
U.S. (Hawaii)	.25*	.20*	.26*
Philippines	.20*	.03	.07
Thailand	.06	.25*	.16*
Continuity, tradition, security (VOC 1)			
Korea	.29*	.25*	.36*
Taiwan	.30*	.20*	.23*
Japan	-.04	.11*	-.04
U.S. (Hawaii)	.27*	.23*	.24*
Philippines	.11*	-.01	.00
Thailand	.10†	.15*	.04
Role motivations (VOC 3)			
Korea	.11*	.16*	.06
Taiwan	.20*	.09†	.12*
Japan	.01	.12*	-.03
U.S. (Hawaii)	.23*	.20*	.20*
Philippines	.09†	.02	.02
Thailand	.08	.08	.03
Happiness, affection (VOC 4)			
Korea	.07	.13*	.04
Taiwan	.18*	.07	.13*
Japan	.06	.15*	.04
U.S. (Hawaii)	.09*	.04	.13*
Philippines	.11†	.08	.08
Thailand	.08	.12*	.11†

Table 5.7 *(continued)*

Dimension	Family size		
	Ideal	Actual	Wanted
Social status (VOC 6)			
Korea	.18*	.18*	.19*
Taiwan	.16*	.15*	.23*
Japan	.03	.08†	-.03
U.S. (Hawaii)	.00	-.06	.03
Philippines	.07	.07	.03
Thailand	.15*	.23*	.15*

NOTE: Consistency is defined by the inclusion of all VOC economic indices and attitude scales for which correlations are of the same sign in five or more countries for each of the three family-size measures.

† $p < .05$.

* $p < .01$.

highest correlations are shown with number of contraceptive methods known. Among countries, correlations are notably low in the Philippines and Japan. Stronger correlations tend to appear for Hawaii and Korea, but not for all combinations of variables.

The family-size measures (Table 5.7) are consistently correlated with a larger number of VOC dimensions than are the family planning indices, all in a positive direction. Thus those who had and wanted large families saw children as a greater burden to educate, but also thought they could afford a large number of children and had greater expectations of economic help from their children. From the attitude scales, large families are associated with emphasis on continuity, tradition, security (VOC 1); role motivations (VOC 3); happiness and affection (VOC 4); and social status (VOC 6).

Among the three family-size indices, there is no consistent finding as to which correlates most strongly with the VOC measures. It may be noted, however, that overall the correlations are somewhat lower for the family-size indices than for the family planning indices, with many low correlations shown particularly for the VOC attitude scales. Among countries, Japan and the Philippines have relatively weak results, as was the case with family planning indices.

From this analysis, it appears that economic dimensions of the value of children, including old-age security, are linked to both family planning and family size. In addition, certain psychological dimensions are important—a traditional view of sex roles, a belief that social status is associated with childbearing, a feeling that childbearing is not a matter of individual choice, and an emphasis on happiness and affection in parent-child relationships. In the sections that follow, these simple correlations are examined within a multivariate framework.

Levels of prediction

To examine the relationships among sociodemographic variables, VOC dimensions, and fertility and family planning indices, multiple regression analyses were conducted. The dependent variables were the eight measures covering various aspects of family planning and family size described earlier. Separate regressions were run to predict each of these measures by sociodemographic variables (block A), by sociodemographic plus VOC economic variables ($A + B$), and by sociodemographic plus VOC economic plus VOC social-psychological variables ($A + B + C$).[6] For the prediction of additional children desired, parity was added as a separate predictor.

To provide an overview of the results of these 150 regression analyses, Table 5.8 shows the variance (R^2) accounted for by each set of predictors for the eight dependent variables. Also shown in Table 5.8 are significance levels (calculated from F-ratios) for the effects of each set of predictors. Highlights of these results are discussed below, after which details of the components of prediction (correlations and regression coefficients for specific variables) are presented for two dependent measures—knowledge of contraception and number of additional children wanted.

The dependent variable best predicted by sociodemographic factors (block A) is, without exception, the one that reflects past behavior: number of living children. In all countries but Japan, second-best prediction by sociodemographic variables is shown for number of contraceptive methods known, a variable that also reflects to a large extent past experience. By contrast, prediction by sociodemographic factors of current attitudes and ideals (that is, attitudes toward birth control and ideal number of children) is generally low. Sociodemographic prediction of current behavior—use of birth control—is also quite weak, except in Korea and Taiwan.

The increment in prediction attributable to VOC economic dimensions (block B) is statistically significant in most cases, but the size of the increment differs substantially across dependent variables and

---

6 For the prediction of actual, desired, and ideal family size, block C was modified by deletion of the summed scores on reasons for wanting/not wanting another child, since these were thought to be conceptually inappropriate in relation to measures of completed family size.

Table 5.8 Prediction of selected birth control and family-size measures (As shown by proportion of variance explained [R^2] in multiple regression analyses)

Dependent variable	Predictors[a]	Korea	Taiwan	Japan	U.S. (Hawaii)	Philip-pines	Thai-land
Number of contraceptive methods known	A	.47*	.30*	.12*	.31*	.22*	.40*
	A+B	.48†	.36*	.13	.38*	.25*	.41
	A+B+C	.52*	.38	.19*	.46*	.27	.45†
General birth control attitude	A	.03	.04*	.05*	.06*	.04*	.16*
	A+B	.07*	.11*	.05	.16*	.06	.22*
	A+B+C	.14*	.18*	.09	.26*	.15*	.26†
Situational birth control attitude	A	.04*	.04*	.02	.26*	.05*	.10*
	A+B	.06	.13*	.04†	.32*	.07	.14†
	A+B+C	.14*	.21*	.10†	.44*	.14*	.20*
Current use of birth control	A	.29*	.20*	.08*	.07*	.04†	.10*
	A+B	.31	.23*	.11*	.11*	.05	.15*
	A+B+C	.35	.28†	.18*	.20*	.07	.18
Number of living children	A	.63*	.52*	.23*	.43*	.57*	.53*
	A+B	.64	.55*	.26*	.52*	.62*	.57*
	A+B+C[1]	.66†	.57†	.29	.54*	.62	.58
Number of children wanted	A	.38*	.19*	.06*	.12*	.36*	.23*
	A+B	.42*	.26*	.10*	.28*	.42*	.30*
	A+B+C[1]	.48*	.28	.14	.33*	.44	.32
Ideal number of children	A	.16*	.15*	.04*	.07*	.15*	.07*
	A+B	.20*	.22*	.09*	.24*	.24*	.23*
	A+B+C[1]	.24	.25*	.12	.28*	.26	.25
Additional number of children wanted	P	.14*	.13*	.04*	.06*	.08*	.07*
	P+A	.32*	.18*	.12*	.13*	.11†	.10†
	P+A+B	.34†	.22*	.16*	.23*	.15*	.18*
	P+A+B+C	.38†	.34*	.25*	.31*	.25*	.29*

NOTE: The significance of each subset of independent variables in explaining the total variance is computed by an F-test modified by the hierarchical order in which each subset was added. The general formula is given below:

$$F = \frac{R^2 \text{ change}/M}{(1 - R^2_{y.12,\ldots,k})/(N - k - 1)}$$

where R^2 change represents a squared part correlation that measures the incremental variance explained with the addition of each new variable, k is the total number of independent variables, M is the number of independent variables in the subset for which the significance test is being made, and N is the total number of cases (Nie et al., 1975:339–340).

a Predictors:
   A = six sociodemographic variables.
   B = five VOC economic dimensions.
   C_1 = twelve VOC social-psychological dimensions.
   C^1 = ten VOC social-psychological dimensions (reasons for wanting/not wanting another child not included).
   P = parity.

† $p < .05$.
* $p < .01$.

countries. The largest increments are shown for wanted and ideal family size in Hawaii (16 percent and 17 percent, respectively) and for ideal family size in Thailand (16 percent). In all countries, wanted and ideal family size are among the variables for which the best prediction from economic dimensions is shown, but the increments are as low as 3–5 percent for Japan and Korea. Prediction of birth control knowledge and attitudes by economic dimensions is relatively strong in Hawaii and Taiwan (with increments of 6–9 percent).

Substantial increments are also shown in many cases for the set of variables labeled VOC social-psychological dimensions (block *C*), but about one-third are not statistically significant. For most countries, the highest level of additional prediction is shown for the variable that reflects current motivations for childbearing—additional children wanted. (The exceptions are Hawaii and Korea, where higher levels are shown mainly for attitudes toward birth control.) The increments in prediction of additional children desired range from 5 percent in Korea to 12 percent in Taiwan.

For all countries, the "prediction" of past reproductive behavior (number of living children) by the broad VOC dimensions is quite low, with increments ranging from 0 to 3 percent. Similar figures are shown for prediction of ideal number of children, while substantially higher increments appear in nearly all cases for measures related to birth control knowledge, attitudes, and use.

When the effects of the two blocks of VOC dimensions (*B* and *C*) are combined with the sociodemographic variables (block *A*) and compared with the sociodemographic variables alone, increments attributable to VOC measures range from 3 to 21 percent, with a mean value of 10.4 percent. Twenty-four comparisons out of a total of 48 show an increment of 10 percent or more attributable to VOC dimensions.

With respect to the total level of prediction by all variables, the dependent variable that is best predicted in all countries is number of living children. As noted above, this is mainly attributable to the strong effects of sociodemographic factors. The total R^2 ranges from .29 in Japan to .66 in Korea. Listed below are the highest and lowest R^2 for the other seven dependent variables.

Country	Highest R^2	Lowest R^2
Korea	Number of methods known (.52)	General and situational birth control attitudes (each .14)
Taiwan	Number of methods known (.38)	General birth control attitude (.18)

Country	Highest R^2	Lowest R^2
Japan	Additional children desired (.25)	General birth control attitude (.09)
U.S. (Hawaii)	Number of methods known (.46)	Current use of birth control (.20)
Philippines	Number of children wanted (.44)	Current use of birth control (.07)
Thailand	Number of methods known (.45)	Current use of birth control (.18)

These data highlight the finding that attitudes toward birth control and current use of birth control are generally not well predicted. The reasons for these two results may be quite different, however. The attitudinal response on birth control is generally favorable everywhere, so correlations are attenuated. Current use of birth control, on the other hand, is a yes-no response affected by many variables that are not taken into account in this analysis—for example, age of the youngest child. It is to be expected, then, that the absolute level of prediction should not be high.

The frequently good prediction of number of contraceptive methods known results mainly from the strong effects of sociodemographic variables, but with substantial increments from VOC dimensions. The sociodemographic variables should reflect in part exposure to information, while VOC dimensions should reflect motivation to learn (that is, demand for family planning information).

Prediction for Japan is quite low overall, compared to other countries. For the Philippines, the prediction of current use of birth control is notably low.

In summary, these data on R^2 show that VOC dimensions do have substantial predictive effects on certain fertility and family planning indices, independent of background and situation. However, these effects are attributable in large part to only a few of the VOC measures and some correlations go in unexpected directions. These factors are discussed in the next section.

Components of prediction

The data presented in this section pertain to two dependent variables: number of contraceptive methods known and number of additional children desired. These variables are chosen for detailed presentation because of their differing psychological implications. Knowledge of contraception may be viewed as an indicator of past learning experience which, as noted earlier, should reflect both exposure to information and motivational factors—that is, the demand for fertility limitation. The number of additional children desired appears to be the best available indicator of current fertility motivations and as such should be closely linked to current perceptions of the value of children. (For detailed analyses of other dependent variables, consult the individual country reports. See also Appendix Table D7, which shows correlations between selected VOC indices and four additional dependent variables.)

The nature of regression analyses suggests a causal relationship that of course is not demonstrated with these cross-sectional data. While it is plausible to assume that the perceived value of children affects fertility motivations and family planning practices, it is equally plausible that motivations and practices that are mainly attributable to other sources of influence have a feedback effect on the perceived (and reported) satisfactions and costs of children. No doubt causality does operate in both directions, and this fact should be borne in mind with respect to the data that follow.

For each dependent variable, three sets of data will be presented: the variance (R^2) accounted for by the three blocks of predictor variables, separately and in combination; the zero-order correlations between the specific variables in each block and the dependent variable; and the regression coefficients (betas) from a multiple regression analysis in which all predictors are considered simultaneously.

Knowledge of contraception. The total variance accounted for in prediction of number of contraceptive methods known ranges from 19 percent for Japan to 52 percent for Korea (Table 5.9). The sociodemographic variables are generally the strongest predictors, although in Hawaii the VOC social-psychological variables are slightly more powerful. For most of the countries, each block has a substantial effect when considered independently. For sociodemographic variables, the variance accounted for ranges from 12 to 47 percent; for VOC economic variables, from 5 to 28 percent; and for VOC social-psychological variables, from 11 to 32 percent.

When VOC dimensions are considered along with sociodemographic variables, their effect diminishes appreciably, confirming that the perceived value of children functions as an intervening element between social factors and reproductive behavior. Each VOC block also shows a certain independent predictive effect, but the size of the increments beyond the sociodemographic predictor is not large for the VOC eco-

Table 5.9 Prediction of knowledge of contraception
(As shown by proportion of variance explained [R^2])

Predictor	Korea	Taiwan	Japan	U.S. (Hawaii)	Philip- pines	Thailand
Sociodemographic	.47	.30	.12	.31	.22	.40
Sociodemographic + VOC economic	.48	.36	.13	.38	.25	.41
Sociodemographic + VOC economic + VOC social- psychological	.52	.38	.19	.46	.27	.45
VOC economic	.28	.27	.05	.25	.13	.23
VOC social- psychological	.29	.14	.11	.32	.11	.29

nomic dimensions, ranging from 1 to 7 percent, and is not significant for Japan and Thailand (see Table 5.8). If the increments attributable to both economic and social-psychological dimensions are considered, the range is from 5 to 15 percent. Substantial independent effects for both VOC blocks were found in Korea, Hawaii, and Thailand.

The regression coefficients from the analysis of all three blocks together are shown in Table 5.10, along with the zero-order correlations between each predictor variable and knowledge of contraception. A comparison of the columns for r's and betas indicates the extent to which correlational variance overlaps among the predictor variables.

Before these results are discussed, it should be reiterated that several VOC dimensions have similar content, especially with respect to economic benefits and costs of children. Interpretations of specific dimensions must therefore be made with caution, since the variance among similar dimensions may be distributed differently across countries.

Among the sociodemographic variables, education shows the most consistently strong predictions across countries. However, each of the other sociodemographic variables also has a substantial independent predictive effect in one or more countries. These varying predictive patterns for sociodemographic variables will of course have an effect on the patterns for VOC variables, since it was shown earlier that there is a considerable amount of shared variance among the blocks.

When background factors are controlled, the strong bivariate relationships for certain VOC economic dimensions are greatly attenuated. Expected economic help, for instance, retains a strong effect only in

Hawaii, where those who expect help (mainly Filipinos) have less knowledge of contraceptive methods. In Taiwan, the perception that larger families are better off economically emerges as an important independent predictor of knowledge of contraception, with the expected inverse relationship.

The social-psychological dimensions also show quite varied patterns across countries in the regression analysis; as with the economic dimensions, many of the beta weights are quite weak. Consistencies across countries that appeared in correlational relationships, such as for VOC Scale 1, tend to disappear when the controls in the regression analysis are introduced. Each country emerges with a distinctive set of social-psychological predictors, the interpretations of which are attempted in the country reports. Here it will simply be noted that only about one-third of the betas are statistically significant and only a few of the variables have betas of .10 or above in two or more countries— namely, happiness and affection (VOC 4); external controls (VOC 7); and reasons for wanting another child.

Overall, these analyses suggest an important observation: while there are certain cross-cultural similarities in relationships between VOC dimensions and fertility and family planning indices, these relationships are affected differently by background and situation in different countries. Such a finding, if replicated and confirmed in other studies, would have important policy implications. For example, it might be universally true that a decrease in expectations of economic help from children would lead to an increase in the demand for fertility limitation. Nevertheless, the social and economic policies to influence expectations of economic help might vary substantially across countries. Thus general recommendations might be made about the significance of certain VOC dimensions and *direct* means to influence them (such as information and persuasion), but such general recommendations might not be feasible for social and economic measures that would influence the perceived value of children *indirectly*.

Additional children desired.   The number of additional children desired, taken by itself, may be regarded as an index of motivations for childbearing at the time of the interview. When considered in conjunction with parity, it may be regarded as an index of motivations for family size. In the analyses that follow, parity is controlled. The purpose of these analyses, then, is to relate the perceived value of children to concurrent motivations for family size.

Table 5.11 shows the variance accounted for in multiple regression

Table 5.10 Zero-order correlations and regression coefficients for (By country)

Predictor	Korea		Taiwan	
	r	beta	r	beta
Age	.19*	.20*	.06	.00
Income	.52*	.16*	.25*	.10*
Education	.62*	.17*	.47*	.16*
Urban experience	.45*	.01	.34*	.08*
Media exposure	.56*	.26*	.46*	.20*
Marriage duration	-.23*	-.17*	-.16*	-.03
Economic burden/education	-.31*	.10*	-.27*	-.04†
Financial ease/large family	.09†	.07*	.13*	.04†
Expected economic help	-.50*	-.05†	-.42*	-.07*
Decreased utility of children	.05	.00	.23*	.10*
Economic benefits/large family	-.13*	-.05*	-.32*	-.21*
Continuity, tradition, security (VOC 1)	-.46*	-.13*	-.33*	.00
Parenthood satisfactions (VOC 2)	.04	.02	-.18*	-.03
Role motivations (VOC 3)	-.20*	-.06*	-.18*	-.03
Happiness, affection (VOC 4)	-.22*	-.12*	-.14*	.05*
Goals, incentives (VOC 5)	.09†	.04*	-.13*	.03
Social status (VOC 6)	-.30*	.08*	-.23*	-.02
External controls (VOC 7)	-.34*	-.11*	-.07	.01
Costs of children (VOC 8)	-.15*	-.02	-.06	.05*
Decision-mindedness in childbearing (VOC 9)	-.05	.01	.10†	.06*
Reasons wanting another child	-.14*	.12*	-.11*	-.04†
Reasons not wanting another child	-.04	.00	-.08	-.06*
Benefit children/large family	.01	-.03*	-.06	-.03†

† $p < .05$.
* $p < .01$.

prediction of knowledge of contraceptive methods

Japan		U.S. (Hawaii)		Philippines		Thailand	
r	beta	r	beta	r	beta	r	beta
-.05	-.06*	-.20*	-.17*	-.03	-.04	.19*	-.01
.12*	.10*	.19*	-.01	.31*	.09*	.47*	.06*
.21*	.12*	.51*	.38*	.43*	.26*	.60*	.34*
.24*	.14*	.18*	-.14*	.33*	.06*	.36*	.07*
.20*	.14*	.18*	.06*	.28*	.09*	.46*	.18*
-.11†	-.04	-.12*	.12*	-.08	-.03	-.18*	.02
.01	.01	-.19*	-.07*	-.09†	.06*	-.25*	-.03†
.02	-.01	.07†	.06*	-.05	-.01	.04	.07*
-.21*	.03	-.49*	-.19*	-.28*	-.06*	-.46*	-.05†
.07	.08*	.06	.02	.25*	.10*	.12*	.00
-.03	-.04†	.06	.09*	-.14*	-.03	-.13*	.01
-.23*	-.01	-.47*	-.06†	-.21*	-.01	-.23*	.05†
-.19*	-.06*	-.28*	.04†	-.02	.01	-.09†	-.02
-.18*	-.02	-.41*	-.04	-.12*	.04	-.13*	.05*
-.26*	-.13*	-.27*	-.10*	-.10†	.03	-.10†	-.08*
-.13*	.01	-.29*	.03	-.02	-.01	.16*	.08*
-.18*	-.06*	-.10*	-.06*	-.19*	-.04	-.31*	-.07*
-.03	.05*	-.28*	-.18*	-.07	.03	-.37*	-.05*
.02	-.03	-.05	.03†	-.07	-.04†	.09†	.19*
-.05	.01	.29*	.11*	-.14*	.02	-.13*	.00
-.20*	-.14*	-.34*	-.04†	-.25*	-.14*	-.16*	-.02
-.05	.03	-.03	.05*	-.10†	.00	-.25*	-.04†
.04	.00	.03	.02	.05	.08*	.12*	-.03

Table 5.11 Prediction of number of additional children desired
(As shown by proportion of variance explained [R^2])

Predictor	Korea	Taiwan	Japan	U.S. (Hawaii)	Philip- pines	Thailand
Parity	.14	.13	.04	.06	.08	.07
Parity + sociodemographic	.32	.18	.12	.13	.11	.10
Parity + sociodemographic + VOC economic	.34	.22	.16	.23	.15	.18
Parity + sociodemographic + VOC economic + VOC social- psychological	.38	.34	.25	.31	.25	.29
VOC economic	.04	.05	.03	.08	.03	.08
VOC social- psychological	.13	.26	.12	.21	.21	.20

analyses, with parity treated separately from other sociodemographic variables. The total variance accounted for, using all predictor variables, ranges from 25 to 38 percent. Considering each block separately, the sociodemographic variables (including parity) and the VOC social-psychological variables are relatively strong, with variance accounted for ranging from 10 to 32 percent and 12 to 26 percent, respectively. Parity has relatively strong effects only in Korea and Taiwan, and the VOC economic variables are relatively weak in all countries.

The incremental effects of VOC dimensions vary substantially across countries. When VOC economic variables are added to parity and other sociodemographic variables, the increments (all of which are statistically significant, as shown in Table 5.8) range from 2 to 10 percent. When VOC social-psychological variables are added to the other three blocks, increments range from 4 to 12 percent (again all statistically significant, as shown in Table 5.8).

The components of these predictive effects are shown in Table 5.12, where both regression coefficients and zero-order correlations are indicated for each predictor variable. While parity is generally an important predictor, duration of marriage is also important in most countries. In Korea, urban experience has a particularly strong negative influence on additional children desired, while in Japan both urban experience and education are positively related to family-size motivations. Income and media exposure have very weak effects in all countries.

With respect to economic aspects of the value of children, the perceived financial ease of raising a large family has a substantial positive relationship with additional children desired in Hawaii, Thailand, and Japan. Other VOC economic indices are weaker, although statistically significant in many cases, and show greater variability across countries.

Among the VOC social-psychological indices, the most powerful by far, in all countries except Korea, are the summed reasons for wanting or not wanting another child. As discussed earlier, these items are closely linked conceptually and methodologically to desired family size and may in fact be regarded as an explanation, in value-of-children terms, for the number of children wanted. Other VOC social-psychological measures have variable predictive effects on additional children desired, with slightly over one-third being statistically significant. The only scales with betas above .10 in two or more countries are continuity, tradition, security (VOC 1) and role motivations (VOC 3).

In view of the strong predictive effects of reasons for wanting and not wanting another child, independent of sociodemographic measures, the components of these summed indices will be examined. Table 5.13 shows the partial correlations, with parity controlled, between each item in these indices and the number of additional children desired.

Among the reasons for wanting another child, the most consistently strong correlation across countries is shown for item 3: "want a boy/ another boy." Also strong in all countries except Korea is item 10: "to provide a companion for my child/children." These findings thus confirm the analyses reported earlier—that sex preference and ideas concerning the social network among children have an important effect on family size. It is of interest that the desire for a girl also shows up quite strongly in Hawaii, the Philippines, Thailand, and (to a lesser extent) Taiwan.

Among the other items that correlate .15 or above in four or more countries are several pertaining to psychological or emotional satisfactions (for example, items 1, 11, 13, 15, and 16). Also important by this standard is item 12: "spouse wants more children."

The correlations between reasons for *not* wanting another child and number of additional children desired are generally lower, but substantial consistency is shown across countries for many items. Considering those that have a correlation of .12 or above in four or more countries, three items emerge as important: "financial burden to family," "would be a lot of work, bother for me," and "would be an emotional strain for me."

Again, it is important to recognize that the summed scores on these items had quite substantial predictive effects on the number of addi-

Table 5.12 **Zero-order correlations and regression coefficients for**
         (By country)

Predictor	Korea		Taiwan	
	r	beta	r	beta
Parity	-.38*	-.36*	-.36*	-.13*
Age	-.33*	.07*	-.24*	-.03
Income	-.21*	.07*	.00	.01
Education	-.13*	-.12*	.02	.03
Urban experience	-.27*	-.32*	-.07	-.10*
Media exposure	-.09†	.01	-.03	-.01
Marriage duration	-.37*	-.26*	-.36*	-.15*
Economic burden/education	.08	.08*	-.02	.03
Financial ease/large family	-.02	.09*	-.04	-.01
Expected economic help	.14*	.12*	.12*	.08*
Decreased utility of children	.06	.04†	-.08†	-.08*
Economic benefits/large family	.10†	.02	.20*	.06*
Continuity, tradition, security (VOC 1)	.12*	.04	.04	-.11*
Parenthood satisfactions (VOC 2)	-.10†	-.02	.04	-.02
Role motivations (VOC 3)	-.14*	-.17*	.07	.04†
Happiness, affection (VOC 4)	-.09†	-.07*	.10	.06*
Goals, incentives (VOC 5)	-.02	.10*	.05	.02
Social status (VOC 6)	.02	.01	.09†	.04†
External controls (VOC 7)	.14*	.05*	-.01	.02
Costs of children (VOC 8)	.01	.09*	-.08†	-.05*
Decision-mindedness in childbearing (VOC 9)	.02	-.05*	.00	-.05*
Reasons wanting another child	.12*	.00	.40*	.30*
Reasons not wanting another child	-.17*	-.10*	-.28*	-.24*
Benefit children/large family	-.01	.00	-.03	-.07*

† p <.05.
* p <.01.

prediction of number of additional children desired

Japan		U.S. (Hawaii)		Philippines		Thailand	
r	beta	r	beta	r	beta	r	beta
-.19*	-.10*	-.25*	-.15*	-.28*	-.22*	-.27*	-.08*
-.07	.06*	-.25*	-.14*	-.02	.12*	-.11†	.05†
-.05	-.05*	-.02	.03	.04	.07*	.12*	.03
.25*	.17*	-.01	-.03	.04	.03	.15*	-.04
.21*	.18*	.01	.02	-.07	-.03	.08	-.03
.08†	-.02	-.05	-.06*	-.03	-.02	.13*	.08*
-.21*	-.10*	-.31*	-.13*	-.18*	.01	-.30*	-.21*
-.06	.03	-.16*	-.03	-.06	.04†	-.13*	.06*
.15*	.14*	.17*	.19*	.02	.02	.18*	.17*
-.05	.08*	.12†	.11*	.07	-.03	-.12†	.01
.05	.08*	-.03	.04†	-.07	-.02	.09†	.11*
.08	.04†	.10†	.02	.12*	.09*	.16*	.11*
-.08	-.11*	.08†	-.05	.04	-.05†	-.12*	-.13*
-.02	.06*	.12*	.05†	.08	.05*	.02	.02
-.08	-.12*	.08†	.00	.03	-.02	-.07	-.01
-.02	.05*	.08†	-.04	.04	.01	-.01	.05†
.01	-.02	.06	-.07*	-.01	-.03	.04	-.04†
-.07	-.06*	.06	.02	.00	-.01	-.10†	-.08*
-.02	-.02	.15*	.11*	.01	.02	-.10†	.02
-.04	.04	-.15*	-.05*	-.14*	-.10*	-.09†	.03
-.03	-.01	-.03	.00	.01	-.02	-.15*	.01
.23*	.30*	.34*	.28*	.36*	.34*	.30*	.30*
-.14*	-.14*	-.22*	-.14*	-.23*	-.16*	-.28*	-.18*
-.06	.01	.04	.06*	.04	.03	-.02	-.01

Table 5.13 Partial correlations (parity controlled) between reasons for wanting/not wanting another child and number of additional children desired

Reasons	Korea	Taiwan	Japan	U.S. (Hawaii)	Philippines	Thailand
Reason for wanting						
1 Enjoy having a small baby	-.09	.26	.02	.18	.15	.20
2 To carry on family name, traditions	.21	.22	.04	.18	.10	.14
3 Want a boy/another boy	.25	.27	.22	.17	.29	.20
4 Want a girl/another girl	.03	.15	.09	.22	.24	.32
5 Relatives feel I should have more children	.10	.18	.08	.10	.15	.18
6 To have a child to help me in my old age	.16	.22	.03	.13	.08	.03
7 My religious duty to have children	.21	.11	-.08	.17	.11	.02
8 To have one more person to help family economically	.12	.18	.03	.17	.12	.07
9 To make my marriage stronger	.00	.30	.11	.22	.11	.07
10 To provide a companion for my children	.02	.29	.23	.32	.26	.28
11 Enjoy caring for, raising children	-.04	.23	.14	.30	.25	.21
12 Spouse wants more children	.05	.23	.06	.26	.26	.17
13 Fun to have children around the house	-.06	.12	.22	.24	.22	.21
14 Raising children helps me learn about life and myself	-.05	.14	.14	.15	.21	.17
15 To have special feeling of love between parent and child	-.07	.18	.10	.25	.18	.20
16 To share what I have and know with children	.07	.16	.09	.17	.15	.20
17 To have enough children survive to adulthood	.17	.21	.00	.16	.13	.11
Reason for not wanting						
1 Financial burden to family	-.10	-.16	-.12	-.09	-.23	-.15
2 Spouse does not want more	-.16	-.09	-.04	-.10	-.10	-.15
3 Would restrict my freedom to do other things I enjoy	-.09	-.11	-.07	-.13	-.09	-.13
4 Would be a lot of work, bother for me	-.06	-.16	-.13	-.12	-.16	-.23
5 Could not spend as much time with spouse	-.14	-.15	.04	-.03	.04	-.07
6 Concern about overpopulation	.08	-.12	.08	-.18	-.12	-.12
7 Would be an emotional strain for me	.02	-.18	-.15	-.12	-.16	-.14
8 Would not be able to give enough attention, care to other children	-.07	-.20	-.10	-.18	-.10	-.22
9 Would cause problems, strains between spouse and me	.02	-.04	-.11	-.02	-.16	-.08

tional children desired, over and above the effects of a broad range of background and situational factors, including parity, income, education, and marriage duration.[7] The statistical evidence thus suggests that these items measure important aspects of fertility motivations that are relatively independent of the traditional sociodemographic indices. Further study of such factors, including their antecedents and their susceptibility to social influence, may provide significant insights into alternative policies to regulate fertility.

---

7 In Korea, there was virtually no relationship for many of the reasons for wanting another child, resulting in a weak combined index and a mystery as to why Korea differed so markedly from the other countries on these measures.

6

discussion
and policy implications

The preceding chapters have presented extensive results of this exploratory study of the value of children. Yet, it should be noted, this volume has also been selective, in relation to the total amount of data collected and analyses performed. The country reports present more detailed analyses, including additional variables and alternative conceptual and methodological approaches.

This concluding chapter integrates the diverse findings of the VOC Study by drawing upon all available material. First some common elements in the descriptive data on the value of children are presented. Then three important aspects of research on the value of children are discussed: structure of values, values and fertility, and values and population policy. Finally, the 15 VOC dimensions described in Chapter 1 are used as a framework within which to review the findings of the study and to discuss the implications of this kind of research for population policies and programs. The varying perspectives taken in different sections of this chapter may produce a certain amount of redundancy in the discussion of findings—but also, it is hoped, these perspectives provide some unifying themes for the study as a whole.

Value profiles for groups

Among the most consistent findings in this study was the emergence of distinctive profiles of values for the three socioeconomic groups that were studied: urban middle class, urban lower class, and rural. The following profiles of values for each group draw upon responses to several questions, both open-ended and structured. Included are the general advantages and disadvantages of children, reasons why people in general want children, reasons for wanting a daughter or a son, positive and negative motivations for wanting another child and a certain family size, and agreement or disagreement with the VOC attitude scales. Some important differences across countries are necessarily obscured in these composite profiles, but those differences are noted elsewhere in this volume. For each group, a profile of positive values is presented first, followed by a profile of costs. Finally, some common elements among groups of countries, which cut across socioeconomic differences, are noted.

In the *urban middle-class group,* psychological or emotional advantages of having children are emphasized. These advantages include happiness for the individual parent or the family, a feeling of personal growth and development of the parent that is associated with child-rearing, and pleasure in the companionship and fun provided by children. Values related to specific aspects of family life, such as continuity of the family name and a strengthening of the bond between husband and wife, are shown to be important for the middle class in some countries but not in others. Economic benefits of children generally are not salient for middle-class respondents.

When middle-class respondents described reasons why other people want children, rather than their own reasons, two interesting differences emerged: continuity of family name was cited as the most important reason in Korea and Taiwan, and in four countries respondents frequently mentioned that it is "instinctive" or "natural" to have children.

Daughters were wanted in the middle class mainly for psychological reasons, especially as companions for the mother and because of their positive personality or behavioral qualities. Sons were wanted mainly for continuity of family name everywhere but in Japan. Middle-class respondents also saw psychological advantages of having sons similar to those of having daughters, but when sons were discussed there was an increase in responses pertaining to economic or practical benefits.

With respect to reasons given as important for wanting another child, the pattern of strong emotional-psychological values and weak economic motivations among the middle class is generally maintained, and continuity of family name and sex preferences are also shown to be important. Values related to the respondent's desired family size include providing companionship for other children or avoiding an only child, as well as sex preference or a desire for balance between sexes.

A common response for the middle class in four countries was "can afford that number or am able to raise that number."

The financial costs of children are very salient, even to the affluent middle class. This finding presumably reflects their desire for children of high "quality" at a greater cost per child, as well as the generally higher costs of raising children in an urban setting. While the level of concern about financial costs tends to be somewhat lower for the middle class than for other socioeconomic groups, the importance of financial considerations in relation to other costs is shown clearly in middle-class responses to questions on the general disadvantages of having children, reasons for not wanting another child, reasons for limiting the family to the desired size, and the perceived financial burden of having three children.

Restrictions of various kinds, or opportunity costs, were important to middle-class respondents in all countries. In tabulations of spontaneous responses by major coding categories, restrictions show up as more salient than financial costs for middle-class respondents in all countries except the Philippines and Thailand. The relative importance of restrictions diminishes, however, in a structured item on reasons for not wanting another child—possibly because opportunity costs are significant in the decision to have children or not have children, but are less so in decisions for more children after the first child has been born.

Emotional strain from rearing children and such associated factors as noise and disorder in the household were salient to middle-class respondents in all countries. Health problems of children and general rearing problems were also important in most countries. In the decision to have another child, parents were also concerned about not being able to give enough care and attention to existing children. Problems of pregnancy and maternal health were cited with modest frequency by middle-class respondents as reasons for restricting family size. In Japan, housing problems were the second most important reason for limiting the number of children, for all urban respondents.

Urban lower-class respondents, like those of the middle class, stressed psychological or emotional benefits provided by children, but there was an increase of economic motivations for this group and some evidence of a stronger orientation toward continuity of family name. The differences in economic dimensions are seen more clearly in the reasons for wanting sons and daughters than in the general advantages; increases are shown for expectations of both economic help from sons and practical help from daughters. Similar to the middle class, the lower-class respondents attributed strongly to others the motivation of continuity of family name and also that it is "instinctive" or "natural" to have children.

In reasons for wanting another child, the similarity between urban middle-class and urban lower-class respondents is again shown on many dimensions, but with the same increased emphasis in the lower class on economic benefits and family continuity. Concerning motivations related to family size, the lower class is distinguished from the middle class mainly by an increase in the specific desire for more boys.

Lower-class respondents in general showed greater concern than the middle class about financial costs of raising children. In fact, in some countries the data suggest a trend toward curvilinearity, with the urban lower class more concerned about costs than either the middle class or the rural group. This is not surprising, since the urban lower-class respondents tended to have more children and lower income than the middle class while being exposed to the same high urban cost factors, and to have higher costs and fewer benefits than the rural group.

Restrictions on alternative activities were also important to the lower class, although generally less important than for the middle class. Rearing and health problems are fairly similar across the middle and lower class, and likewise there is little difference with respect to emotional costs.

For the *rural group,* the economic utility of children comes to the fore, with respect to current economic contributions and to security in the parents' old age. This emphasis shows up in a variety of items: the general advantages of having children, the reasons for wanting both sons and daughters, the perceived motivations of others for having children, the reasons for wanting another child, and in responses to specific questions on old-age support. Economic motivations were thus most salient for the rural group, somewhat less so for the urban lower class, and least salient for the middle class. The "traditional" value of family continuity shows this same trend, again reflected in responses to several types of questions, including the attitude scale labeled "continuity, tradition, security."

Emotional benefits remained salient to rural respondents in all countries, but their significance diminished both in relation to other benefits and also by absolute frequency of mention. This does not mean, of course, that rural parents do not enjoy their children; it does seem to suggest that, given their socioeconomic setting, the emotional benefits of children are much less important than the economic benefits. It is of interest that two related psychological benefits emerged as important for rural respondents in three East Asian countries: "pride in children's accomplishments" and "children to carry out the parents' hopes and aspirations." Perhaps these rural parents were especially frustrated by their own life circumstances and hoped their children would fare better.

Rural respondents in all countries showed a strong awareness of the financial burden of children. Although the costs of raising children should be low in rural areas, rural respondents tended to have many children to raise on relatively low incomes. Restrictions on alternative activities of the parents were less salient in rural areas, but restrictions on work did rank as somewhat important among rural respondents in Taiwan and Thailand, and other restrictions were cited in Japan and by Filipinos in Hawaii.

Rural respondents in several countries mentioned physical work, tiredness, and emotional strain caused by children as a general disadvantage and also as a reason for restricting family size. This pattern of response is probably related to the greater amount of physical labor required of both husbands and wives in rural areas.

Most striking in the profiles described above is the contrast between psychological benefits of children emphasized by the middle class and economic benefits emphasized by the rural respondents, with the urban lower class falling between. This finding may be a function of different styles of response related to the education of respondents, but the pervasiveness of the trend in different types of questions suggests that the three groups have genuinely different orientations toward the value of children. The difference in expected economic benefits is, of course, quite consistent with explanations of the demographic transition that have been advanced in the theoretical literature on population.

The similarities of comparable socioeconomic groups are more impressive than similarities among groupings of countries. Still, there are discernible patterns that seem to reflect similarities in cultural influences or levels of socioeconomic development. Meaningful similarities among countries and ethnic groups are apparent for Korea and Taiwan; for Thailand, the Philippines, and Filipinos in Hawaii; and for Japan, Japanese in Hawaii, and Caucasians in Hawaii.

For Korea and Taiwan, the most striking similarity is the emphasis on the linked dimensions of son preference and continuity of family name. In both countries, family ties are very strong and continuity of name and family tradition flows from the male lineage. Filial piety is among the highest virtues in both countries and, in the Chinese tradition, sons are essential for the rituals of ancestor worship. In Korea and Taiwan, then, the value of children is dominated by these cultural traditions that place such great emphasis on family continuity through sons.

In the Philippines and Thailand, influences specifically tied to religious systems are important. In both the Catholic and the Buddhist religions, for example, abortion is rejected as a method of birth control. Catholicism also fosters a general pronatalist orientation which must be partly responsible for the strongly positive value orientations regarding children that have been shown for the Philippines, but this study contains only weak evidence for the linkage with religion. Buddhism, while not generally pronatalist, does encourage son preference since sons are needed to "make merit" for the parents. In this respect Thailand is close to Taiwan and Korea, rather than the Philippines, but the effects on son preference are weaker in Thailand.

Filipino and Thai respondents were also distinctively similar to each other and different from other respondents on several specific dimensions—for example, greater emphasis on economic benefits and security from children (especially among urban lower-class and rural respondents), greater concern about child mortality, greater concern about marital problems from children. These similarities between the Philippines and Thailand are a mixed lot and appear to reflect the similar level of socioeconomic development of the two countries, as well as such factors as strong religious commitment.

The pattern shown in Japan and among Japanese and Caucasians in Hawaii appears also to be a reflection of socioeconomic development, in this case at the higher end of the scale. These more affluent respondents living in more modern societies were more concerned about opportunity costs of having children, for instance, which is presumably indicative of the greater range of alternative satisfactions available to them. They also tended to place greater emphasis on the psychological benefits to the parent in rearing children and showed very little concern for the economic benefits from children. Preference for sex of children is also less strong among Japanese and Caucasian respondents, perhaps reflecting societal differences in sex roles and such factors as higher educational levels for the samples.

Structure of values

The preceding profiles focused on certain common elements in the findings of this study, but it is important to recognize also that different value domains were revealed by different types of questions.

For example, questions dealing with children versus no children, reasons for wanting or not wanting another child, the advantages and disadvantages of specific family sizes, and the importance of children generally all revealed different (although overlapping) sets of values. In retrospect this outcome is perhaps not surprising, but in any event the results have important implications for future studies.

One way to organize these findings is to conceptualize different aspects of values. In the Philippines report (Volume 2) in this series, for instance, a scheme is introduced in which "each value is assumed to have three chief characteristics: salience, or frequency of reference to the value . . . ; centrality, or closeness to a person's basic concerns; and differential effect, or prominence in highlighting particular contrasts, such as boys versus girls or the first child versus the fifth child" (Bulatao, 1975:197). Such a scheme is helpful in interpreting the variations in results across questions; it also implies differences in sources of influence, resistance to change, and impact on fertility decisions, for values that comprise a different mix of characteristics.

Another approach to the structure of values relies on empirical clustering of data and attempts to interpret the clusters found. This approach is used in each country report, particularly in connection with factor analysis of the 45 VOC attitude items. For comparative analysis, a set of nine VOC dimensions that had substantially similar structures across countries was constructed by this method. In addition, the 15 comprehensive VOC dimensions described in the introduction to this volume were derived through an integration, partly empirical and partly judgmental, of the total set of data for all questions across the six countries.

Beyond the labeling of clusters of values, which makes the results more manageable, *types* of values may be identified, based largely on presumed linkages to broader theoretical or conceptual systems. The scheme of Hoffman and Hoffman (1973), which was developed prior to this study, organizes the positive values of children in relation to a set of nine individual psychological needs. That scheme is described in Chapter 1 of this volume. A simpler distinction that has been found useful by several investigators in this study is "extrinsic" versus "intrinsic" values. These categories are defined somewhat differently by each investigator, but the basic distinction appears to be costs and rewards that are external to the individual (social approval, financial aspects) versus those that are internal (feeling needed, a sense of security).

In a project memorandum prepared in 1974, Bulatao suggested the following classification of "values and disvalues":

Values

1. Instrumental assistance from children
2. Rewarding aspects of interaction with children
3. Psychological appreciation of children

Disvalues

1. Direct financial costs
2. Opportunity costs
3. Childrearing demands
4. Costs to social relationships

These categories are offered as part of a model of child production, in which "values are the ultimate ends of the production process [while] the disvalues involve the resources that must be spent in the process . . . or the opportunity costs of child production." (For an elaboration of the model, see Bulatao, 1975.)

In various ways, then, the experience of this exploratory study has led the investigators toward (1) the development of a meaningful conceptual scheme for the perceived satisfactions and costs of children and (2) the integration of that scheme within models that incorporate social influences and reflect the reciprocal relationship between values and behavior. The testing and refinement of such models is a major aim of the second phase of the VOC Study, initiated in 1975, which applies improved measures to larger samples in a wider variety of cultures.

Values and fertility

Significant statistical relationships between VOC dimensions and indices of fertility and family planning have been shown in this study. The study has been less successful, however, in demonstrating cause-and-effect relationships, including changes over time. While this weakness is to some extent inevitable in a cross-sectional study, much can still be learned from improved and expanded studies, whether cross-sectional or longitudinal.

Of particular importance will be the testing of hypotheses that relate specific VOC dimensions to different stages of the family-building process. For example, it is reasonable to expect that, for some couples, opportunity costs of children play a major part in the decision to have the first child but may be relatively unimportant at later stages. And, as suggested by the phrase "some couples," it is necessary to include in the hypotheses statements about the relationship between the VOC dimension and the situation for specified individuals or groups. For example, either real or perceived opportunities within the social setting should be specified—that is, alternatives to having the first child or another child.

Another area that deserves further work is the specification of relationships between types of values and number of children. Certain positive values, such as personal development, may be satisfied by fewer rather than more children, while others, such as old-age security, may be satisfied only by a large family. Certainly it is too simplistic to assume that there should be a linear positive association between the strength or salience of a specific positive value and fertility.

Likewise, there is a need for clear conceptualization of the role of negative values, including their interaction with positive values. Economic costs, for instance, should be interpreted in relation to both the availability of economic resources and expected economic benefits. And the time dimension should be taken into account, particularly with respect to the issue of current costs versus long-term benefits. Perhaps hypotheses can be developed too about anticipatory factors— that is, the extent to which a cost may or may not be recognized without being learned through the experience of childrearing. If a cost is learned mainly through experience, a question naturally arises as to the point at which it begins to influence fertility decisions.

The diversity of values and the contrasts across socioeconomic groups shown in this study highlight the need to deal with differences in values (preferences, tastes) within the context of microeconomic theories. As pointed out by Edwards (1975:18):

A fundamental weakness of [Becker's] approach, and indeed of others, is its assumption that basic tastes and preferences do not change with income. . . . It is a major lacuna in the social sciences that we lack a theory of preferences and must therefore base our theories of choice on the assumption of given tastes. The cost in terms of our understanding of what determines family size and how it can be reduced seems very great indeed. If we knew more about preferences, perhaps policy variables could be manipulated in ways which would have direct effects on them.

Values and population policy

Population policies are developed by governments because demographic behavior is not a purely private affair. Demographic events, such as the move of a rural household to the city or the birth of a third child, have an impact on others in the society, as well as on the individuals directly concerned. If these effects on others, or externalities, are thought to be important, then a rationale exists for developing a public policy to regulate demographic events in the collective interest. Such policies are usually viewed as complementary to broader policies for socioeconomic development.

All the countries in this study, along with many other countries around the world, have shown in the past decade a serious concern about population policy issues. The focus in most countries has been on means to reduce fertility and thus retard rates of population growth. In some countries, however, such as Japan, attention has also been given to the question of policies to increase fertility rates.

Fertility policies, whether antinatalist or pronatalist, often are designed to change the balance of satisfactions and costs associated with children. Such changes may be brought about by social policies (child care facilities, jobs for women), economic policies (tax exemptions for children, costs of education), or information and persuasion (facts about the costs of rearing children, messages that smaller numbers of children are better for the family and the society). Information about the perceived value of children obviously is relevant for the formulation and implementation of such fertility policies. (See also the discussion of population policy in Chapter 1.)

If the policy goal is antinatalist, then satisfactions of children that are positively related to family size should be curtailed or reduced in importance, linked to small rather than large families, or satisfied by means other than children (that is, alternatives to children). Costs of children that are negatively related to family size should be increased in strength or made salient at earlier stages of the family-building cycle.

A major problem of such antinatalist policies is to design them in such a way as to avoid penalizing children. Increasing the costs of children, for instance, may serve as a deterrent to some parents, but others will still have many children and find it harder to provide for them. This difficulty may be avoided by policies that increase information about, and salience of, current costs, rather than increasing the actual costs. Penalization of children can also be avoided by focusing on satisfactions, including the provision of alternative satisfactions. But that is easier said than done, because it often requires major social changes.

Few countries have introduced social or economic policies designed explicitly to alter the satisfactions and costs of children, although such policies have been discussed frequently in the population literature. Rather, the easier approach of reducing the costs of birth control, for those who wish to restrict family size, has been widely adopted, often accompanied by some element of persuasion. This persuasion, however, has usually been in the form of general appeals for smaller families, directed to the total population. This approach is useful for facilitating the adoption of birth control among those who have already achieved their desired family size, but there is little evidence that it will bring about a significant reduction in the number of children wanted. To achieve that end, persuasion programs (and other aspects of population policies) should be linked to specific motivations of the target audience. For example, a program directed to a rural population should focus on the economic functions of children and should raise, in the local context, such issues as the decreasing economic utility of children and emerging alternatives to children as a source of income and security. Such an approach is consistent with the theoretical and empirical literature on attitude formation and change (see, for example, Smith, Bruner, and White, 1956; Crawford, 1974), but it has yet to be systematically incorporated in population programs.

In view of the diversity of satisfactions that children provide, and because of the complex interaction of satisfactions and costs, no single program or policy is likely to be sufficient. The following section relates the findings of this study to specific policy measures. Particular attention is given to information and persuasion programs, since the results do provide clear guidelines for improving the content of population messages. Moreover, it is easier to make cross-cultural generalizations in this area because communications provide a means for directly influencing specific dimensions of the value of children. Indirect influence, through social and economic policies, may be more important and has the potential of being more effective in the long run, but it is not easy to generalize about such policies because of the differences across countries in linkages between social and economic factors and the value of children. A few policy recommendations of this kind are suggested in this volume and in the country reports, but with considerable caution in view of the obvious limitations of a study based on small and nonrepresentative samples. As research on the value of children progresses, providing validation and further elaboration of the intervening and independent effects of specific values, it should become possible to recommend a broader array of policies to influence the value of children and fertility.

Dimensions of values

As a means of summarizing the results of this study, each of the 15 VOC dimensions described in Chapter 1 will be discussed here. Highlights of the findings for each dimension will be presented, followed by comments about the implications for population policies and pro-grams. Only antinatalist measures are discussed, since that is the em-phasis in most countries with explicit population policies. It should be noted, however, that information about the value of children could equally well be used to suggest policies to increase fertility, if that were determined to be a social goal.

Emotional benefits.   Perhaps the least surprising finding of this study is the emphasis given by parents to the emotional satisfactions of hav-ing children. Although children may have been viewed as "little adults" in some societies in earlier eras, they are not so regarded by present-day parents in the countries in this study. For many parents, the ex-pressions of love between parent and child and the fun of having chil-dren around the house are perhaps the major sources of happiness and satisfaction in the parents' lives. Not only do parents personally ex-perience the pleasure of having children, but they are also led to expect such pleasure and their feelings are reinforced by the modern media and by traditional folk sayings and literature. Small wonder, then, that "emotional benefits" showed up as important in a questionnaire about the value of children.

Yet the emotional benefits are not always the most important posi-tive values. A good many parents, especially in rural areas, gave a higher ranking to other values. The main competitor was economic benefits and security, but respondents sometimes gave priority to fa-milial and social or religious values over emotional benefits. Urban re-spondents, however, tended to give prominence to emotional aspects of childrearing. Perhaps they were more prone to think in "psycho-logical" terms, but perhaps also they were more appreciative of family emotional ties in the midst of an impersonal urban setting.

The emotional dimension is probably a powerful element in the de-sire to have the first child, but this study of persons who were already parents can offer no evidence on that point. The data do show emo-tional benefits as being among the strongest reasons for wanting an-other child, in all countries and in all socioeconomic groups. Moreover, with parity controlled, various aspects of emotional benefits are sig-nificantly correlated with the number of additional children desired. (The attitude scale of happiness and affection, however, shows mainly weak correlational and predictive relationships with fertility and fam-ily planning indices.)

Presumably family size would be affected particularly by the enjoy-ment of having a small baby, compared with the enjoyment of children in general, since another baby would be wanted when previous children grow older. The results of the current study are ambiguous on this point. Relatively few respondents, except for Filipinos, rated the enjoyment of babies as an important reason for wanting another child; at the same time, in several countries scores on this item are significantly correlated with the number of additional children desired.

Even if emotional benefits were related only to the desire to have *some* children, rather than a certain number, they would still be important for policy purposes. If many people believe that critical emotional satisfactions can be gained only by having children, then few will choose not to have children. Yet, from a policy point of view, an argument can be made in favor of programs to increase the proportion of childless women as a means of reducing the average number of children per woman, since this policy allows some women to have many children and preserves a diversity of family sizes that may be socially beneficial.

The major policy approach in this area would be to provide alternatives that can offer some of the same emotional satisfactions that people expect from children. Presumably attention should be focused on alternative interpersonal relationships. In some societies, for instance, there is an emerging belief that husband-wife relationships can be deeper and more satisfying without children, particularly when both spouses are employed in meaningful ways. There are also those who prefer to care for other people's children, either occasionally or in a professional role such as a teacher, and who view this as a substitute for having their own children. And there are communal living arrangements, as in the Israeli kibbutz, where children are shared among a group of adults. In a variety of ways, then, it is possible to obtain at least some of the emotional benefits associated with having children without becoming a parent.

Moreover, programs can be developed to connect emotional benefits with small rather than large families. This is in fact already being done in many family planning campaigns: "A small family is a happy family." The approach could be made more specific. In the present study, it was found that a majority of parents believed that "a child who has a very close relationship with his parents" is likely to come from a small family. This belief could be reinforced, with an emphasis on the gratifications for the parent of such close relationships.

Economic benefits and security.   The findings of this study lend support to the notion that changes in the economic benefits of children, which are associated with modernization and urbanization, are a major cause of the demographic transition. Throughout the study it has been demonstrated that rural parents emphasized strongly the economic benefits and security from children, while urban lower-class parents showed a similar but weaker orientation and the educated, modern middle class showed little concern about economic benefits. This trend holds for all countries, although in the Philippines the differences across socioeconomic groups are relatively small; all Filipino groups showed a high level of concern about economic benefits and security from children. The results also show that, for rural and lower-class urban parents, expected economic benefits were a relatively strong reason for wanting another child. Old-age support, rather than current economic contributions, appears to be the major concern. In every country in this study, at least 70 percent of rural parents expected to rely at least somewhat on their children for financial support in old age.

At the same time, the evidence points to emotional security as an important component of old-age support. Some respondents were explicit about this; many others gave general responses, such as "I want to have children to take care of me when I am old." It is perhaps artificial to separate the economic and noneconomic forms of security that people associate with children, but each has somewhat different policy implications.

Measures of expectations of economic benefits from children are negatively related to family planning indices and positively related to family-size indices. In most countries, for example, economic motives for wanting another child are positively correlated with the number of additional children wanted. Also, economic motives show some independence of other factors that were measured. Spontaneous mention of economic benefits, in an open-ended question on advantages of children, is significantly correlated with desired family size in four countries.

In this area the policy recommendations are clear and have often been cited: governments should implement credible and adequate old-age pension programs as well as programs providing housing and physical care for the elderly. These would appear to be the nearest substitutes that governments can provide for the security of having children, although such programs obviously lack the element of emotional support that may be critical for many parents.

Another policy approach, somewhat more subtle, is to devise programs that ensure higher "quality" for children from small families and thus, presumably, greater earning potential and ability to support parents in their old age. This can be accomplished mainly through the educational system. In Singapore, for example, only the first three children have priority in choice of schools, and in Taiwan an educational bond system that ensures better education for children from small families is being tried experimentally. Through means such as these, and perhaps through information programs, parents may be persuaded that adequate security can be obtained with a small number of children. Relevant information, for instance, would include statistics on the high probability of survival for children beyond a certain age, which would be helpful in demonstrating to parents that only a few children are needed to ensure survival of a son or daughter in the parents' old age. Public health programs to reduce infant and child mortality should, of course, be continued and strengthened.

The results of this study pertaining to reasons for wanting sons show that it is mainly sons, rather than daughters, who are relied on for old-age support. This selectivity presumably is the result of many social, cultural, and legal factors in each country, and any policies developed to bring about changes would have to be country-specific. With respect to information programs, however, it may be noted that persuasive efforts are under way in some countries to show that daughters are more faithful to their parents than sons. ("A son is a son till he gets a wife; a daughter is a daughter all her life.") Moreover, as more and more women enter the wagepaying labor market, parents may realistically expect their daughters to provide economic support. This too is being emphasized in information programs, and it is reinforced by the general social trend toward equal rights for women.

Self-enrichment and development.   This positive value, which encompasses the social role of parenthood and the psychological satisfactions of childrearing, was frequently articulated by the better-educated middle class, but elements of it were also rated as important by other groups in response to structured items and attitude scales.

Having children is of course the only way to become a parent, and in many societies parenthood and adulthood are virtually synonymous. Children are therefore wanted by young adults in order to demonstrate maturity and to be accepted as a member of the adult community. In some societies, concepts of masculinity and femininity may be associated with large numbers of children.

Also included in this value are the ideas that a parent learns about life through raising children, that childrearing is an important avenue to self-fulfillment, and that a parent (particularly the mother) can demonstrate competence through successful childrearing. These appear to be rather sophisticated concepts, and they are in fact most often expressed by the better-educated respondents. Emphasis on these specific values is assumed to be related to the absence of alternative means for self-fulfillment and self-expression.

There is some evidence in this study that the values of self-fulfillment and self-enrichment, which were combined in one category, have different fertility implications and should be treated separately. Although the roles related to parenthood can in fact be ascribed to people as soon as the first child is born, it appears that those who regard such roles as important tend to desire large families. By contrast, many parents who emphasize learning, incentives, and competence believe these values can best be met through small families.

At a conceptual level, the roles of adulthood and parenthood reflect the pronatalist values and social structures that are an integral part of most societies. Parenthood is normal; nonparenthood is abnormal. Men find satisfaction in their jobs; women find satisfaction in their children. Children give meaning to life; a life without children is empty. Because these values and beliefs are so deeply ingrained in social and cultural systems, there are no simple policy measures to counteract them. Rather, as has been pointed out often in the literature on population policy, fundamental social changes that will alter familial and occupational roles are required. Such changes are in fact occurring in many societies, but relatively slowly in the developing countries. And, of course, changes in the family structure are often regarded as undesirable, since the family is viewed as the cornerstone of traditional values and morality.

With such barriers to change in mind, perhaps the most realistic aim for population policies is to encourage in every way possible the idea of individual freedom in the choice of life-styles. Not every person is suited for parenthood, and societies should offer a genuine alternative of nonparenthood without social and economic penalties. The pronatalist pressures in the society should, in effect, be relaxed. Although there can be no single formula for accomplishing this, an example would be to publicize as models actual cases of women who have found satisfaction in careers, along with continuing efforts for legal and other changes to make such careers a realistic alternative to parenthood. Primary school textbooks, for instance, should portray both men and women in a variety of nonparental roles.

Identification with children.   This value pertains to the vicarious pleasures involved in having children, which are related to the processes by which parents tend to identify themselves with their children. Thus the accomplishments of the child become a source of pride to the parents, and the parents can perceive their own values, preferences, traits, and even physical features in the child and his or her development. Also included here would be the reliving of one's childhood through children. This constellation of values represents the social expression of a profound emotional attachment, which may also have biological roots.

Identification with children was salient to parents in all socioeconomic groups in Korea, Taiwan, and Japan and was also important to Japanese and Caucasians in Hawaii. These values were not often expressed by Filipino and Thai respondents, however, at least in response to open-ended questions. Although this category was not adequately covered by the structured items in the questionnaire, a related item on the enjoyment of caring for and raising children is positively correlated with the number of additional children desired (with parity controlled) in all countries except Korea.

As noted earlier, "pride in children's accomplishments" and "children to carry out parents' hopes and aspirations" were particularly salient for the rural groups, perhaps reflecting the parents' dissatisfaction with their own lot in life and their hopes for better prospects for their children. Other elements of the value category, such as "pleasure from watching growth and development of children," appear to involve a modern, individualistic approach to childrearing. These elements were in fact most prominent in Japan and Hawaii.

With respect to population policies, there appears to be no substitute for one's own child as an object for identification, except perhaps an adopted child. Possibly some aspects of this value can be satisfied through other creative acts, as in art, or even through lasting contributions to the society or community, as in business entrepreneurship or participation in community development. But for most people in most societies, children are likely to remain the most valued objects for personal identification.

The most useful policy approach in this area, as with several other positive values, may be to emphasize the quality of the child in relation to small family size. In small families, children will have a better chance in life and will be better able to realize their parents' hopes and aspirations, thus being a greater source of pride and providing greater satisfaction through identification.

Family cohesiveness and continuity. To a great extent, children are viewed as an essential part of marriage, and having children is a major motivation for getting married. Without children, a marriage is not "complete"; without children, there is no sense of "family." Children are often seen as creating a stronger bond between husband and wife. Moreover, the continuity of the family and the family name is possible only through having children.

These motivations are obviously powerful ones, particularly in traditional societies with strong familial values. Even in modern societies like Japan and Hawaii, however, aspects of family cohesiveness and continuity are strong. For example, continuity of family name was an important reason for wanting sons for all groups in Hawaii, and the concept of children as a bond between spouses was in several countries more common among the modern, urban respondents than among rural respondents. The primary group ties of the nuclear family were important to parents living in the impersonal social context of large cities, while the value-related concepts of carrying on the family name and traditions were important to parents in rural societies. In nearly all countries, "children to make the marriage stronger" and "children to carry on the family name and traditions" are positively related to the number of additional children wanted.

It is hardly feasible to recommend as a population policy that family ties should be loosened, since there is considerable sentiment in most countries to reverse the existing secular trend in that direction. Rather, the policy emphasis should be on aspects of this value that may be changed without weakening the family. Changes in inheritance laws and practices might in some instances affect the linkage between family continuity and family size; for example, requirements for equal distribution of wealth among all male and female children could strengthen motivations for smaller families. Moreover, changes in the practices for transmitting the family name should reduce the desire for sons, since continuity of family name is a major reason for wanting sons, and a reduction in son preference would have a substantial impact on fertility. The aim of such policies would not be to weaken the family as a social unit but to weaken the linkages between familial motivations and large family size.

Emotional costs. Parents' feelings toward children are ambivalent; emotional costs, as well as emotional satisfactions, are clearly recognized. Children are a nuisance, and they create worry and emotional strain for parents. It is necessary to discipline children and see that they behave properly, but parents are not sure how to do that and they worry about "bad" influences from outside the home.

Emotional costs were highly salient to respondents in all countries and all socioeconomic groups, and were generally more salient than economic costs as a disadvantage of having children compared with not having children. In considering the costs of another child or a large family, most respondents stressed economic rather than emotional costs.

Urban respondents rated emotional costs higher than did rural respondents, and it appears that emotional costs were felt with particular strength in Japan and Korea. In all countries except Taiwan, emotional costs are negatively related to the number of additional children wanted (with parity controlled).

It is likely that the emotional costs of childrearing are not fully anticipated by prospective parents, although this study provides no evidence on that since all respondents had at least one child. The study does show that emotional costs are salient to couples with children, however, and the strength of these responses is impressive.

Population policies concerning costs of children are quite different from those concerning satisfactions, since the concept of substitution does not apply. Rather, policies should aim to increase the awareness and salience of costs (if not the actual costs), particularly in the early childbearing years.

With respect to policies to increase emotional costs, this effect appears to be accomplished, deliberately or otherwise, through housing policies. With less living space and play space, it is almost inevitable that the emotional costs of children will increase with family size. In Japan, where housing costs are high and are closely linked to the amount of space, urban respondents regarded housing problems as second only to financial costs as a reason for limiting family size. In some countries public housing policies are used with apparent effect for pronatalist or antinatalist purposes. In Singapore, for instance, a large part of the population lives in public housing and priority for additional space is not given for children after the second child.

It seems likely that delays in the birth of the first child could be encouraged through public education about the emotional costs of childrearing and the need for newlyweds to establish themselves financially and emotionally before taking on this additional burden. For some couples, greater awareness of emotional costs would also facilitate decisions not to have children.

Economic costs. Much of the discussion and experimentation in the area of population policy has centered on means to increase the financial costs of having children. The findings of the present research project support the relevance of this policy approach. Respondents were very much aware of the financial costs of children, and such costs were given as the primary reason for restricting family size in all countries in this study. At the same time, however, the data suggest that most respondents thought they could afford more than the number of children they planned to have. Moreover, many parents, particularly in rural areas, expected to obtain long-range economic benefits from having children. When these factors are considered in relation to the powerful social and emotional motivations for having children, it appears that increases in costs might have to be very substantial to bring about significant declines in fertility.

It should be noted that although parents were aware in a general way of the economic costs of children, they lacked specific knowledge. When asked to estimate the amount of money they had spent on their children in the past year, not surprisingly, many could give no answer and those who did respond produced widely varying figures. It is in fact difficult to separate expenditures on children from other family expenditures, and even economists cannot readily assess the effects of substituting lower quality goods, housing, and so forth as the family increases in size. Nonetheless, economists in a number of countries are trying to devise realistic estimates of the costs of children. The availability of such data could be useful in public education programs, since long-term costs of children could be related explicitly to prospective earnings. While total economic rationality in childbearing decisions cannot be expected, at least the empirical basis for that component of decisions could be provided. The costs of raising children in urban areas are quite high in many countries, and prospective parents should at least be aware of those costs, particularly if they have high educational aspirations for their children. Such information would not be irrelevant for rural parents, but the impact presumably would be less because of lower costs of children and greater expected economic benefits.

A review of all of the data from this study suggests that there is a threshold effect involving economic costs of children. While such costs are generally recognized, they do not become a controlling element until some minimum family size has been achieved. Normative influences and emotional needs operate strongly for at least the first and second child, and values such as son preference may push the minimum number substantially higher. For most parents, however, a point is reached at which consideration is given to preventing further pregnancies, and it is then that economic costs become highly salient. The aim of population policies concerning costs of children should be to increase the strength of negative economic considerations and to shift the awareness and salience of costs to earlier stages of the family-building cycle.

Restrictions or opportunity costs.   The life-style of a couple, particularly the wife, is changed substantially when the first child is born. Children demand time and attention, so other activities must be foregone. Respondents sometimes expressed this in fairly specific terms, such as less time for recreation or social life, but more often they saw it as a general lack of flexibility and freedom ("children tie you down"). For many women, jobs and careers are abandoned, or at least interrupted, with the birth of the first child.

These opportunity costs were felt most strongly by urban parents, and in many countries this disadvantage of having children was as important as, or more important than, financial or emotional costs. Opportunity costs were most salient in Japan and least salient in the Philippines and Thailand, in the responses to the open-ended question about having children compared to no children. Curiously, however, this pattern changes substantially in responses to a structured question about reasons for not wanting another child. For the item "restrict my freedom to do other things I enjoy," responses were strongest among respondents in Taiwan, Thailand, and the Philippines and were stronger for the lower class and rural group than for the middle class. The same pattern is observed for an item on another child being "a lot of work and bother for me," perhaps reflecting a combination of high parity and a high degree of workforce activity by females. In all groups, however, opportunity costs were less important than financial costs as a reason for not wanting another child.

Statistical analyses show that in a majority of countries spontaneous mention of opportunity costs has an inverse significant relationship with ideal and desired family size. "Restriction of freedom" as a reason for not wanting another child is negatively correlated in all countries with the number of additional children desired, but at relatively low levels.

As with other costs, population policies may aim to increase the actual opportunity costs or to enhance the awareness and salience of such costs. Actual costs could be increased in two ways: by making alternative activities more available and more attractive or by increasing the extent to which children interfere with such alternative activities. Meaningful jobs for women are of course a major attractive alternative, and there is substantial evidence to show that the availability of such jobs does affect fertility. Other opportunities to compete with childbearing include recreational and social activities outside the home and involvement in community development or welfare activities of various kinds. Opportunities for continuing education can also be important.

Means for increasing the extent to which children interfere with alternative activities include reducing the availability of child care facilities and shortening school hours for children. These options are obviously undesirable on other grounds, however, and so are not really feasible.

On the other hand, it would be feasible to increase the awareness and salience of opportunity costs. It is clear that most prospective parents do not fully anticipate the changes in their life-style that will occur with the birth of the first child. Nor do they appreciate the practical advantages to be gained by a delay in the first birth—such as accumulation of savings, job advancement and higher earnings before a child is born, opportunity for higher education, and job mobility. Public education programs in population should emphasize such opportunity costs with particular stress on the advantages of delaying the first birth.

Physical demands. Children do create a lot of work for parents, particularly the mother, but the amount of work depends on the availability of household help or laborsaving devices, and the relative importance probably varies with other physical demands made on the mother, such as manual employment. Substantial differences across countries were found for this factor. Parents in Thailand and Taiwan, particularly rural parents, showed the strongest concern about physical demands. Physical demands were of relatively little concern in Japan and Hawaii. Except in Taiwan, "a lot of work and bother" as a reason for not wanting another child is negatively correlated with the number of additional children wanted.

There appear to be no particularly important policy implications for this dimension of the costs of children, although it might be effectively used as part of persuasion campaigns for small families in certain countries where the physical demands of childrearing have been shown to be salient for parents.

Family costs.   While children were sometimes seen as creating a stronger bond between husband and wife, they were also seen as creating marital problems: arguments about the rearing of children, less time for husband and wife to spend with each other, the children replacing the spouse as an object of love and affection. These concerns were not among the most significant costs of children, but they were cited as a disadvantage of having children by about one out of four middle-class parents in Korea and were of some importance also to the middle class in Japan and among Japanese and Caucasians in Hawaii. Two specific reasons for not wanting another child—"not able to spend as much time with spouse" and "cause problems, strains between me and spouse"—were cited as very important by only modest numbers of respondents in most countries; also, the correlations of these items with additional children desired tend to be weak.

As with physical demands, there appear to be no clear-cut policy recommendations related to this dimension. However, family costs should be cited when recommending delays in the birth of the first child; that is, couples should adjust to each other before they assume the additional strains of coping with children.

The positive and negative values discussed above have effects both on the desire to have children and on family size. The values discussed in the following paragraphs are related mainly to family size.

Sibling relationships.   Respondents in all countries appeared to have strong feelings about interpersonal relationships among siblings, and these feelings influenced their decisions about family size. The most striking example of this is the desire to avoid having an only child, based on the belief that a lack of sibling relationships has harmful effects on a child's personality. Perhaps equally important, however, are feelings about the special sibling relationship that will bind children together throughout life and ideas about the social network of the family—that is, that a certain number of members are needed to create a "proper family." Also connected with this are beliefs related to sex roles: that it is good for a child to have a sibling of the same sex or the opposite sex or both.

As discussed earlier, the general category of "companionship for other children" appeared most frequently among the reasons for not wanting fewer children than the desired family size given by the respondent. Moreover, "to provide a companion for my child/children" was among the stronger reasons for wanting another child, even for parents who already had two or more children. With parity controlled, in all countries except Korea this item shows quite strong correlations with the number of additional children desired.

Although children undoubtedly need companionship, research suggests that it may make little difference whether that companionship comes from siblings or peers. Despite the stereotype of the spoiled only child, for instance, there is no consistent evidence for significant personality differences between only children and other children. Nor is there any striking evidence for personality differences related to large and small families, although this study shows that belief in such differences is prevalent. There is, however, evidence that children from small families (including only children) tend to have greater verbal abilities, higher academic achievement, and better social adjustment than those from large ones. While research in this area is far from adequate, there does seem to be a discrepancy between empirical knowledge and popular beliefs concerning the effects on children of sibling relationships and family size (see Clausen and Clausen, 1973; Thompson, 1974).

Two directions for policy are indicated: to provide facilities for nonsibling companionship for children, and to gather new knowledge and disseminate existing knowledge about the effects of sibling and nonsibling relationships on the social and intellectual development of children. The former can be accomplished through institutions and facilities—nursery schools, day care centers, after-school recreation programs, communal play areas in housing developments. The latter can be accomplished through support for research on this topic and efforts to translate research findings into information programs.

Although strongly held beliefs in this area are not likely to be changed by information programs, that influence combined with facilities to provide children with companionship may reinforce trends toward smaller families. It is encouraging to note that in some societies, such as in Eastern Europe, even the extreme case of the only child has come to be accepted by many parents.

The evidence from this study suggests that beliefs about sibling relationships have a powerful influence on family size, yet this source of influence has been a neglected area of population policy. If parents can be persuaded that the number and sex of siblings has little effect on the child, they may be more free to make decisions for smaller families based on economic considerations, on aspirations for their children's education and general prospects in life, or on the basis of their own preferences and awareness of alternative sources of satisfaction.

Sex preference.   Few parents in this study were indifferent to the sex composition of their family. Boys were preferred over girls and most parents wanted their first child to be a boy, but they also wanted at least one girl. In some countries, such as Korea and Taiwan, it was common to want at least two sons.

The existence and strength of sex preferences have been shown by several measures in this study and the reasons behind those preferences have been explored. A frequent reason for wanting another child was to have a son or a daughter or to attain a certain sex ratio among the children. Many parents said that if they had only daughters, they would keep having children until a son was born. The preference for sons was strongest among rural and lower-class respondents, especially in Korea and Taiwan. Sons were wanted in most countries to continue the family name and for the economic help and security they were expected to provide. In some countries, sons were wanted for religious reasons and for rituals connected with the afterlife. Girls were wanted for immediate psychological and practical benefits—as companions for the mother, to help in housework and taking care of other children, because girls have attractive personalities—and because they were needed to provide a balance of sexes among the children.

The effect of sex preference on family size is obvious, and it is substantial when such preferences are strong. Even if only one child of each sex is wanted, many parents will need to have more than two children to attain that goal; the effects are compounded when at least two sons are wanted. In all countries, "to have a boy/another boy" as a reason for wanting another child is positively correlated with the number of additional children wanted; the desire for a girl also shows strong correlations in several countries.

The policy measures to reduce sex preferences are to a large extent country-specific, since they involve changes in inheritance laws and practices, customs and laws concerning transmission of the family name, and possibly changes in religious practices and beliefs. At the same time, however, the underlying reasons for sex preferences for sons and daughters show that these preferences are closely linked to traditional sex roles for adult men and women. It is reasonable to expect, then, that public policies leading toward equalization of sex roles should have the important side effect of reducing the strength of son or daughter preference—that is, fostering indifference to the sex of the child. This will come about because of changes in adult roles (for example, daughters as well as sons will be able to offer parents financial support) and because of eventual changes in socialization practices to match those adult roles (for example, sons as well as daughters will help with housework and child care). Changes of this kind are occurring in most societies, but at vastly different rates and mainly in the cities.

Public policies providing equal rights for men and women are of course desirable on grounds unrelated to population, but it is useful to note that among the several population effects of such policies should be a reduction in fertility motivations that are based on the sex of the child.

The results of this study also underline the significance of current research into methods for increasing the probability of having a child of a given sex. The development of techniques for sex predetermination will of course affect not only fertility but also a wide array of social customs and practices. The availability of such techniques could also provoke severe personal and familial conflicts, especially in societies where sex roles are undergoing rapid transformation. Additional research on the differential value of sons and daughters can provide useful data for analysis of the likely consequences of sex predetermination.

Child survival. Parents are aware that children may die and they want to have enough children so that some will survive to adulthood. This desire may have a very practical basis if the parents expect to be supported by their children in old age; or it may be emotional, such as the wish to have grandchildren or the feeling that the family name must be continued. It may also involve powerful religious motivations, as when sons are needed to perform burial rites or rituals involving ancestor worship.

The concern over mortality of children was shown in this study to be strongest in the Philippines and Thailand and generally to be stronger among rural and lower-class respondents than among the middle class. However, a substantial number of respondents in all countries thought that "to have enough children to survive to adulthood" was a very important reason to have another child, indicating that this concern is not limited to areas where mortality is high. This item is positively correlated with the number of additional children desired in all Asian countries, and in fact the correlation is strongest in Japan (where parents also had the smallest number of living children).

The major public policy to deal with this question is of course a health policy, and substantial efforts are under way in most countries to reduce infant and child mortality. It may be surmised, however, that there is a cultural lag between actual decreases in mortality and public perceptions of that change. For this and other reasons, subjective probabilities for child survival may be considerably lower than actual probabilities, suggesting that public information programs could help allay fears about mortality of children and thus influence fertility motivations.

Maternal health.   In response to an open-ended question about reasons for not wanting more children than the number given as desired, maternal health considerations were cited by respondents in Korea, Japan, the Philippines, Thailand, and Hawaii (Filipinos). Awareness of maternal health problems appeared to be greater among urban respondents, but this factor was also mentioned by rural respondents in some countries. It is surprising to note that maternal health was cited by a moderate number of respondents in all three socioeconomic groups in Japan, where health care standards are high and fertility levels are low. Perhaps there is a greater public awareness of health issues in Japan. It is also possible that responses coded as "maternal health" and responses coded as "physical work, tiredness caused by children" really reflect the same concern on the part of the parents. The questionnaire contained no structured items on maternal health, so no check on the open-ended responses can be made.

In any event, the data show that, for many respondents, health problems of the mother were a salient concern in deciding to limit family size. Since population policies obviously would not aim to increase such health problems, the relevant option is to increase awareness and salience of the maternal health complications associated with higher parities and higher ages. There is good empirical evidence in this area, and evidence too on health and mortality effects on children born at later stages of the reproductive cycle (see Nortman, 1974; Wray, 1971), and these facts might be given greater attention in public education programs. The evidence from this study suggests that sufficient awareness exists so that interest in this topic should be high, and those who are aware do connect this concern with family-size decisions. Also relevant in this context is the availability of legal, safe, and simple abortion, which can provide a low-risk alternative to delivery for women who have reason to be concerned about their health.

Social costs.   Concern about overpopulation was a salient reason for not wanting more than the desired number of children for some respondents in Korea and Taiwan and for Japanese and Caucasians in

Hawaii. The level of concern was particularly high among middle-class Caucasians in Hawaii, where more than one-third gave this response to the open-ended question. In a structured question about reasons for not wanting another child, however, the strongest response to an item on overpopulation was given by respondents in the Philippines (in all three socioeconomic groups). This response may be attributable to the generally high level of responses in the Philippines; but perhaps it is also relevant that urban Filipinos already had more children than urban respondents in other countries, so that information campaigns about overpopulation might have had more impact on them. The relationship between this item on overpopulation and the number of additional children wanted varied substantially across countries, with the strongest negative correlation (with parity controlled) shown for Korea.

Overall, the results indicate that overpopulation and other social costs are not major factors in decisions about family size; rather, personal costs and family economic considerations are the controlling influence in decisions to stop having children. Similar findings have been shown in other studies and, partly because of those findings, population policies and persuasion programs have been directed mainly to the personal and familial benefits of smaller families. The danger of this approach is of course that what is best for the individual or family is not likely to be best for the society in the long run. A need exists, therefore, to find ways to bridge the gap between the individual and society with respect to demographic behavior.

McNicoll (1975) has argued for the development of community-level population policies, on the grounds that for most people the community rather than the nation is the major source of social identification and social influence, particularly in rural areas where fertility is highest. With this approach, the harmful social consequences of population growth would be expressed in terms meaningful at the local level, rather than in national aggregates, and programs would encourage communities to set their own demographic goals and to develop means for achieving them. Such efforts could also include community-level incentive programs (Kangas, 1970).

To develop effective community-level population policies, knowledge is needed about the motivations and aspirations of the groups to be affected. In this study, for instance, it was shown that rural parents in some countries were especially concerned about upward mobility for their children. Information about local population growth as an impediment to improving the quality of local education and increasing the number of years of free schooling presumably would be meaningful to these parents and would help to develop community awareness of population problems and a community atmosphere of social responsibility in childbearing. Likewise, research on the value of children could identify the aspects of old-age security that are important to parents in the community and local programs might be devised to meet those needs through means other than children, where necessary, thus providing a credible alternative to large families as a means of assuring old-age support.

Micro-level research on such topics as the value of children can facilitate the development of population policies that take into account the needs of people, as well as the needs of the society. It may be argued that policies developed on this basis will not only be more acceptable but also more effective. Ultimately ways must be found to bring self-interest and societal interest into congruence, so that demographic events will contribute to, rather than detract from, the goal of improving the common welfare.

appendices

Appendix A   Core questionnaire

Sample number	Block number	Household number

Name: _____

Address:

Street _____

City/town _____

State/province _____

Name of interviewer: _____

	Number of visits				
	1	2	3	4	5
Date					
Time started					
Time ended					
Time spent					
Result*					
Appointment date and time					

* Codes: 1. Interview completed.
2. Interview partly completed—appointment made.
3. Appointment made for interview later.
4. Refusal—no interview obtained.
5. No one at home.
6. Eligible respondent(s) not home.
7. Other *(specify):* _____

Field supervisor: _____ Date: _____

Editor: _____ Date: _____

Coder: _____ Date: _____

Keypuncher: _____ Date: _____

Serial number

INTRODUCTION BY INTERVIEWER

My name is _____ .

I am conducting a survey for _____ *(sponsoring organization)* _____ .

This is a scientific research project and your answers will be kept confidential.

Screening for eligibility

To begin with, we would like to have a few statistics about yourself and your family.

		Eligibility criteria
S1.	Are you currently married? ☐ Yes ☐ No *(Go to S6.)*	☐ Currently married
S2.	Is your (husband/wife) living with you now? ☐ Yes ☐ No *(Go to S6.)*	☐ Living with spouse
S3.	How many children do you have? _____ children *(If no children, go to S6.)*	☐ Couple has at least one child
S4.	How old are you now? _____ years old	☐ Wife is ☐ Husband 20–34 is 20–44
S5.	And how old is your (husband/wife)? _____ years old	years years old old
S6.	Where were you born? City/town _____ State/province _____ Country _____	

☐ Respondent eligible if <u>all 5</u> eligibility boxes are checked.
   (Read purpose of study, below.)

☐ Respondent ineligible if <u>any</u> of the eligibility boxes is <u>not</u> checked.
   (Skip rest of interview, thank respondent for assistance, and leave.)

Purpose of study

(Read to eligible respondents): We are conducting this survey to find out how parents, like yourself, feel about children. The questions deal mainly with your own feelings toward children and the role that children play in your life. We believe you will find it interesting.

Your answers will be used only by the researchers at the university conducting this study. To make the study successful, please be entirely frank and open in your comments and answer each question as fully as you can.

Sex of respondent

Respondent is:

   1 ☐ Wife   2 ☐ Husband

INTERVIEW PROPER

A. Number of children

1. Please tell me the names of all of your own children who are now alive, whether they are living here or away. Starting with the oldest, what are their names? *(Ask sex of child and date of birth.)*

Names of children	Sex B = boy G = girl	Date of birth	
		Month	Year
(1)			
(2)			
(3)			
(4)			
(5)			
(6)			
(7)			
(8)			

2. Do you and your (husband/wife) have any other children, such as adopted children, living with you as part of your family?

   1 ☐ Yes   2 ☐ No *(Go to 3.)*

   (Ask name, sex, age, relationship to respondent.)

Names of children	Sex B = boy G = girl	Age	Relationship to respondent
(1)			
(2)			
(3)			
(4)			
(5)			
(6)			
(7)			
(8)			

B. Influences from home

3. There are certain things that children learn in school, and other things they usually learn at home.

   In your opinion, what are some of the important things that children learn at home?

   (1) _____

   (2) _____

   (3) _____

C. Children compared with no children

4. I would like to know what you think are some of the good things or advantages about having children, <u>compared with not having children at all</u>.

   These might include the pleasures and benefits you get from having children now and those that you expect in the future.

   What would you say are some of the good things or advantages about having children, compared with not having children?

   Rank

   (1) _____ _____
   (2) _____ _____
   (3) _____ _____
   (4) _____ _____
   (5) _____ _____
   (6) _____ _____

   (If blank spaces, ask): Can you think of any other good things or advantages about having children?

5. Of the good things and advantages that you just mentioned, which would you say is <u>most important</u> to you personally, and which is <u>second most important?</u>
   (Enter 1 and 2 in rank column.)

6. Now I would like to know about some of the difficulties or disadvantages connected with having children, <u>compared with not having children at all</u>.

   These might include, for instance, various problems or stresses related to raising children, or things that you cannot do or have to give up because you have children.

   What would you say are some of the difficulties or disadvantages connected with having children, compared with not having children?

   Rank

   (1) _____ _____
   (2) _____ _____
   (3) _____ _____
   (4) _____ _____
   (5) _____ _____
   (6) _____ _____

   (If blank spaces, ask): Can you think of any other difficulties or disadvantages connected with having children?

7. Of the difficulties and disadvantages that you just mentioned, which would you say is <u>most important</u> to you personally, and which is <u>second most important?</u>
   (Enter 1 and 2 in rank column.)

D. Desired family size

8. (Are you/Is your wife) pregnant now?

    1 ☐ Yes   2 ☐ No   3 ☐ Uncertain

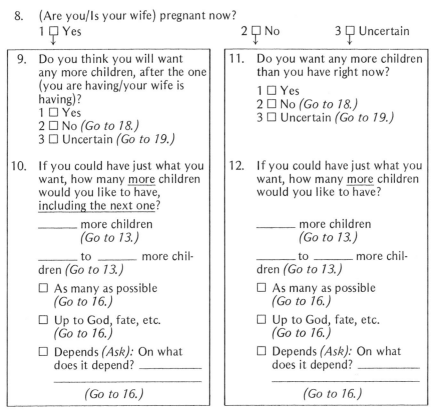

| 9. Do you think you will want any more children, after the one (you are having/your wife is having)?

1 ☐ Yes
2 ☐ No *(Go to 18.)*
3 ☐ Uncertain *(Go to 19.)* | 11. Do you want any more children than you have right now?

1 ☐ Yes
2 ☐ No *(Go to 18.)*
3 ☐ Uncertain *(Go to 19.)* |
| 10. If you could have just what you want, how many <u>more</u> children would you like to have, <u>including the next one?</u>

_____ more children
     (Go to 13.)

_____ to _____ more children *(Go to 13.)*

☐ As many as possible
   (Go to 16.)

☐ Up to God, fate, etc.
   (Go to 16.)

☐ Depends *(Ask):* On what does it depend? _____
_____
     (Go to 16.) | 12. If you could have just what you want, how many <u>more</u> children would you like to have?

_____ more children
     (Go to 13.)

_____ to _____ more children *(Go to 13.)*

☐ As many as possible
   (Go to 16.)

☐ Up to God, fate, etc.
   (Go to 16.)

☐ Depends *(Ask):* On what does it depend? _____
_____
     (Go to 16.) |

13. Let's see if I have this right:

    You now have _____ children of your own. *(See 1.)*

    You would like to have (_____ more children/ _____to_____ more children). *(See 10 or 12.)*

    So you want a <u>total</u> of (_____ children/ _____ to _____ children of your own.

    Is this right? *(If error, revise preceding items as required.)*

14. Can you tell me some of the reasons why you would <u>not</u> want <u>fewer</u> than _____children? *(See total in 13, use lowest number if range.)*

    (1) _____

    (2) _____

    (3) _____

15.   Can you tell me some of the reasons why you would <u>not</u> want <u>more</u> than
_____ children? *(See total in 13, use highest number if range.)*

(1) _____

(2) _____

(3) _____

(Go to 16.)

(16–17 for respondents who want more children)

16. Now I want to ask about some specific reasons why you may want another child. Here is a list of reasons people sometimes give for wanting another child. For each one, please tell me whether, for you, the reason is very important, somewhat important, or not important at all.	Very impor- tant 1	Some- what impor- tant 2	Not impor- tant 3
(1) Because I enjoy having a small baby.			
(2) To help carry on our family name and traditions.			
(3) Because I want to have (a boy/another boy).			
(4) Because I want to have (a girl/another girl).			
(5) Because some relatives feel that I should have more children.			
(6) To be sure that in my old age I will have a child to help me.			
(7) Because it is my religious duty to have children.			
(8) So that there will be one more person to help our family economically.			
(9) Because having another child will make my marriage stronger.			
(10) To provide a companion for my (child/ children).			
(11) Because I enjoy caring for and raising children.			
(12) Because my (husband/wife) wants more children.			
(13) Because it is fun to have children around the house.			
(14) Because raising children helps me to learn about life and myself.			
(15) Because I want the special feeling of love that develops between a parent and child.			
(16) Because I want to share what I have and what I know with children.			
(17) Because I want to be sure to have enough children survive to adulthood.			

17. Often people feel two ways at the same time. They may have decided that they want another child, but still there are some reasons they would <u>not</u> like to have another child.			
Here is a list of reasons people sometimes give for not wanting another child. For each one, please tell me whether, for you, the reason is very important, somewhat important, or not important at all.	Very important 1	Some-what important 2	Not important 3
(1) Because having another child would be a financial burden for our family.			
(2) Because my (husband/wife) does not want any more children.			
(3) Because another child would restrict my freedom to do other things I enjoy.			
(4) Because another child would be a lot of work and bother for me.			
(5) Because I could not spend as much time together with my (husband/wife).			
(6) Because I am concerned about the problem of overpopulation.			
(7) Because caring for another child would be an emotional strain for me.			
(8) Because I would not be able to give enough care and attention to my other (child/children).			
(9) Because having another child would cause problems and strains between me and my (husband/wife). *(Go to 21.)*			

18. *(For respondents who do not want more children)*
    Can you tell me some of the reasons why you do not want any more children?

    (1) _____
    _____

    (2) _____
    _____

    (3) _____
    _____

(19–20 for respondents who do not want more children or are uncertain)

	Very impor- tant 1	Some- what impor- tant 2	Not impor- tant 3
19. Now I want to ask about some specific reasons why you may not want another child. Here is a list of reasons people sometimes give for not wanting another child. For each one, please tell me whether, for you, the reason is very important, somewhat important, or not important at all.			
(1) Because having another child would be a financial burden for our family.			
(2) Because my (husband/wife) does not want any more children.			
(3) Because another child would restrict my freedom to do other things I enjoy			
(4) Because another child would be a lot of work and bother for me.			
(5) Because I could not spend as much time together with my (husband/wife).			
(6) Because I am concerned about the problem of overpopulation.			
(7) Because caring for another child would be an emotional strain for me.			
(8) Because I would not be able to give enough care and attention to my other (child/ children).			
(9) Because having another child would cause problems and strains between me and my (husband/wife).			
20. Often people feel two ways at the same time. They may have decided that they do not want another child, but still there are some reasons why they would like to have another child. Here is a list of reasons people sometimes give for wanting another child. For each one, please tell me whether, for you, the reason is very important, somewhat important, or not important at all.	Very impor- tant 1	Some- what impor- tant 2	Not impor- tant 3
(1) Because I enjoy having a small baby.			
(2) To help carry on our family name and traditions.			
(3) Because I want to have (a boy/another boy).			
(4) Because I want to have (a girl/another girl).			
(5) Because some relatives feel that I should have more children.			
(6) To be sure that in my old age I will have a child to help me.			

20. (continued)

	1	2	3
(7) Because it is my religious duty to have children.			
(8) So that there will be one more person to help our family economically.			
(9) Because having another child will make my marriage stronger.			
(10) To provide a companion for my (child/children).			
(11) Because I enjoy caring for and raising children.			
(12) Because my (husband/wife) wants more children.			
(13) Because it is fun to have children around the house.			
(14) Because raising children helps me to learn about life and myself.			
(15) Because I want the special feeling of love that develops between a parent and child.			
(16) Because I want to share what I have and what I know with children.			
(17) Because I want to be sure to have enough children survive to adulthood. *(Go to 21.)*			

E. Ideal family size and composition

21. The answers to the questions I asked before about the number of children you want depend somewhat on the number of children you already have. Now I want you to answer as if you had just gotten married and <u>did not yet have any children.</u>

Would you want to have any children?

1 □ Yes   2 □ No   3 □ Depends   4 □ Don't know
            (Go to 32.)   *(Go to 26.)*   *(Go to 26.)*

22. How soon after your marriage would you want to have your first child? _____

23. Would you want your first child to be a boy or a girl, or wouldn't it matter?

1 □ Boy   3 □ Wouldn't matter
2 □ Girl   4 □ Up to God, fate, etc.

24. In your ideal family, if you were starting all over, how many children would you want to have altogether?

☐ One *(Go to 32.)*   ☐ Five

☐ Two   ☐ Six or more *(specify):* _____

☐ Three   ☐ Up to God, fate, etc. *(Go to 27.)*

☐ Four   ☐ Don't know *(Go to 27.)*

25. Of these, how many boys and how many girls would you like, if you could have just what you want?

_____ boys   _____ children of either sex

_____ girls   ☐ No preference *(Go to 27.)*

26. I would like to get a picture of your ideal family.

    (Show chart to respondent.) Please help me complete this chart, showing <u>B</u> for boy and <u>G</u> for girl, up to the number of children you consider ideal. *(Use <u>X</u> for no preference, depends, not sure.)*

1st	2nd	3rd	4th	5th	6th	7th	8th

27. How important is it to you to have at least one girl among your children? Would you say it is *(read choices):*

    1 ☐ Very important   2 ☐ Somewhat important   3 ☐ Not important at all *(Go to 29.)*

    28. Why is it important to you to have a girl?
    _____
    _____

29. How important is it to you to have at least one boy among your children? Would you say it is *(read choices):*

    1 ☐ Very important   2 ☐ Somewhat important   3 ☐ Not important at all *(Go to 32.)*

    30. Why is it important to you to have a boy?
    _____
    _____

    31. If you didn't have any sons and you kept having daughters, what would you do? Would you continue having babies until you had a boy, or would you stop after a certain number of girls?

    ☐ Continue until a   ☐ Up to God, fate,
      boy comes   etc.

    ☐ Stop after _____ girls ☐ Uncertain
      (Write number of girls.)

32. Now I will mention two things that sometimes affect the number of children people want. Please tell me whether each would affect the number of children you want.

    Suppose your family income increased, to double what it is now, would that affect the number of children you want?

    1 ☐ Yes   2 ☐ No *(Go to 34.)*   3 ☐ Don't know *(Go to 34.)*

    > 33. How might it affect the number you want? _____
    > _____

34. Suppose the government decided to provide free education for all children, up to and including college. Would that affect the number of children you want?

    1 ☐ Yes   2 ☐ No *(Go to 36.)*   3 ☐ Don't know *(Go to 36.)*

    > 35. How might it affect the number you want? _____
    > _____

36. Have you ever discussed with your (husband/wife) the number of children (he/she) wants?

    1 ☐ Yes   2 ☐ No *(Go to 39.)*

    > 37. Can you tell me how many children (he/she) wants altogether?
    > _____ children altogether   ☐ Don't know *(Go to 39.)*
    > *(range or exact number)*
    >
    > 38. Can you tell me how many boys and how many girls (he/she) wants?
    > _____ boys   _____ children of either sex
    > _____ girls   ☐ Don't know

39. We often talk about small and large families, but people have different ideas about what that means.

    When you think of a small family, how many children would be in it?

    _____ children *(range or exact number)*

40. When you think of a large family, how many children would be in it?

    _____ children *(range or exact number)*

41. Some people feel that children who grow up in small families tend to be different from children who grow up in large families.

    For each of the following items, please tell me if you think the description applies to a child from a small family or a child from a large family.

	Small family 1	Large family 2	Don't know 3
(1) A child who is very open and loving toward other people	☐	☐	☐

41. (continued)

		1	2	3
(2)	A child with high intellectual ability	☐	☐	☐
(3)	A child who is very popular with other children	☐	☐	☐
(4)	A child who has a very close relationship with his parents	☐	☐	☐
(5)	A child who always wants to have his own way	☐	☐	☐
(6)	A child who has great confidence in himself	☐	☐	☐
(7)	A child who is very happy	☐	☐	☐

F. Opinions about children

42. Now I am going to ask for your opinion about different aspects of having children.

(Point to items.) For each of these statements about children, I want you to tell me if you agree or disagree. Some of the statements are similar to what we have discussed before and some are different.

(Point to response categories.) These are the kinds of answers you can give. First, decide if you agree or disagree with the statement. Then, tell me if you hold that opinion strongly, moderately, or slightly.

> *(Optional instruction)*
> If your opinion is very certain or strong, say strongly.
> If your opinion is not quite so certain or strong, say moderately.
> If your opinion is uncertain or weak, say slightly.

Here is the first statement. Tell me which answer comes closest to your general feeling about it.

(Repeat instructions or add optional instruction if necessary.)

Item	Agree			Disagree		
	Strong	Moderate	Slight	Strong	Moderate	Slight
(1) Caring for children is a tedious and boring job.						
(2) A good reason for having children is that they can help when parents are too old to work.						
(3) Raising children is an act of virtue.						
(4) It is only with a child that a person can feel completely free to express his love and affection.						
(5) Most married couples would be happier if they did not have any children.						

42. (continued)

Item	Agree			Disagree		
	Strong	Mod-erate	Slight	Strong	Mod-erate	Slight
(6) Having children gives a person a special incentive to succeed in life.						
(7) It is important to have children so that the family traditions will live on.						
(8) It is only natural that a man should want children.						
(9) A couple ought to think seriously about the inconveniences caused by children before they have any.						
(10) Always having children around is a great mental strain.						
(11) Considering the pressures from family and friends, a person really doesn't have much choice about whether or not to have children.						
(12) It is a person's duty to society to have children.						
(13) All the efforts a parent makes for his children are worthwhile in the long run.						
(14) Having children makes a stronger bond between husband and wife.						
(15) One of the highest purposes of life is to have children.						
(16) A girl becomes a woman only after she is a mother.						
(17) It is the parents' fault if their children are not successful in life.						
(18) Having children is the most important function of marriage.						
(19) Children limit you in what you want to do and where you want to go.						
(20) Life for most people would be pretty dull without children.						
(21) A young couple is not fully accepted in the community until they have children.						
(22) After becoming a parent, a person is less likely to behave immorally.						
(23) The first thing a couple should think about when deciding to have children is whether or not they can afford it.						

42. (continued)

Item	Agree			Disagree		
	Strong	Moderate	Slight	Strong	Moderate	Slight
(24) For most people, it is inevitable to have children.						
(25) One of the best things about having children is the true loyalty they show to their parents.						
(26) Having children causes many disagreements and problems between husband and wife.						
(27) A person with children is looked up to in the community more than a person without children.						
(28) It is only natural that a woman should want children.						
(29) Just the feeling a parent gets of being needed is enough to make having children worthwhile.						
(30) A person who has been a good parent can feel completely satisfied with his achievements in life.						
(31) The family with children is the basis for all that is good in our society.						
(32) Before having a child, a couple should consider whether they would rather use their money for something else.						
(33) One of the best things about being a parent is the chance to teach children what they should do and what they should not do.						
(34) A man has a duty to have children to continue the family name.						
(35) A person can feel that part of him lives on after death if he has children.						
(36) One of the best things about having children is that you are never lonely.						
(37) Raising children is a heavy financial burden for most people.						
(38) It isn't right for a couple to interfere with nature by deciding to limit the number of children they will have.						

42. (continued)

Item	Agree			Disagree		
	Strong	Mod-erate	Slight	Strong	Mod-erate	Slight
(39) When you have children, you have to give up a lot of other things that you enjoy.						
(40) The really important things in life can be learned only from the experience of raising children.						
(41) Before having a child, a couple should consider whether it would interfere with the wife's work or not.						
(42) Having children is a sign of blessing on a marriage.						
(43) The family with children is the only place in the modern world where a person can feel comfortable and happy.						
(44) A person who has no children can never really be happy.						
(45) A boy becomes a man only after he is a father.						

G. Birth control

43. Some people practice birth control or family planning, either to delay a pregnancy or to stop having children.

Have you ever heard of birth control or family planning?

1 □ Yes *(Go to 46.)*

2 □ No →

> 44. Do you know of any ways to prevent or delay a pregnancy?
>
> 1 □ Yes   2 □ No *(Go to 64.)*
>
> 45. What ways do you know about?
>
> _____
>
> _____
>
> *(If contraception mentioned, define birth control and proceed to 46; otherwise, go to 64.)*

46. *(If wife pregnant, go to 50.)*
At the present time, are you or your (husband/wife) practicing birth control?

1 □ Yes   2 □ No *(Go to 50.)*

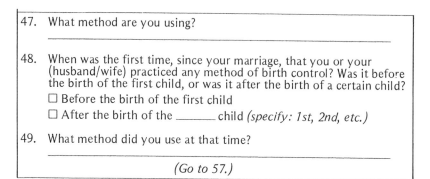

47. What method are you using?
_____

48. When was the first time, since your marriage, that you or your (husband/wife) practiced any method of birth control? Was it before the birth of the first child, or was it after the birth of a certain child?
☐ Before the birth of the first child
☐ After the birth of the _____ child *(specify: 1st, 2nd, etc.)*

49. What method did you use at that time?
_____

(Go to 57.)

50. Have you or your (husband/wife) ever practiced birth control in the past?
1 ☐ Yes   2 ☐ No *(Go to 53.)*

51. When was the first time, since your marriage, that you or your (husband/wife) practiced birth control? Was it before the birth of your first child, or was it after the birth of a certain child?
☐ Before the birth of the first child
☐ After the birth of the _____ child *(specify: 1st, 2nd, etc.)*

52. What method did you use at that time?
_____

(Go to 53.)

53. What about in the future? Do you think you or your (husband/wife) might want to practice birth control later on?

1 ☐ Yes →
54. When might that be? Would it be after the birth of a certain child, or when?
☐ After the birth of the _____ child *(specify 2nd, 3rd, 4th, etc.)*
☐ Other *(specify):* _____
_____
☐ Don't know
(Go to 57.)

2 ☐ No →
55. Then do you plan to continue having children until you can't have any more?
1 ☐ Yes *(Go to 57.)*
2 ☐ No

56. *(Ask only if wife not pregnant.)* As far as you know, (are you/is your wife) physically able to become pregnant again?
1 ☐ Yes   2 ☐ No   3 ☐ Uncertain

53. (continued)

    3 ☐ Depends → On what does it depend? _____

    4 ☐ Don't know

57. Now I want to ask about some specific methods of birth control.
Have you ever heard about _____ ?
Do you know how it is used?
Have you or your (husband/wife) ever used it?

(Skip methods respondent has used; write yes *or* no *in each box for other methods.)*

Method	Have you heard about this method?	Do you know how it is used?	Have you or your spouse ever used it?
(1) IUD or loop			
(2) Birth control pill			
(3) Condom or rubber			
(4) Diaphragm			
(5) Rhythm or calendar method			
(6) Withdrawal			
(7) Vasectomy or male sterilization			
(8) Tubal ligation or female sterilization			

58. What is your opinion generally about married couples' doing something to prevent pregnancy, that is, using some method of birth control? Do you approve or disapprove?

    ☐ Approve →
> 59. Would you say you approve strongly or just slightly?
>   ☐ Strongly   ☐ Slightly
>   *(Go to 61.)*

    ☐ Disapprove →
> 60. Would you say you disapprove strongly or just slightly?
>   ☐ Strongly   ☐ Slightly

    ☐ Depends →   On what does it depend? _____

    ☐ Don't know

61. Even if people hold certain opinions about birth control generally, they sometimes feel differently about birth control in certain circumstances. In the following situations, do you approve or disapprove of birth control?

	Approve 1	Dis-approve 2	Don't know 3
(1) To delay the birth of the first child	☐	☐	☐

61. (continued)

		1	2	3
(2)	To control the spacing or timing of births after the first child	☐	☐	☐
(3)	To prevent further pregnancies after having all the children wanted	☐	☐	☐

62. Have you and your (husband/wife) ever talked about contraception or family planning?

   1 ☐ Yes   2 ☐ No

63. Do many of your close friends and relatives use contraception?

   1 ☐ Yes   2 ☐ No   3 ☐ Not sure

64. Have you ever heard of abortion?

   1 ☐ Yes   2 ☐ No *(Go to 70.)*

---

65. In general what is your opinion about a married woman's getting an abortion to prevent an unwanted birth. Do you approve or disapprove?

   ☐ Approve → | 66. Would you say you approve strongly or just slightly?
                | ☐ Strongly   ☐ Slightly
                | *(Go to 68.)*

   ☐ Disapprove → | 67. Would you say you disapprove strongly or just slightly?
                  | ☐ Strongly   ☐ Slightly

   ☐ Depends →   On what does it depend? _____
                  _____

   ☐ Don't know

---

68. Even if people hold certain opinions about abortion generally, they sometimes feel differently about abortion in certain circumstances. In the following situations, do you approve or disapprove of abortion?

		Approve 1	Dis- approve 2	Don't know 3
(1)	If the doctor says it will be dangerous for the wife to give birth again	☐	☐	☐
(2)	If the couple cannot afford to have another child	☐	☐	☐
(3)	If the pregnancy will interfere with the wife's work or career	☐	☐	☐
(4)	If the pregnancy resulted from rape	☐	☐	☐

69. Do many of your close friends and relatives feel it is shameful to have an abortion?

    1 ☐ Yes   2 ☐ No   3 ☐ Not sure

70. About how many children do you think a typical couple in this community has by the time they stop having children?

    _____ children *(range or exact number)*

    ☐ Don't know

71. Do you know any married couples around here who have decided not to have any children?

    1 ☐ Yes   2 ☐ No *(Go to 73.)*

    > 72. About how many such couples do you know personally?
    > _____ couples

73. In your opinion, what are the main reasons why people around here want children?

    (1) _____

    (2) _____

    (3) _____

    (If blank spaces, ask): Can you think of any other reasons why people around here want children?

H. Economic considerations

I would like to know what kind of economic or practical help you expect from your children, either while they are growing up or after they are adults.

Please think not only of the sons and daughters you now have but those you might have in the future.

74. Do you expect some economic or practical help from your sons?

    1 ☐ Yes   2 ☐ No *(Go to 76.)*   3 ☐ Uncertain *(Go to 76.)*

    > 75. What kinds of help would you expect?
    > _____
    > _____
    > _____

76. Do you expect some economic or practical help from your daughters?

    1 ☐ Yes   2 ☐ No *(Go to 78.)*   3 ☐ Uncertain *(Go to 78.)*

    > 77. What kinds of help would you expect?
    > _____
    > _____
    > _____

78.   What means of financial support do you think you and your (husband/wife) might have when you get old?
(Record in first column below; for each item mentioned, ask): Do you expect to rely on _____ a good deal or only a little, when you get old?

Means of financial support	Rely a good deal	Rely only a little	Uncertain/depends
(1)			
(2)			
(3)			
(4)			
(5)			
(6)			

(If children not mentioned, ask 79; if children mentioned, go to 80.)

79.   When you get old, do you expect to rely on financial support from your children a good deal, only a little, or not at all?
1 ☐ Rely a good deal
2 ☐ Rely only a little
3 ☐ Not rely at all
4 ☐ Depends →   On what does it depend? _____
_____
5 ☐ Uncertain

80.   Now let's talk about the time before you retire or stop working. Do you think your children will give you some money from time to time *(read first 3 choices):*
1 ☐ Regardless of whether they live with you
2 ☐ Only if they live with you
3 ☐ Not at all
4 ☐ Depends →   On what does it depend? _____
_____

81.   Some parents live together with their children at some time after the children are married. Others do not live together with their children at all.
How do you think it will be in your case? Would you expect to *(read first 4 choices):*
1 ☐ Not live together at all
2 ☐ Live together only for a few years after children's marriage
3 ☐ Live together only when you are old
4 ☐ Live together with children the rest of your life
5 ☐ Other, including combinations of the above *(specify):*
_____
_____

82–89. Thinking of the changes that have taken place since you grew up, do you think that children nowadays are more willing, just as willing, or less willing to do each of the following:

82. To live with their parents after they are married.
☐ More willing
☐ Just as willing
☐ Less willing →
  ☐ Depends
  ☐ Don't know

83.	Do you like to see this kind of change taking place?
	☐ Yes ☐ No ☐ Doesn't matter

84. How about giving part of their wages to their parents when they start earning. Are children nowadays *(read first 3 choices):*
☐ More willing
☐ Just as willing
☐ Less willing →
  ☐ Depends
  ☐ Don't know

85.	Do you like to see this kind of change taking place?
	☐ Yes ☐ No ☐ Doesn't matter

86. How about supporting their parents in their old age. Are children nowadays *(read first 3 choices):*
☐ More willing
☐ Just as willing
☐ Less willing →
  ☐ Depends
  ☐ Don't know

87.	Do you like to see this kind of change taking place?
	☐ Yes ☐ No ☐ Doesn't matter

88. And how about helping with chores around the house or on the family farm or in the family business. Are children nowadays *(read first 3 choices):*
☐ More willing
☐ Just as willing
☐ Less willing →
  ☐ Depends
  ☐ Don't know

89.	Do you like to see this kind of change taking place?
	☐ Yes ☐ No ☐ Doesn't matter

90. Some couples feel that the more children they have, the better off the family will be economically. Others feel that having a lot of children will make their family less well-off.
How do you personally feel about this? _____
_____

91. We would like to know how much of a financial burden it is to raise children, for a family in your circumstances.
   (1) If you were to raise only <u>one</u> child, would it be fairly easy economically, somewhat of a financial burden, or a heavy financial burden?

91. (continued)

	Fairly easy economically	Somewhat of a financial burden	A heavy financial burden
	□ → *Ask (2)*	□ → *Ask (2)*	□ → *Go to 92*

(Read response choices after each item.)

(2) How about <u>two</u> children? □ → *Ask (3)*   □ → *Ask (3)*   □ → *Go to 92*

(3) How about <u>three</u> children? □ → *Ask (4)*   □ → *Ask (4)*   □ → *Go to 92*

(4) How about <u>four</u> children? □ → *Ask (5)*   □ → *Ask (5)*   □ → *Go to 92*

(5) How about <u>five</u> children? □ → *Ask (6)*   □ → *Ask (6)*   □ → *Go to 92*

(6) How about <u>six</u> children? □ → *Ask (7)*   □ → *Ask (7)*   □ → *Go to 92*

(7) What do you feel is the largest number of children you could raise without their becoming a heavy financial burden to you?

_____ children

92. About how much money in all do you think it has cost you to raise your child(ren) over the last twelve months?

_____ Total amount

□ Don't know

I. Education and educational aspirations for children

93. What is the highest grade of schooling you completed? *(Circle one.)*

None	Primary	Intermediate/ high school	College
0	1	7	13
	2	8	14
	3	9	15
	4	10	16+
	5	11	
	6	12	

Other type of schooling *(specify):* _____

(Ask 94 only if 4 or fewer years of education; for others, go to 96.)

94. Are you able to read, for example, a newspaper?

□ Yes →

□ No

95. Are you able to read easily, or with some difficulty?

□ Easily   □ Some difficulty

96. And how about your father? Did he ever attend school?

☐ Yes →

☐ No

☐ Don't know

97. How many years of schooling did he complete? *(Ask approximate number if respondent not sure.)*
_____ years   ☐ Don't know

98. And your mother? Did she ever attend school?

☐ Yes →

☐ No

☐ Don't know

99. How many years of schooling did she complete? *(Ask approximate number if respondent not sure.)*
_____ years   ☐ Don't know

100. We'd like to know how much schooling you expect your children to have. Consider the children you already have and also any children you might have in the future. First, let's talk about sons. What is the highest level of school which you would expect any of your sons to attend?

1 ☐ Primary school (grades 1–6)

2 ☐ Intermediate or junior high school (grades 7–9)

3 ☐ Senior high school (grades 10–12)

4 ☐ College or university

5 ☐ Graduate school

6 ☐ Other schooling *(specify):* _____

7 ☐ Depends *(Go to 102.)*

8 ☐ Don't know *(Go to 102.)*

101. How certain are you that any of your sons will get that much education? Would you say *(read choices):*

1 ☐ Certain

2 ☐ Fairly certain

3 ☐ Just a chance

102. And how about any daughters you might have? What is the highest level of school you would expect any of them to attend?

1 ☐ Primary school (grades 1–6)

2 ☐ Intermediate or junior high school (grades 7–9)

3 ☐ Senior high school (grades 10–12)

4 ☐ College or university

5 ☐ Graduate school

6 ☐ Other schooling *(specify):* _____

7 ☐ Depends *(Go to 104.)*

8 ☐ Don't know *(Go to 104.)*

103. How certain are you that any of your daughters will get that much education? Would you say *(read choices):*

1 ☐ Certain

2 ☐ Fairly certain

3 ☐ Just a chance

104. For a family like yours, do you think that providing education for your children will be a very heavy financial burden, a somewhat heavy burden, or fairly easy?
    1 □ Very heavy burden
    2 □ Somewhat heavy burden
    3 □ Fairly easy
    4 □ Don't know

J. Background: age, marriage, residence

105. In what year and month were you born?
    _____ year   _____ month

106. Some people become widowed or divorced and then marry again. Has this ever happened to you?
    1 □ Yes   2 □ No

107. How old were you when you (first) got married?
    _____ years

108. In what year and month was that?
    _____ year   _____ month

109. (Respondent lives *[check one]*):
    □ Rural area (farm or small town)   □ Urban area (large town or city)

110. How long have you lived in this area?	113. How long have you lived in this area?
_____ years □ All my life *(Go to 116.)*	_____ years □ All my life *(Go to 116.)*
111. Have you ever lived in a large town or city? 1 □ Yes 2 □ No *(Go to 116.)*	114. Have you ever lived on a farm or in the country? 1 □ Yes 2 □ No *(Go to 116.)*
112. For how many years? _____ years *(Go to 116.)*	115. For how many years? _____ years

116. Now I have some questions about your parents. Does your father or mother, or both, live with you here in this house?
    1 □ Father only
    2 □ Mother only
    3 □ Both
    4 □ Neither

117. Including yourself, how many sons and daughters did your mother have who lived to be at least ten years old?

_____ number of sons   _____ number of daughters

118. How many of these were older than you? *(Ask about brothers and sisters separately.)*

_____ number of older brothers _____ number of older sisters

K. Family decision-making

119. Here is a list of some things that families often have to make decisions about. In your family, who usually has more influence, the husband or wife, in making decisions about the following things:

	Hus-band 1	Wife 2	Both equally 3	Don't know 4
(1) What type of job or work the husband should have.				
(2) What doctor to have when a child is not well.				
(3) How many children to have.				
(4) Whether to purchase an important object like a _____ .*				

120. In your family, who would you say has the stronger desire to have children, you or your (husband/wife)?

1 ☐ Husband stronger
2 ☐ Wife stronger
3 ☐ Both equally
4 ☐ Other *(specify):* _____

L. General opinions

Now I want to ask a few different kinds of questions about yourself and your opinions. For each question, choose the one answer you feel is best.

121. Which is most important for the future of _____ ? *(name country in which interview is taking place and read choices):*

1 ☐ The hard work of the people
2 ☐ Good planning on the part of the government
3 ☐ God's help in man's activities
4 ☐ Good luck in daily activities

---

* Major consumer product appropriate to country setting supplied by each investigator.

122. What should most qualify a person to hold high office? *(read choices):*
    1 ☐ Coming from a distinguished family background
    2 ☐ Devotion to the old and time-honored ways
    3 ☐ Being the most popular among the people
    4 ☐ High education and special knowledge

123. Scientists are studying such things as what determines whether a baby is a boy or girl and why earthquakes occur. Do you think that these kinds of studies are *(read choices):*
    1 ☐ All very harmful   3 ☐ All somewhat beneficial
    2 ☐ All somewhat harmful   4 ☐ All very beneficial

124. Which one of the following kinds of information or news interests you most? *(read choices):*
    1 ☐ Local events   4 ☐ Sports or entertainment events
    2 ☐ National events   5 ☐ Religious events
    3 ☐ World events

125. Some people think it is useful to discuss ideas about new and different ways of doing things. Other people think that it is not worthwhile since the traditional and familiar ways are best. How useful do you think it is to discuss new and different ways of doing things? *(read choices):*
    1 ☐ Rarely useful   3 ☐ Usually useful
    2 ☐ Only useful at times   4 ☐ Almost always useful

126. Do you prefer to meet new people or to see people you already know?
    1 ☐ Meet new people
    2 ☐ See people already known

127. How often do you usually get news and information from newspapers? *(read choices):*
    1 ☐ Every day   3 ☐ Rarely
    2 ☐ A few times a week   4 ☐ Never

128. How often do you usually get news and information from radio or television? *(read choices):*
    1 ☐ Every day   3 ☐ Rarely
    2 ☐ A few times a week   4 ☐ Never

M. Religion and religiosity

129. *(To be added in each country. Use decimals for subquestions on religiosity.)*

N. Occupation

(130–135 for husbands only; for wives go to 136.)

130. Now we would like to find out what you do to earn a living. Are you working now?

☐ Yes →

> 131. What kind of work do you do? Please tell me as fully as you can.
> Title of occupation: _____
> Description of work: _____
> _____
> _____
>
> *(Go to 134.)*

☐ No →

> 132. Have you had a job at any time in the past year?
> 1 ☐ Yes   2 ☐ No *(Go to 135.)*
>
> 133. What is the main kind of work you have done?
> _____
> _____

134. During the past twelve months, about how much money have you earned from the work you've done?

_____ money earned

135. What kind of work did <u>your father</u> do most of the time until you were sixteen?

Occupation of father: _____ *(Go to 155.)*

☐ Inapplicable because father dead while (respondent) was growing up *(Go to 155.)*

☐ Don't know *(Go to 155.)*

(136—154 for wives only)

136. Aside from keeping house, are you working now?

1 ☐ Yes   2 ☐ No *(Go to 142.)*

(137—141 for wives currently working)

137. What kind of work do you do? Please tell me as fully as you can.
Title of occupation: _____
Description of work: _____
_____

138. Do you work full-time or part-time?
1 ☐ Full-time   2 ☐ Part-time

139. In this job, are you able to take care of your (child/children) while you are at work or do you have to make other arrangements?

☐ Care for them while working

☐ Other arrangements

(For wives currently working, continued)

140. In all, how many years have you worked since you first got married?
_____ years

141. During the past 12 months, about how much money have you earned from the work you've done?
_____ money earned
(Go to 147.)

(142–146 for wives not currently working)

142. Have you worked at any time since you first got married?
1 ☐ Yes   2 ☐ No *(Go to 147.)*

143. What is the main kind of work you have done? _____
_____

144. In all, how many years have you worked since you first got married?
_____ years

145. Have you worked at all during the past 12 months?
1 ☐ Yes   2 ☐ No *(Go to 147.)*

146. During the past 12 months, about how much money have you earned from the work you've done?
_____ money earned
(Go to 147.)

(147–154 for all women)

147. Before your marriage, did you ever work for wages or a salary?

1 ☐ Yes →

2 ☐ No

148. How long did you work altogether before your marriage?
_____ years

149. What kind of work did your father do most of the time until you were sixteen years old?
Occupation of father: _____
☐ Inapplicable because father dead while (respondent) was growing up
☐ Don't know

150. You mentioned before that you have _____ children you gave birth to *(see 1)*. I want to ask you now about other pregnancies you may have had.
Some pregnancies end in stillbirth, miscarriage, or abortion. Have you ever had any pregnancies that ended in these ways?

1 ☐ Yes →

2 ☐ No

151. *(Ask how many of each):*
_____ stillbirths
_____ miscarriages
_____ abortions

152. Have you ever had any children who died after birth?

1 ☐ Yes →

2 ☐ No

153. *(Ask how many):*

_____ children who died

154. Then you have had _____ pregnancies in all *(number of living children plus events listed in 151, 153).* Is that right?
(If error, revise 1, 151, or 153 as required.)

O. Family economic status

155. Here is a card showing different amounts of income. What would you say the total income of your family has been during the past twelve months? Just tell me the category, not the exact amount. *(Categories to be added in each country. Check category.)*

156. Would you say that your present income level is just about adequate for the things your family needs, or would you say it is more than adequate or less than adequate?

1 ☐ Adequate

2 ☐ More than adequate

3 ☐ Less than adequate

157. Now we would like to know your ideas about saving. For a family like yours, do you feel that saving for the future is *(read choices):*

1 Very important →

2 Somewhat important →

3 Not important

158. In your case, what would be the main purpose of saving?

_____

_____

_____

159. During the last year have you been able to save any money or was there no money left for saving?

1 ☐ Saved some money

2 ☐ Did not save money

160. Compared with other families in this community, do you think that the economic status of your family is *(read choices):*

1 ☐ Better than most

2 ☐ Same as most

3 ☐ Worse than most

(161—162 for husbands only; for wives, go to 164.)

161. Do you have in this household any of the following items? *(Categories of major consumer products to be added in each country. Check, if yes.)*

162. Do you own the (house/apartment) in which you are living, or do you rent it, or what arrangements do you have for housing?
    1 □ Own
    2 □ Rent
    3 □ Other → *(specify):* _____
    _____

P. Rural socioeconomic status

(For rural husbands only; for others, go to 164.)

163. *(Questions to be added in each country. Use decimals for multiple questions.)*

Q. Effects of having children

164. I would like to know how your feelings about children may have changed as a result of the experience of having children of your own.

    Thinking back to the time just before you were married, would you say you feel differently about children now than you did then?
    1 □ Yes   2 □ No   3 □ Don't know

    > 165. Can you tell me how your feelings about children have changed?
    > _____
    > _____
    > _____

This is the end of the interview. Thank you very much for your help and cooperation. Your answers will be very useful to us in this research project.

APPOINTMENT TO INTERVIEW SPOUSE

Date: _____

Time: _____

INTERVIEWER NOTES

1. Apart from the respondent and yourself, was there anyone else present during the interview?

   ☐ Yes   ☐ No → *(Go to 3.)*

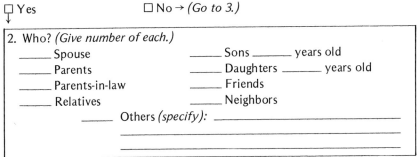

2. Who? *(Give number of each.)*

   _____ Spouse   _____ Sons _____ years old
   _____ Parents   _____ Daughters _____ years old
   _____ Parents-in-law   _____ Friends
   _____ Relatives   _____ Neighbors
               _____ Others *(specify):* _____
   _____
   _____

3. How often was the respondent distracted?
   1 ☐ Continually distracted
   2 ☐ Several times during the interview
   3 ☐ A few times during the interview
   4 ☐ Not at all

4. What was the degree of <u>rapport</u> between yourself and the respondent?
   1 ☐ Poor
   2 ☐ Fair
   3 ☐ Good
   4 ☐ Excellent

5. What was the degree of <u>cooperation</u> of the respondent?
   1 ☐ Very uncooperative
   2 ☐ Uncooperative
   3 ☐ Cooperative
   4 ☐ Very cooperative

6. What was the respondent's degree of <u>interest</u> in the content of the interview?
   1 ☐ Very interested
   2 ☐ Somewhat interested
   3 ☐ Not interested

7. Was the respondent offended by any questions in the interview?
   1 ☐ Yes   2 ☐ No

   Which questions? *(Give section and number.)*
   _____
   _____
   _____

8. Do you think the respondent gave inaccurate or misleading answers to any of the questions?

    ☐ Yes   ☐ No

    Please give the following information for each item:

Section	Item no.	Type of inaccuracy	Reasons for doubt
————	————	—————————	————————————————
			————————————————
			————————————————
————	————	—————————	————————————————
			————————————————
			————————————————
————	————	—————————	————————————————
			————————————————
			————————————————
————	————	—————————	————————————————
			————————————————
			————————————————

9. Other comments:

Appendix B Composition and description of constructed variables and indices

Index and source | *Description and range of index values*

Total number of children wanted

Source: Core questions 1, 2, and 10 or 12

1–50 = sum of the actual number of children respondent has plus the additional number of children desired

(Note: If the additional number desired is expressed as a range, from x to y, then $\frac{x + y}{2}$ is used for computation.)

55 = as many as possible

66 = up to God, fate

77 = depends or uncertain

99 = no response

Ideal number of children

Source: Core question 24

0 = if answer is no to question 21

1–50 = ideal number of children (if answer is yes to question 21)

55 = depends or uncertain

66 = up to God, fate

77 = don't know

99 = no response

Difference between wanted and ideal number of children

Source: Core questions 1, 2, 10 or 12, 24

(Total number of children wanted minus ideal number of children plus 10)

0– 9 = wanted less than ideal

10 = wanted same as ideal

11–60 = wanted greater than ideal

88 = depends, up to God, or don't know, for either total number of children wanted or ideal number of children

99 = no response

Size of family wanted

Source: Core questions 39, 40

1 = small family wanted (total number of children wanted is less than or equal to the number of children in "small" family)

Index and source	*Description and range of index values*

Size of family wanted
(continued)

2 = medium family wanted (total number of children wanted is less than the number of children in "large" family and greater than the number of children in "small" family)

3 = large family wanted (total number of children wanted is greater than or equal to the number of children in "large" family)

9 = no response

Ideal family size

Source: Core questions 24, 39, 40

1 = small-family ideal (ideal number of children is less or equal to the number of children in "small" family)

2 = medium-family ideal (ideal number of children is less than the number of children in "large" family and greater than number of children in "small" family)

3 = large-family ideal (ideal number of children is greater than or equal to number of children in "large" family)

9 = no response

Typical family size

Source: Core question 70

0–20 = number of children a typical couple in the community has, as perceived by respondent

99 = don't know, no response

Desired number of children relative to norms

Source: Core questions 1, 2, 10 or 12, 70

(Total number of children wanted minus typical family size plus 10)

0– 9 = wanted number of children is less than typical family size

10 = wanted number of children is equal to typical family size

11–20 = wanted number of children is greater than typical family size

99 = all other codes

Ideal number of children relative to norms

Source: Core questions 24, 70

(Ideal number of children minus typical family size plus 10)

0– 9 = ideal number of children is less than typical family size

10 = ideal number of children is equal to typical family size

11–20 = ideal number of children is greater than typical family size

99 = all other codes

Index and source	*Description and range of index values*
Size of respondent's family of orientation Source: Core question 117	0–40 = total number of brothers and sisters respondent grew up with 99 = no response
Benefits for children of large families Source: Core question 41 (1–4, 6, 7)	(Linear combination of selected items relating to benefits of belonging to "small" or "large" family) 1 = great benefits for children of "small" family ↓ 13 = great benefits for children of "large" family
Ideal number of children—sequential Source: Core question 26	(This index is similar to the ideal number of children index, page 193, except that it is constructed from another item showing also the sequence of family-building viewed as ideal by the respondent) 0–12 = sum of the number of children as given in question 26 (or if response to question 24 is one child, "up to God, fate," or "don't know," or if response to question 25 is "don't know") 66 = up to God, fate 77 = don't know 99 = no response
Boy preference—importance Source: Core questions 23, 27, 29	(Combination of selected questions: First child, girl or boy? How important to have a girl? How important to have a boy?) 1 = strong girl preference ↓ 5 = strong boy preference 9 = no response
Boy preference—composition Source: Core questions 23, 24, 25	(Combination of selected items on sex composition of ideal family) 1 = strong preference for number of girls ↓ 7 = strong preference for number of boys 9 = no response
Boy preference—combined Source: Core questions 23, 24, 25, 26	(Sum of the two indices on boy preference above) 1 = strong girl preference ↓ 11 = strong boy preference 9 = no response

Index and source	*Description and range of index values*

Reasons for wanting another child

Source: Core question 16 or 20

(Sum of 17 reasons, each weighted 1 = not important, 2 = somewhat important, or 3 = very important)

   0 = no response

   1 = weak positive value of children

   ↓

  51 = strong positive value of children

Reasons for not wanting another child

Source: Core question 17 or 19

(Sum of 9 reasons, each weighted 1 = not important, 2 = somewhat important, or 3 = very important)

   0 = no response

   1 = weak negative value of children

   ↓

  27 = strong negative value of children

Number of contraceptive methods known

Source: Core question 57

(Appropriate sub-items from question 57)

  0– 8 = number of contraceptive methods known

Number of contraceptive methods know how to use

Source: Core question 57

(Appropriate sub-items from question 57)

  0– 8 = number of contraceptive methods know how to use

Number of contraceptive methods used

Source: Core question 57

(Appropriate sub-items from question 57)

  0– 8 = number of contraceptive methods used

Contraceptive use

Source: Core questions 46, 50, 53, 56

(This index differs from preceding in that it specifically concerns present, past, and future use of contraceptive methods by respondent)

   1 = presently using birth control

   2 = wife not able to conceive

   3 = not using birth control now but have used it in past and plan to use it in future

   4 = have not used birth control before but plan to use it in future

   5 = not presently using birth control, have used it before, and no definite plan to use it in future

   6 = not presently using birth control, have not used it before, and no definite plan to use it in future

   7 = wife pregnant, have used birth control in past, and plan to use it in future

   8 = wife pregnant, have not used birth control in past, but plan to use it in future

Index and source	*Description and range of index values*
Contraceptive use *(continued)*	9 = wife pregnant, used birth control before, but no definite plans to use it in future
	10 = wife pregnant, have not used birth control before, and no definite plan to use it in future
	99 = no response
First birth interval (months) Source: Core questions 1, 108	Negative = first birth took place before date of marriage
	0–800 = number of months first birth occurred after date of marriage
	888 = respondent married more than once or no children reported
	999 = no response
Second birth interval (months) Source: Core question 1	0–800 = number of months second birth occurred after first birth
	888 = respondent married more than once or no children reported
	999 = no response
Third birth interval (months) Source: Core question 1	0–800 = number of months third birth occurred after second birth
	888 = respondent married more than once or no children reported
	999 = no response
General birth control attitudes Source: Core questions 43, 58, 59, 60	0 = has not heard of birth control
	1 = disapproves strongly of birth control
	2 = disapproves slightly of birth control
	3 = all other responses
	4 = approves slightly of birth control
	5 = approves strongly of birth control
Situational birth control attitudes Source: Core questions 43, 61	0 = has not heard of birth control
	1 = strongest disapproval
	↓
	7 = strongest approval
Combined birth control attitudes Source: Core questions 43, 58, 59, 60, 61	(Combination of general birth control attitudes and situational birth control attitudes)
	1 = strongest disapproval
	↓
	11 = strongest approval

Index and source	*Description and range of index values*
General abortion attitudes Source: Core questions 64, 65, 66, 67	0 = has not heard of abortion 1 = disapproves strongly of abortion 2 = disapproves slightly of abortion 3 = all other responses 4 = approves slightly of abortion 5 = approves strongly of abortion
Situational abortion attitudes Source: Core questions 64, 68	0 = has not heard of abortion 1 = strongest disapproval of abortion ↓ 9 = strongest approval of abortion
Combined abortion attitudes Source: Core questions 64, 65, 66, 67, 68	(Combination of general abortion attitudes and situational abortion attitudes) 0 = has not heard of abortion 1 = strongest disapproval of abortion ↓ 13 = strongest approval of abortion
Small-family press Source: Core questions 16(5) or 20(5), 63, 70, 71	(Sum of questions 16(5), 63, 70, and 71 minus 3) 0 = has not heard of birth control (in this case, question 63 is inapplicable) 1 = large family press (strong) ↓ 9 = small family press (strong)
Small-family press— attitudinal Source: Core question 42 (11, 21, 27)	(This index differs from preceding one in being constructed from selected items from question 42) 1 = large-family press (strong) ↓ 7 = small-family press (strong)
Small-family press— combined Source: Core questions 16(5) or 20(5), 42(11, 21, 27), 63, 70, 71	(Linear sum of items included in the two indices on family press, given above) 1 = very strong large-family press ↓ 15 = very strong small-family press
Decision-mindedness in childbearing Source: Core question 42 (9, 23, 32, 38, 41)	(Sum of selected items from question 42 on attitudes toward children and childbearing) 1 = predisposition to avoid decisions ↓ 31 = predisposition to make decisions

Index and source	*Description and range of index values*
Fatalism score Source: Core questions 10 or 12, 23, 24, 31	(Sum of selected items to which respondent gives fatalistic response, such as "up to God")
Fatalism attitude index Source: Core question 42 (11, 24, 38)	(Sum of selected items from question 42 on attitudes toward children and childbearing) 1 = very low fatalism ↓ 19 = very high fatalism
Expected economic help Source: Core questions 16(6, 8), 74, 76, 79	(Linear sum of items measuring respondent's expectation of some economic help from children) 0 = no economic help expected ↓ 8 = great deal of economic help expected
Expected economic help—combined Source: Core questions 16(6, 8), 42(2), 74, 76, 79	(Linear combination of index on expected economic help, above, plus an attitudinal item from question 42 on same topic) 0 = no economic help expected ↓ 17 = great deal of economic help expected
Decreased utility of children Source: Core questions 82, 84, 86, 88	(Linear combination of selected items on decreasing utility of children) 1 = great increase in utility of children ↓ 9 = great decrease in utility of children
Decreased utility of children—weighted Source: Core questions 82–89	(Linear combination of preceding index weighted by additional items) 1 = great increase in utility of children ↓ 13 = great decrease in utility of children and does not like this state of affairs
Number of children somewhat of a financial burden Source: Core question 91	(Smallest number of children that would be somewhat of a financial burden; score of 7 means more than 6 children would be somewhat of a burden)
Number of children a heavy financial burden Source: Core question 91	(Smallest number of children that would be a heavy financial burden) 66 = could raise any number of children without their becoming a heavy burden 99 = no response

Index and source	Description and range of index values

Economic burden of wanted family

Source: Core questions 1, 2, 10 or 12, 91

(Comparison of questions on total number of children wanted and the economic burden of children)

1 = wanted number of children is no burden

2 = wanted number of children is a slight burden

3 = wanted number of children is somewhat of a burden

4 = wanted number of children is a heavy burden

9 = no response

Economic costs

Source: Core questions 1, 2, 10 or 12, 17(1), 91, 104

(Combination of preceding index plus additional items pertaining to costs of children)

1 = children perceived to entail minimal economic cost

↓

8 = children perceived to entail heavy economic cost

9 = no response

Economic costs— combined

Source: Core questions 1, 3, 10 or 12, 17(1), 42(37), 91, 104

(Combination of index on economic costs plus one item taken from the attitude items on children and childbearing)

1 = children perceived to entail minimal economic cost

↓

15 = children perceived to entail heavy economic cost

99 = no response

Propensity to save

Source: Core questions 157, 159

(Combination of two questions on whether saving is important and whether respondent was able to save money during past year)

1 = saving not important and did not save anything last year

↓

5 = saving very important and did save money last year

Relative economic status

Source: Core questions 156, 160

(Combination of two questions on whether present income of respondent is adequate for family needs and the respondent's perception of his/her status compared with others)

Index and source	*Description and range of index values*
Relative economic status *(continued)*	1 = income perceived to be less than others' and inadequate 5 = income perceived to be better than others' and more than adequate
Husband's influence in decision-making Source: Core questions 119(1), 119(2), 119(4)	(Linear combination of items on different decision-making situations: type of job husband should have, what doctor to have when child is not well, whether to purchase an important consumer good or not) 1 = decisions made mostly by wife 7 = decisions made mostly by husband
Wife's employment since marriage Source: Core questions 140, 142, 144	0–50 = years wife worked since marriage 88 = respondent is husband 99 = no response
Overall modernity scale Source: Core questions 121–126	(Linear combination of items to measure modernity, using brief form of Smith and Inkeles scale) 1 = extremely traditional 15 = extremely modern
Media exposure Source: Core questions 127, 128	1 = never gets news from papers, radio, or television 9 = gets news daily from papers, radio, or television
Literacy Source: Core questions 94, 95	0 = has more than 4 years of schooling 1 = can read easily 2 = can read with some difficulty 3 = illiterate
Urban-rural residence Source: Core questions 110, 111, 113, 114	(Combination of items to evaluate length of respondent's exposure to urban or rural life) 1 = has always lived in rural area 2 = now lives in rural area but has lived in large town or city 3 = has always lived in urban area

Index and source	*Description and range of index values*
Urban-rural residence (continued)	4 = now lives in urban area but has lived on a farm or in the country
	9 = no response
Urban experience	(Percentage of respondent's life spent in urban area)
Source: Core questions 110–115	0 = has lived in rural area all his/her life
	↓
	100 = has lived in urban area all his/her life
	999 = no response

Appendix C Examples of responses included under major and specific code categories for advantages and disadvantages of children

ADVANTAGES

Happiness, love, companionship

Companionship, avoidance of loneliness
  Examples: "Children are companions"
  "It is lonely without children"
  "One is free from loneliness"

Love, affection
  Examples: "Somebody to love"
  "Somebody who loves you"
  "Feeling of love"
  "Someone to care about you"

Play, fun with children; avoidance of boredom
  Examples: "Play with them"
  "They're fun"
  "Dull or boring without them"
  "Children are exciting"
  "Nice to come home to"
  "Children are amusing"
  "Watch cute things children do"
  "Children as 'playthings,' as pets"
  "Children (girls) to dress up"

Relief from strain, distraction from problems
  Examples: "Distraction from problems of work"
  "Lessen your problems, tiredness"
  "Children relieve mental strain"
  "They are relaxing"

Happiness for individual parent (general)
  Examples: "Happiness in life"
  "Children bring happiness to parents"
  "Joy of children"

Happiness for the family[1]

---

1 Responses in this category emphasize the happiness children bring for the entire family.

Uniqueness, specialness in parent-child relationship
  Examples: "Children are unique"
            "Special relationship"
            "Cannot be compared to anything else"

Personal development of parent

Character development, responsibility, maturity, morality
  Examples: "Parents/husband more responsible"
            "Helps you mature"
            "Helps you settle down"
            "Helps you lead a normal life"

Incentives to succeed, striving to provide for children
  Examples: "Gives parents a goal"
            "Reason to want to succeed in life"
            "Somebody to live for"
            "Work hard to provide for children"
            "Gives meaning to work, life"

Fulfillment of self, completeness as person
  Examples: "Gives a feeling of completeness"
            "Makes you a whole person/woman, man"
            "Feeling of self-fulfillment"

Extension of self
  Examples: "Seeing yourself in your children"
            "Children as part of yourself"
            "Your own flesh and blood"

Learning from experience of childrearing
  Examples: "Learn about the nature of children/child development/
            how to raise children"
            "Learn about life"
            "Experience to learn more"

Motherhood, fatherhood; adulthood
  Examples: "Makes you an adult"
            "Pleasure in being a father/mother"
            "Being respected as a parent"

Proof of fertility, masculinity, femininity
  Examples: "To show that you can have children"
            "Demonstrating your masculinity/femininity"

Childrearing satisfactions

Pride in children's accomplishments
  Examples: "Pride in child's success"
            "Accomplishment of children in school"
            "Careers of children"
            "Children's abilities, talents"

Pleasure from growth, development of children
    Examples: "Nice to watch them grow"
             "Different stages of development are interesting"

Children to carry out parent's hopes, aspirations
    Examples: "Children do what parents could not"
             "Fulfillment of parent's ambitions"

Opportunity to teach, guide, instill values
    Examples: "Telling them how to behave"
             "Passing on values to them"
             "Bring them up the way you want"

Satisfaction in one's childrearing ability, accomplishment
    Examples: "Feeling of competence from raising children"
             "Doing a good job as a parent"

Satisfaction in providing for children
    Examples: "Giving your children the best you can"
             "The pleasure of giving to someone else, sharing"

Economic benefits, security

Economic help in old age
    Examples: "They look after me financially when I'm old"
             "Financial, economic help in old age"

Companionship, comfort, care in old age
    Examples: "Help old parents when they get sick"
             "Companionship, reassurance, knowing there is someone who
             will care for you when you get old"

Unspecified help in old age
    Examples: "Help in old age"
             "For old age"
             (Other general responses similar to the above)

Economic help (old age not mentioned)
    Examples: "To contribute to family finances"
             "For tax deduction"

Comfort, care (old age not mentioned)
    Examples: "Protect parents"
             "Help in life, help in family affairs"
             "Care for parents when they get sick"

Help in housework, family chores; practical help
    Examples: "Somebody to run errands"
             "To wash the car, mow the lawn, help with dishes"
             "Somebody to send to the store"

Sharing financial responsibility; insurance, security
    Examples: "Someone else to share family responsibility"
             "Help from children in case you need it"

Help in family business, farm
    Examples: "Someone to take my place when I retire"
             "Work in the business, on the farm"
Help in taking care of other children
    Example: "Look after the younger children"
Unspecified help (old age not mentioned)
    Examples: "Provide help to parents"
             "Children are useful"
             "Children bring luck"

Benefits to family unit

Children as bond between spouses
    Examples: "Bond in marriage, more stable marriage"
             "Less tendency to separate"
             "Make love stronger"
             "Bring husband and wife closer together"
Children as reason for, fulfillment of marriage
    Examples: "Having children is purpose of marriage"
             "Children bless marriage; as blessing on marriage"
             "Children are essential to marriage"
Children as family life, complete or close-knit family
    Examples: "Children complete the family"
             "Presence of children makes home a *real* home"
             "Children make the family more close together"

Kin group benefits

Continuity of family name
    Examples: "To spread the family name"
             "To preserve our clan"
             "To bear my name"
Continuity of family traditions
    Examples: "To inherit family traditions"
             "To carry on the achievement of family"
Enhancement of reputation of family
    Examples: "To make family more prominent in community"
             "To give family prestige"
Having future grandchildren
    Examples: "Having grandchildren is fun when you are old"
             "You will be lonely without grandchildren when you are old"
Children as heirs, someone to inherit family wealth
    Example: "To have someone to inherit my property"
Religious rituals, ancestor worship
    Example: "To have children to worship me when I die"

To satisfy desires of other kin
    Examples: "Grandparents/parents/in-laws want children"
              "Family expects us to have children"

Social, religious influences

Conformity to social norms
    Examples: "Most people expect me to have children"
              "People would think it strange if I did not have children"

Conformity to religious norms
    Examples: "Obligation, duty to God to have children"
              "Religious obligation to have children"
              "I'm Catholic, you know"

Children as benefits to society
    Examples: "Contribution to humanity/national development"
              "Future services to the country"

General, intrinsic value of children

Children as treasure, wealth, assets
    Examples: "Children are wealth"
              "Future assets; guide and hope to parents"
              "The more boys, the wealthier"
              "No hope for the future without children"

Instinctive, natural to have children
    Examples: "You are bound to have children when you get married"
              "It's better to have children"
              "Everyone should have children"

General wanting, liking children
    Examples: "I like children"
              "Children are just adorable"
              "I want children"

Other advantages

(Responses that did not fit any of the above categories were coded in this category.)

DISADVANTAGES

Financial costs

Educational costs
    Example: "Hard to provide education for children"

General financial costs
    Examples: "Cost of living is high"
              "Children are expensive"
              "Hard to raise children when one is jobless and has no money"

General financial costs *(continued)*
>"Financial problems during pregnancy"
>"Medical costs are high"
>"Can't buy children the things they need"

Emotional costs

Responsibility of parenthood
>Example: "Heavy responsibility; the more children you have, the more responsibility you have as a parent"

Discipline, moral behavior
>Examples: "Worry over bringing children up right"
>"Children may get in trouble"
>"Children are always fighting"

Health problems of children
>Examples: "Physical and emotional strain when child is sick, worry over children's sickness"
>"Burden increases when child gets sick"
>"Can't work when child is sick"

Concern over children's future success, happiness
>Examples: "Children might have hard time in life"
>"Concern about their future"
>"Children may not have a good chance in life"
>"Children may not be lucky in life"

Concern about satisfying children's present wants
>Examples: "Worry about trying to provide for children's desires"
>"If you have to get something for one, you have to get it for the others"

Noise, disorder, nuisance
>Examples: "Children are noisy; never any peace when children are around"
>"House is messy with children around"
>"Children are a lot of bother"

General rearing problems
>Examples: "Hard to raise children"
>"Parent doesn't know what to do to raise children"

General emotional strain
>Examples: "Children make me nervous"
>"Always worrying about children"
>"Children drive me crazy"
>"Worry about leaving children with baby-sitter"

Physical demands on parents

Health hazard of pregnancy; maternal health
>Examples: "Difficulty or danger in pregnancy/nursing children"
>"Hard to take care of children when parents are sick"
>"Pregnancy is bad for the mother's health"

Physical work, tiredness caused by children
    Examples: "Extra housework to take care of children"
                "You have to wake up at night"
                "Physical strain caring for children"
                "Always tired"

Restrictions on alternative activities

Restrictions on time
    Examples: "Children use up time"
                "No time to do anything else when you have children"

Restrictions on travel
    Example: "Can't take trip/go places"

Restrictions on social life, recreation
    Examples: "Don't have much entertainment"
                "Can't spend as much time with friends"
                "No recreation"
                "Can't fulfill social obligations"

Restrictions on job, career
    Examples: "Can't work when you're raising children"
                "Not enough time for work or business"

Restrictions on personal wants
    Examples: "Can't buy some things for yourself"
                "Children come first in using family's money"
                "Cannot follow your personal wishes any more"

Restrictions on privacy
    Examples: "Can't be by yourself"
                "Never alone, no privacy"

General lack of flexibility, freedom
    Examples: "Cannot leave the house"
                "Children tie you down"
                "Can't go to church"
                "Can't do the things you used to do"
                "Can't do things spontaneously; have to plan ahead of time"

Marital problems

Less time, interaction between spouses
    Examples: "Not enough time with husband/wife"
                "Too busy with children to enjoy husband/wife"

Disagreements over children
    Examples: "Children cause quarrels"
                "Disagreements about raising children"

General marital problems
    Example: "Marriage has not been happy since we had children"

Kin group costs, problems of inheritance

Disadvantages relating to, affecting kin group
      Example: "Division of property, wealth among children; hard to divide
               property equally, not enough inheritance to go around"

Societal costs, overpopulation

Disadvantages relating to, affecting society
      Examples: "Concern about population problem"
                 "Too many children is bad to society"
                 "Pollution, too crowded"

Other disadvantages

      Examples: "Children not useful"
                 "No help in earning a living"

Table D1 Advantages of having children
(Percentage of respondents mentioning each advantage, by socioeconomic group and country)

Advantage and SES group	Korea	Taiwan	Japan	U.S. (Hawaii)			Philippines	Thailand
				Japanese	Caucasian	Filipino		
Companionship, avoidance of loneliness								
Urban middle	14.2	21.6	11.0	37.8	24.3	na	5.1	38.3
Urban lower	17.5	38.7	14.2	46.7	28.7	27.6	13.5	22.5
Rural	14.3	15.4	12.0	na	na	64.3	11.8	12.5
Love, affection								
Urban middle	14.2	10.4	2.3	10.2	30.6	na	4.4	7.5
Urban lower	10.6	14.0	8.2	6.7	17.2	4.3	4.8	9.1
Rural	8.7	3.5	2.8	na	na	7.1	3.1	5.8
Play, fun with children; avoidance of boredom								
Urban middle	20.0	44.0	2.2	31.6	23.2	na	19.1	3.3
Urban lower	37.2	52.8	3.7	42.6	27.6	15.6	19.0	3.3
Rural	30.2	32.3	6.3	na	na	6.0	17.3	0.8
Relief from strain, distraction from problems								
Urban middle	13.3	7.6	2.9	1.0	1.1	na	12.5	2.5
Urban lower	13.6	7.0	10.4	2.7	0.0	6.9	13.5	0.8
Rural	6.4	1.4	5.6	na	na	2.4	5.5	1.6
Happiness for individual parent (general)								
Urban middle	5.8	12.5	9.6	20.4	21.1	na	34.5	14.2
Urban lower	3.0	10.5	11.2	18.6	18.2	45.3	40.5	4.2
Rural	4.0	9.2	9.8	na	na	63.1	31.5	5.8

Table D1 (*continued*)

Advantage and SES group	Korea	Taiwan	Japan	U.S. (Hawaii)			Philippines	Thailand
				Japanese	Caucasian	Filipino		
Happiness for family								
Urban middle	42.4	13.3	42.6	6.1	1.1	na	29.4	19.2
Urban lower	32.6	4.2	49.3	6.7	2.3	26.5	23.8	10.0
Rural	19.1	2.8	45.8	na	na	6.0	19.7	5.8
Uniqueness, specialness in parent-child relationship								
Urban middle	3.3	6.3	4.4	4.1	5.3	na	0.0	1.7
Urban lower	1.5	3.5	3.4	4.0	2.3	0.0	0.0	1.7
Rural	1.6	2.8	2.8	na	na	1.2	1.6	0.0
Character development, responsibility, maturity, morality								
Urban middle	14.9	5.6	12.5	18.4	25.3	na	9.6	23.4
Urban lower	6.9	1.4	6.7	24.0	14.9	9.4	7.1	3.4
Rural	2.4	1.4	2.8	na	na	1.2	1.6	0.8
Incentives to succeed, striving to provide for children								
Urban middle	25.0	3.5	2.2	8.1	10.5	na	22.0	20.0
Urban lower	27.3	0.0	3.7	16.0	14.9	10.3	19.1	2.5
Rural	7.9	1.4	4.9	na	na	14.3	12.6	1.7
Fulfillment of self, completeness as person								
Urban middle	0.8	0.7	5.1	6.1	9.5	na	4.4	7.5
Urban lower	1.5	0.0	1.5	8.0	10.3	2.6	0.8	0.8
Rural	4.0	0.0	2.8	na	na	0.0	1.6	0.0

Extension of self								
Urban middle	2.5	0.7	6.6	8.1	21.1	na	1.5	2.5
Urban lower	0.8	0.0	4.4	10.7	14.9	0.9	0.0	0.0
Rural	0.0	0.0	4.9	na	na	1.2	0.8	0.0
Learning from experience of childrearing								
Urban middle	7.5	2.1	9.5	25.5	28.5	na	2.9	1.7
Urban lower	0.0	0.7	7.4	18.6	21.8	4.3	4.8	0.0
Rural	0.8	0.0	4.2	na	na	0.0	0.8	0.0
Motherhood, fatherhood; adulthood								
Urban middle	5.8	0.0	3.6	7.1	4.2	na	0.7	0.8
Urban lower	3.0	0.7	2.2	6.7	0.0	0.0	1.6	0.0
Rural	4.0	0.0	2.8	na	na	1.2	0.0	0.8
Proof of fertility, masculinity, femininity								
Urban middle	0.0	0.0	1.5	0.0	3.2	na	0.7	0.0
Urban lower	3.0	0.0	0.0	0.0	0.0	0.0	0.8	0.8
Rural	7.1	0.0	0.0	na	na	1.2	0.8	0.0
Pride in children's accomplishments								
Urban middle	5.8	6.9	0.0	8.2	13.7	na	7.4	2.5
Urban lower	12.9	15.6	0.0	1.3	5.7	5.1	7.9	0.8
Rural	15.9	16.2	0.7	na	na	4.8	7.1	0.0
Pleasure from growth, development of children								
Urban middle	23.4	0.0	23.5	27.6	38.9	na	6.6	1.7
Urban lower	19.0	0.0	19.4	28.0	37.9	4.3	5.6	0.0
Rural	18.3	0.0	21.8	na	na	0.0	4.7	0.0

Table D1 *(continued)*

Advantage and SES group	Korea	Taiwan	Japan	U.S. (Hawaii) Japanese	Caucasian	Filipino	Philippines	Thailand
Children to carry out parent's hopes, aspirations								
Urban middle	17.5	0.0	13.9	7.1	8.4	na	2.2	3.3
Urban lower	7.6	0.7	14.2	8.0	5.7	0.9	2.4	0.8
Rural	7.1	0.0	22.5	na	na	0.0	3.9	0.0
Opportunity to teach, guide, instill values								
Urban middle	3.3	2.1	0.7	9.2	23.2	na	2.2	0.8
Urban lower	3.8	2.1	1.4	10.7	14.9	2.6	3.2	0.0
Rural	4.8	0.7	0.7	na	na	0.0	2.4	0.0
Satisfaction in one's child-rearing ability, accomplishment								
Urban middle	25.0	0.7	0.0	7.1	11.6	na	0.0	0.0
Urban lower	12.9	0.0	0.7	5.3	6.9	0.9	0.0	0.8
Rural	10.3	1.4	0.7	na	na	0.0	0.0	0.0
Satisfaction in providing for children								
Urban middle	3.3	1.4	10.3	5.1	8.4	na	1.5	1.7
Urban lower	8.3	0.0	5.2	5.3	5.7	1.7	3.2	0.0
Rural	4.0	0.7	10.6	na	na	0.0	6.3	2.5
Economic help in old age								
Urban middle	0.8	0.0	0.7	0.0	0.0	na	5.1	2.5
Urban lower	2.3	0.0	0.7	1.3	0.0	0.9	2.4	4.2
Rural	7.9	2.1	0.7	na	na	17.9	0.8	10.0

Companionship, comfort, care in old age									
Urban middle	0.8	1.4	2.9	6.1	3.2	na	19.1	2.5
Urban lower	6.8	0.7	3.7	8.0	1.1	26.5	20.6	5.0
Rural	15.1	0.0	4.2	na	na	31.0	22.8	42.5
Unspecified help in old age									
Urban middle	0.8	3.5	0.7	1.0	2.1	na	33.9	7.5
Urban lower	3.8	23.9	3.0	1.3	1.1	16.2	33.3	49.2
Rural	6.3	39.4	5.6	na	na	41.7	35.4	11.7
Economic help (old age not mentioned)									
Urban middle	0.0	0.0	0.0	3.0	2.1	na	15.4	1.7
Urban lower	0.8	0.7	0.0	2.7	3.4	17.1	21.4	2.5
Rural	3.2	2.1	0.7	na	na	14.3	26.8	10.0
Comfort, care (old age not mentioned)									
Urban middle	9.2	0.7	1.5	1.0	1.1	na	7.3	2.5
Urban lower	12.1	0.7	0.0	2.7	2.3	6.8	5.6	9.2
Rural	15.1	0.0	4.9	na	na	16.7	4.7	13.3
Help in housework, family chores; practical help									
Urban middle	0.8	2.1	0.7	2.0	3.2	na	22.3	0.0
Urban lower	3.1	5.6	1.5	1.3	3.4	37.6	42.9	16.7
Rural	8.7	5.6	2.8	na	na	65.5	48.0	10.0
Sharing financial responsibility; insurance, security									
Urban middle	0.8	0.0	0.0	0.0	2.1	na	0.0	0.8
Urban lower	2.3	1.4	1.5	1.3	0.0	0.0	0.0	0.0
Rural	0.8	0.7	0.7	na	na	2.4	0.0	0.0

Table D1 *(continued)*

Advantage and SES group	Korea	Taiwan	Japan	U.S. (Hawaii) Japanese	Caucasian	Filipino	Philippines	Thailand
Help in family business, farm								
Urban middle	0.0	0.7	0.0	0.0	0.0	na	2.2	0.8
Urban lower	0.0	0.0	0.0	0.0	0.0	0.0	0.0	1.7
Rural	0.8	3.5	1.4	na	na	0.0	7.1	3.3
Help in taking care of other children								
Urban middle	0.0	0.0	0.0	1.0	1.1	na	0.0	0.0
Urban lower	0.8	0.7	0.0	2.7	0.0	0.9	0.0	0.8
Rural	1.6	0.0	0.0	na	na	9.5	0.0	2.5
Unspecified help (old age not mentioned)								
Urban middle	0.0	0.7	0.0	3.1	2.1	na	16.2	5.0
Urban lower	0.8	1.4	0.0	4.0	2.3	17.9	11.9	21.7
Rural	3.2	6.9	7.0	na	na	9.5	16.5	17.5
Children as bond between spouses								
Urban middle	19.2	9.7	22.1	18.3	14.7	na	19.9	27.5
Urban lower	25.7	0.0	26.8	11.9	20.7	11.2	15.1	5.8
Rural	2.4	2.1	9.9	na	na	1.2	9.5	1.7
Children as reason for, fulfillment of marriage								
Urban middle	2.5	0.0	0.0	9.2	8.4	na	6.6	3.3
Urban lower	1.5	0.0	0.7	4.0	2.3	3.5	2.4	0.0
Rural	0.8	0.0	0.0	na	na	1.2	1.6	0.0

Children as family life, complete or closeknit family								
Urban middle	10.8	11.2	9.5	29.6	25.3	na	4.4	19.2
Urban lower	3.0	2.8	15.7	25.3	20.6	8.6	1.6	0.0
Rural	2.4	4.2	7.0	na	na	3.6	3.2	2.5
Continuity of family name								
Urban middle	10.0	18.8	0.0	9.2	10.5	na	3.7	20.0
Urban lower	17.4	45.0	0.0	10.7	8.0	15.4	10.3	14.2
Rural	24.6	33.0	0.0	na	na	7.1	4.7	28.3
Continuity of family traditions								
Urban middle	2.5	0.0	1.5	2.0	0.0	na	0.0	0.8
Urban lower	1.5	0.0	0.0	0.0	1.1	0.9	2.4	0.0
Rural	0.8	0.0	2.1	na	na	0.0	0.0	0.0
Enhancement of reputation of family								
Urban middle	0.0	0.0	0.0	0.0	0.0	na	0.7	3.3
Urban lower	0.0	0.0	0.0	0.0	0.0	0.0	0.0	1.7
Rural	0.0	0.0	0.0	na	na	0.0	0.0	8.3
Having future grandchildren								
Urban middle	5.0	0.0	0.0	7.1	11.6	na	2.2	0.0
Urban lower	1.5	0.0	0.0	8.0	4.6	1.7	0.8	0.0
Rural	2.4	0.0	0.0	na	na	3.6	0.0	0.0
Children as heirs, someone to inherit family wealth								
Urban middle	0.8	0.0	1.5	0.0	1.1	na	2.9	0.0
Urban lower	0.0	0.0	3.0	0.0	3.4	4.3	3.2	0.8
Rural	3.2	0.0	8.5	na	na	0.0	0.0	1.7

218

Table D1 (continued)

Advantage and SES group	Korea	Taiwan	Japan	U.S. (Hawaii) Japanese	Caucasian	Filipino	Philippines	Thailand
Religious rituals, ancestor worship								
Urban middle	0.0	0.0	0.0	0.0	0.0	na	0.0	0.0
Urban lower	0.0	0.0	0.0	0.0	0.0	0.0	0.0	0.0
Rural	5.6	0.0	0.0	na	na	0.0	0.0	1.7
To increase strength, power of kin group								
Urban middle	0.0	0.0	0.0	2.0	0.0	na	0.0	0.8
Urban lower	0.0	0.0	0.0	2.7	1.1	0.0	0.8	0.0
Rural	2.4	0.7	0.0	na	na	0.0	0.8	0.8
To satisfy desires of spouse								
Urban middle	0.0	0.0	0.0	1.0	0.0	na	0.0	0.8
Urban lower	1.5	0.0	0.0	0.0	0.0	1.7	0.0	0.0
Rural	0.0	0.0	0.0	na	na	0.0	0.0	0.0
To satisfy desires of other kin								
Urban middle	0.0	1.4	0.0	3.1	2.1	na	0.0	0.0
Urban lower	2.3	2.8	0.7	0.0	0.0	1.7	0.0	0.8
Rural	1.6	0.7	0.0	na	na	1.2	0.0	0.0
Conformity to social norms								
Urban middle	0.8	2.1	2.2	2.0	2.1	na	0.0	2.5
Urban lower	1.5	2.1	0.7	0.0	1.1	0.0	0.0	0.0
Rural	4.0	1.4	1.4	na	na	0.0	0.0	0.8

	C1	C2	C3	C4	C5	C6	C7	C8
Conformity to religious norms								
Urban middle	0.8	0.0	0.7	0.0	1.1	na	0.7	0.0
Urban lower	0.0	0.0	0.7	0.0	0.0	0.0	4.0	4.2
Rural	0.0	0.0	0.0	na	na	0.0	0.0	5.8
Children as benefits to society								
Urban middle	3.3	1.4	1.4	2.0	5.3	na	5.1	2.5
Urban lower	0.8	1.4	0.0	0.0	0.0	0.0	4.0	1.7
Rural	7.1	3.5	0.0	na	na	0.0	3.9	9.1
Children as treasure, wealth, assets								
Urban middle	0.0	4.9	0.0	1.0	0.0	na	5.1	0.8
Urban lower	0.0	2.1	1.5	0.0	1.1	0.0	5.6	0.0
Rural	1.6	1.4	2.1	na	na	2.4	3.1	0.0
Instinctive, natural to have children								
Urban middle	5.0	1.4	0.0	4.1	6.3	na	0.0	0.0
Urban lower	0.8	4.2	0.0	1.3	2.3	0.0	0.0	0.0
Rural	4.8	2.1	0.0	na	na	1.2	1.6	0.0
General wanting, liking children								
Urban middle	0.0	0.0	0.7	12.2	8.5	na	0.7	0.0
Urban lower	0.0	0.7	0.7	16.0	16.0	3.5	0.8	0.8
Rural	0.0	0.0	0.7	na	na	0.0	1.6	0.8
Other advantages								
Urban middle	0.8	0.0	0.0	7.1	5.3	na	0.0	6.7
Urban lower	0.8	2.1	0.0	0.0	4.6	1.7	0.0	4.2
Rural	2.4	0.7	0.0	na	na	0.0	0.0	0.0

na—not applicable because subsample did not include persons in this socioeconomic group.

Table D2 Most important advantages of having children
(Percentage of respondents who assigned first ranking to each advantage, by socioeconomic group and country)

Advantage and SES group	Korea	Taiwan	Japan	U.S. (Hawaii)			Philippines	Thailand
				Japanese	Caucasian	Filipino		
Companionship, avoidance of loneliness								
Urban middle	5.0	8.3	2.9	6.1	7.4	na	0.7	16.7
Urban lower	8.3	9.7	3.0	12.0	7.0	1.7	1.6	5.8
Rural	4.8	2.1	2.8	na	na	0.0	0.8	5.0
Love, affection								
Urban middle	1.7	5.6	1.5	4.1	16.0	na	1.5	2.5
Urban lower	1.5	4.2	2.2	4.0	11.6	0.9	0.8	2.5
Rural	0.8	1.4	0.7	na	na	3.6	0.8	2.5
Play, fun with children; avoidance of boredom								
Urban middle	3.3	21.5	0.0	5.1	3.2	na	3.7	0.8
Urban lower	6.8	15.3	0.7	5.3	8.1	1.7	3.2	0.8
Rural	11.1	6.9	1.4	na	na	2.4	3.1	0.0
Relief from strain, distraction from problems								
Urban middle	5.0	3.5	1.5	0.0	1.1	na	2.9	1.7
Urban lower	6.1	2.8	3.7	0.0	0.0	2.6	0.8	0.0
Rural	3.2	0.0	0.7	na	na	0.0	0.0	0.0
Happiness for individual parent (general)								
Urban middle	0.8	8.3	2.2	6.1	7.4	na	16.2	3.3
Urban lower	0.0	3.5	3.7	4.0	4.7	34.2	9.5	0.8
Rural	0.0	4.9	2.8	na	na	18.1	9.4	4.2

Happiness for family								
Urban middle	18.3	9.7	19.9	3.1	1.1	na	12.5	9.2
Urban lower	16.7	2.1	29.1	2.7	1.2	20.5	7.9	5.0
Rural	6.3	1.4	21.1	na	na	1.2	8.7	2.5
Uniqueness, specialness in parent-child relationship								
Urban middle	0.0	4.2	1.5	1.0	1.1	na	0.0	0.0
Urban lower	1.5	0.7	0.7	1.3	1.2	0.0	0.0	0.0
Rural	0.0	2.1	0.7	na	na	0.0	0.0	0.0
Character development, responsibility, maturity, morality								
Urban middle	0.8	1.4	4.4	8.2	3.2	na	1.5	9.2
Urban lower	0.8	0.7	2.2	8.0	5.8	0.9	0.8	1.7
Rural	1.6	0.7	1.4	na	na	0.0	0.8	0.8
Incentives to succeed, striving to provide for children								
Urban middle	5.8	1.4	0.0	2.0	2.1	na	8.8	4.2
Urban lower	4.5	0.0	1.5	0.0	2.3	2.6	7.1	0.8
Rural	2.4	0.7	2.1	na	na	3.6	4.7	0.8
Fulfillment of self, completeness as person								
Urban middle	0.0	0.7	2.9	2.0	3.2	na	0.0	3.3
Urban lower	0.8	0.0	0.7	1.3	4.7	0.0	0.8	0.8
Rural	1.6	0.0	1.4	na	na	0.0	0.8	0.0
Extension of self								
Urban middle	0.0	0.0	0.0	0.0	3.2	na	0.0	0.0
Urban lower	0.8	0.0	1.5	1.3	2.3	0.0	0.0	0.0
Rural	0.0	0.0	0.0	na	na	0.0	0.0	0.0

Table D2 (continued)

Advantage and SES group	Korea	Taiwan	Japan	U.S. (Hawaii) Japanese	Caucasian	Filipino	Philippines	Thailand
Learning from experience of childrearing								
Urban middle	3.3	0.0	3.7	4.1	5.3	na	0.7	0.0
Urban lower	0.0	0.0	1.5	2.7	2.3	0.0	0.0	0.0
Rural	0.0	0.0	0.7	na	na	0.0	0.0	0.0
Motherhood, fatherhood; adulthood								
Urban middle	0.0	0.0	2.9	2.0	3.2	na	0.0	0.0
Urban lower	0.8	0.7	0.7	2.7	0.0	0.0	0.0	0.0
Rural	0.8	0.0	0.7	na	na	0.0	0.0	0.0
Proof of fertility, masculinity, femininity								
Urban middle	0.0	0.0	0.7	0.0	1.1	na	0.0	0.0
Urban lower	0.0	0.0	0.0	0.0	0.0	0.0	0.0	0.8
Rural	2.4	0.0	0.0	na	na	0.0	0.0	0.0
Pride in children's accomplishments								
Urban middle	0.0	2.8	0.0	3.1	1.1	na	1.5	1.7
Urban lower	3.0	2.8	0.0	0.0	2.3	1.7	1.6	0.0
Rural	6.3	10.4	0.0	na	na	1.2	1.6	0.0
Pleasure from growth, development of children								
Urban middle	8.3	0.0	10.3	10.2	10.6	na	0.7	0.0
Urban lower	6.1	0.0	4.5	10.7	11.6	0.9	1.6	0.0
Rural	3.2	0.0	5.6	na	na	0.0	1.6	0.0

Children to carry out parent's hopes, aspirations								
Urban middle	1.7	1.5	na	0.0	0.0	2.9	0.0	5.8
Urban lower	0.0	1.6	0.9	1.2	1.3	5.2	0.0	3.0
Rural	0.0	0.8	0.0	na	na	5.6	0.0	2.4
Opportunity to teach, guide, instill values								
Urban middle	0.0	0.0	na	2.1	1.0	0.0	0.7	0.0
Urban lower	0.0	0.8	0.0	1.2	5.3	0.0	0.7	0.0
Rural	0.0	0.8	0.0	na	na	0.0	0.0	1.6
Satisfaction in one's childrearing ability, accomplishment								
Urban middle	0.0	0.0	na	2.1	3.1	0.0	0.7	15.0
Urban lower	0.8	0.0	0.0	2.3	1.3	0.7	0.0	3.0
Rural	0.0	0.0	0.0	na	na	0.0	0.7	3.2
Satisfaction in providing for children								
Urban middle	0.0	0.7	na	0.0	1.0	5.9	0.7	0.0
Urban lower	0.0	1.6	0.0	0.0	2.7	0.7	0.0	2.3
Rural	0.0	2.4	0.0	na	na	2.1	0.0	1.6
Economic help in old age								
Urban middle	0.0	2.9	na	0.0	0.0	0.0	0.0	0.0
Urban lower	4.2	1.6	0.9	0.0	1.3	0.0	0.0	0.8
Rural	9.2	0.8	7.2	na	na	0.0	2.1	3.2
Companionship, comfort, care in old age								
Urban middle	0.0	4.4	na	1.1	1.0	0.7	0.7	0.0
Urban lower	3.3	11.1	6.8	0.0	1.3	1.5	0.0	1.5
Rural	23.3	15.7	14.5	na	na	2.1	0.0	5.6

Table D2 *(continued)*

Advantage and SES group	Korea	Taiwan	Japan	U.S. (Hawaii) Japanese	Caucasian	Filipino	Philippines	Thailand
Unspecified help in old age								
Urban middle	0.0	0.7	0.0	0.0	0.0	na	12.5	3.3
Urban lower	1.5	6.3	0.0	0.0	0.0	0.9	18.3	31.7
Rural	1.6	25.7	2.1	na	na	25.3	20.5	5.8
Economic help (old age not mentioned)								
Urban middle	0.0	0.0	0.0	0.0	0.0	na	3.7	0.8
Urban lower	0.8	0.7	0.0	0.0	0.0	1.7	6.3	0.8
Rural	0.0	1.4	0.0	na	na	7.2	8.7	3.3
Comfort, care (old age not mentioned)								
Urban middle	2.5	0.7	0.7	0.0	0.0	na	0.7	0.0
Urban lower	6.1	0.0	0.0	0.0	2.3	0.9	1.6	5.0
Rural	6.3	0.0	2.1	na	na	2.4	0.8	2.5
Help in housework, family chores; practical help								
Urban middle	0.0	0.0	0.0	0.0	0.0	na	2.9	0.0
Urban lower	0.0	0.7	0.7	0.0	0.0	0.9	4.8	5.0
Rural	1.6	1.4	0.7	na	na	4.8	9.4	0.8
Sharing financial responsibility; insurance, security								
Urban middle	0.0	0.0	0.0	0.0	1.1	na	0.0	0.8
Urban lower	0.0	0.7	0.0	0.0	0.0	0.0	0.0	0.0
Rural	0.8	0.7	0.0	na	na	1.2	0.0	3.3

Help in family business, farm								
Urban middle	0.0	0.0	na	0.0	0.0	0.0	0.0	0.0
Urban lower	0.8	0.0	0.0	0.0	0.0	0.0	0.0	0.0
Rural	0.8	0.0	0.0	na	na	0.0	2.1	0.0
Help in taking care of other children								
Urban middle	0.0	0.0	na	0.0	0.0	0.0	0.0	0.0
Urban lower	0.8	0.0	0.0	0.0	0.0	0.0	0.7	0.0
Rural	0.8	0.0	0.0	na	na	0.0	0.0	0.0
Unspecified help (old age not mentioned)								
Urban middle	0.8	2.9	na	0.0	0.0	0.0	0.7	0.0
Urban lower	13.3	2.4	3.4	0.0	0.0	0.0	0.0	0.0
Rural	9.2	3.9	1.2	na	na	0.7	2.1	0.8
Children as bond between spouses								
Urban middle	16.7	8.1	na	3.2	7.1	8.1	4.2	3.3
Urban lower	3.3	6.3	5.1	8.1	5.3	5.2	0.0	6.8
Rural	1.7	0.8	0.0	na	na	1.4	1.4	0.0
Children as reason for, fulfillment of marriage								
Urban middle	1.7	1.5	na	3.2	4.1	0.0	0.0	0.8
Urban lower	0.0	0.0	2.6	0.0	1.3	0.0	0.0	0.8
Rural	0.0	0.8	1.2	na	na	0.0	0.0	0.8
Children as family life, complete or closeknit family								
Urban middle	9.2	2.2	na	7.4	9.2	2.9	8.3	5.0
Urban lower	0.0	0.8	3.4	8.1	13.3	8.2	2.8	0.0
Rural	1.7	0.0	2.4	na	na	2.1	2.1	0.8

Table D2 *(continued)*

Advantage and SES group	Korea	Taiwan	Japan	U.S. (Hawaii)			Philippines	Thailand
				Japanese	Caucasian	Filipino		
Continuity of family name								
Urban middle	5.8	10.4	0.0	1.0	1.1	na	0.7	8.3
Urban lower	9.1	38.9	0.0	1.3	1.2	1.7	3.2	5.8
Rural	11.9	24.3	0.0	na	na	1.2	0.0	11.7
Continuity of family traditions								
Urban middle	2.5	0.0	0.7	0.0	0.0	na	0.0	0.0
Urban lower	0.8	0.0	0.0	0.0	0.0	0.0	0.0	0.0
Rural	0.0	0.0	1.4	na	na	0.0	0.0	0.0
Enhancement of reputation of family								
Urban middle	0.0	0.0	0.0	0.0	0.0	na	0.7	0.8
Urban lower	0.0	0.0	0.0	0.0	0.0	0.0	0.0	0.8
Rural	0.0	0.0	0.0	na	na	0.0	0.0	4.2
Having future grandchildren								
Urban middle	0.8	0.0	0.0	0.0	0.0	na	0.0	0.0
Urban lower	0.8	0.0	0.0	0.0	0.0	0.0	0.0	0.0
Rural	0.8	0.0	0.0	na	na	0.0	0.0	0.0
Children as heirs, someone to inherit family wealth								
Urban middle	0.0	0.0	1.5	0.0	0.0	na	0.0	0.0
Urban lower	0.0	0.0	0.7	0.0	1.2	0.0	0.0	0.0
Rural	1.6	0.0	3.5	na	na	0.0	0.0	0.8

	1	2	3	4	5	6	7	8
Religious rituals, ancestor worship								
Urban middle	0.0	0.0	na	0.0	0.0	0.0	0.0	0.0
Urban lower	0.0	0.0	0.0	0.0	0.0	0.0	0.0	0.0
Rural	0.0	0.0	0.0	na	na	0.0	0.0	1.6
To increase strength, power of kin group								
Urban middle	0.0	0.0	na	0.0	0.0	0.0	0.0	0.8
Urban lower	0.0	0.0	0.0	0.0	0.0	0.0	0.0	0.0
Rural	0.0	0.0	0.0	na	na	0.0	0.7	0.0
To satisfy desires of spouse								
Urban middle	0.0	0.0	na	0.0	0.0	0.0	0.0	0.0
Urban lower	0.0	0.0	0.0	0.0	0.0	0.0	0.0	0.0
Rural	0.0	0.0	0.0	na	na	0.0	0.0	0.8
To satisfy desires of other kin								
Urban middle	0.0	0.0	na	0.0	0.0	0.0	0.0	0.0
Urban lower	0.8	0.8	0.0	0.0	0.0	0.0	0.7	0.8
Rural	0.0	0.0	0.0	na	na	0.0	0.0	0.0
Conformity to social norms								
Urban middle	0.0	0.0	na	0.0	0.0	0.0	0.7	0.0
Urban lower	0.0	0.0	0.0	1.2	0.0	0.7	0.7	0.0
Rural	0.0	0.0	0.0	na	na	0.7	0.0	1.6
Conformity to religious norms								
Urban middle	0.0	0.0	na	1.1	0.0	0.0	0.0	0.0
Urban lower	1.7	0.0	0.0	0.0	0.0	0.7	0.0	0.0
Rural	0.0	0.0	0.0	na	na	0.0	0.0	0.0

Table D2 *(continued)*

Advantage and SES group	Korea	Taiwan	Japan	U.S. (Hawaii) Japanese	Caucasian	Filipino	Philippines	Thailand
Children as benefits to society								
Urban middle	0.8	1.4	0.7	1.0	0.0	na	1.5	1.7
Urban lower	0.0	0.0	0.0	0.0	0.0	0.0	0.8	0.0
Rural	1.6	2.1	0.0	na	na	0.0	2.4	3.3
Children as treasure, wealth, assets								
Urban middle	0.0	2.1	0.0	0.0	0.0	na	1.5	0.8
Urban lower	0.0	0.0	0.0	0.0	0.0	0.0	1.6	0.0
Rural	0.8	0.0	1.4	na	na	1.2	0.0	0.0
Instinctive, natural to have children								
Urban middle	3.3	0.0	0.0	2.0	1.1	na	0.0	0.0
Urban lower	0.8	1.4	0.0	0.0	0.0	0.0	0.0	0.0
Rural	0.8	1.4	0.0	na	na	0.0	0.0	0.0
General wanting, liking children								
Urban middle	0.0	0.0	0.0	7.1	2.1	na	0.7	0.0
Urban lower	0.0	0.7	0.0	4.0	1.2	1.7	0.0	0.0
Rural	0.0	0.0	0.0	na	na	0.0	0.0	0.0
Other advantages								
Urban middle	0.0	0.0	0.0	2.0	0.0	na	0.7	0.8
Urban lower	0.8	1.4	0.0	0.0	0.0	0.0	0.0	0.8
Rural	0.0	0.0	0.0	na	na	0.0	0.0	0.0

na—not applicable because subsample did not include persons in this socioeconomic group.

Table D3 Disadvantages of having children
(Percentage of respondents mentioning each disadvantage, by socioeconomic group and country)

Disadvantage and SES group	Korea	Taiwan	Japan	U.S. (Hawaii) Japanese	U.S. (Hawaii) Caucasian	U.S. (Hawaii) Filipino	Philippines	Thailand
Educational costs								
Urban middle	7.5	2.1	2.3	5.1	3.2	na	27.2	5.8
Urban lower	25.0	3.0	0.7	6.7	3.5	14.5	21.4	7.5
Rural	38.1	3.5	3.7	na	na	1.2	18.1	17.5
General, other costs								
Urban middle	39.2	31.6	20.7	30.6	48.5	na	47.8	39.1
Urban lower	57.6	45.1	20.8	35.9	37.2	64.9	47.6	60.8
Rural	43.6	66.4	21.9	na	na	90.5	44.1	41.7
Responsibility of parenthood								
Urban middle	5.8	8.4	4.6	14.2	9.5	na	6.6	9.2
Urban lower	0.8	10.5	2.2	4.0	7.0	6.0	5.6	2.5
Rural	0.8	7.1	3.0	na	na	1.2	4.7	0.0
Discipline, moral behavior								
Urban middle	5.0	7.0	1.5	11.2	12.7	na	44.9	4.2
Urban lower	3.8	11.2	1.5	16.0	17.2	29.9	42.9	7.5
Rural	18.3	5.7	14.3	na	na	31.0	36.3	17.5
Health problems of children								
Urban middle	22.5	16.1	15.3	8.1	11.6	na	29.4	5.8
Urban lower	19.7	15.7	19.4	6.7	14.9	6.9	27.0	5.8
Rural	29.4	24.2	23.4	na	na	57.1	26.0	6.6
Concern over children's future success, happiness								
Urban middle	10.8	0.0	1.5	6.1	6.4	na	5.9	5.8
Urban lower	6.0	5.2	5.2	0.0	4.6	6.0	3.2	0.8
Rural	5.6	2.8	8.3	na	na	2.4	3.9	1.6

Table D3 (continued)

Disadvantage and SES group	Korea	Taiwan	Japan	U.S. (Hawaii)			Philippines	Thailand
				Japanese	Caucasian	Filipino		
Concern about satisfying children's present wants								
Urban middle	6.7	0.0	0.0	1.0	0.0	na	3.7	0.0
Urban lower	5.3	2.2	0.7	4.0	2.3	3.4	3.2	0.0
Rural	6.4	0.0	3.7	na	na	1.2	0.8	0.8
Noise, disorder, nuisance								
Urban middle	21.7	27.4	9.2	5.1	6.4	na	15.4	3.3
Urban lower	34.9	40.6	13.4	5.3	8.0	23.1	24.6	0.8
Rural	31.7	22.8	12.8	na	na	8.3	20.5	4.2
General rearing problems								
Urban middle	5.8	8.4	3.0	14.2	22.1	na	24.2	28.3
Urban lower	17.5	12.0	11.9	13.3	13.7	32.5	12.7	20.0
Rural	8.7	7.1	7.5	na	na	21.4	22.1	7.5
General emotional strain								
Urban middle	14.2	14.7	16.1	21.4	24.2	na	11.0	18.3
Urban lower	18.9	11.2	13.4	10.7	9.1	16.4	7.1	14.2
Rural	16.7	3.5	12.8	na	na	16.7	5.5	7.5
Health hazard of pregnancy; maternal health								
Urban middle	5.8	0.0	0.0	1.0	1.1	na	5.1	2.5
Urban lower	0.8	0.7	0.7	0.0	1.1	3.4	6.3	0.0
Rural	2.4	0.0	0.7	na	na	0.0	3.1	2.5
Physical work, tiredness caused by children								
Urban middle	9.2	11.2	6.1	12.2	11.6	na	9.5	12.5
Urban lower	6.8	10.5	9.7	13.3	2.3	20.5	5.6	9.2
Rural	6.3	17.8	4.5	na	na	29.8	8.7	30.8

231

Restrictions on time								
Urban middle	21.7	19.7	26.9	19.3	10.5	na	10.3	0.0
Urban lower	3.8	6.7	29.1	12.0	6.9	2.6	4.8	0.8
Rural	5.6	4.2	15.9	na	na	0.0	2.4	1.7
Restrictions on travel								
Urban middle	19.2	0.0	3.8	6.1	11.6	na	0.7	4.2
Urban lower	7.6	0.0	1.5	4.0	3.4	4.3	0.0	4.2
Rural	6.3	0.0	2.2	na	na	16.7	0.0	7.5
Restrictions on social life, recreation								
Urban middle	13.3	4.2	13.0	18.4	7.4	na	10.3	1.7
Urban lower	0.8	1.5	8.2	16.0	5.7	2.6	19.9	5.0
Rural	2.4	2.1	8.3	na	na	2.4	6.3	0.0
Restrictions on job, career								
Urban middle	7.5	7.7	10.0	7.1	13.7	na	12.5	8.3
Urban lower	6.8	5.2	12.7	21.3	8.0	0.9	6.3	7.5
Rural	15.9	14.2	12.1	na	na	3.6	11.0	10.8
Restrictions on personal wants								
Urban middle	3.3	0.0	10.7	8.2	6.4	na	8.1	0.8
Urban lower	0.0	0.0	9.0	9.3	16.1	6.8	11.9	1.7
Rural	0.0	0.0	6.0	na	na	4.8	2.4	0.0
Restrictions on privacy								
Urban middle	4.2	4.2	3.0	3.1	4.2	na	0.0	3.3
Urban lower	0.0	0.7	1.5	4.0	8.0	0.0	0.0	0.8
Rural	1.6	0.0	1.5	na	na	8.3	0.0	0.8
General lack of flexibility, freedom								
Urban middle	15.0	17.6	12.3	45.9	64.2	na	14.0	5.0
Urban lower	14.4	18.0	12.7	61.3	49.4	40.2	11.1	7.5
Rural	0.8	5.0	9.0	na	na	33.3	4.7	5.0

Table D3 *(continued)*

Disadvantage and SES group	Korea	Taiwan	Japan	U.S. (Hawaii)			Philippines	Thailand
				Japanese	Caucasian	Filipino		
Less time, interaction between spouses								
Urban middle	21.7	2.8	5.3	3.1	5.3	na	0.7	0.0
Urban lower	3.0	1.5	1.5	4.0	3.4	0.0	2.4	0.0
Rural	1.6	0.0	1.5	na	na	0.0	0.0	0.0
Disagreements over children								
Urban middle	0.8	0.7	1.5	3.1	6.3	na	0.0	0.0
Urban lower	1.5	0.0	0.0	4.0	1.1	0.0	0.8	0.0
Rural	0.0	0.0	0.7	na	na	0.0	0.0	0.8
General marital problems								
Urban middle	2.5	0.0	4.6	1.0	5.3	na	1.5	0.0
Urban lower	1.5	0.0	0.7	0.0	3.4	0.9	0.0	0.0
Rural	2.4	0.0	0.7	na	na	0.0	0.0	0.0
Disadvantages relating to, affecting kin group								
Urban middle	0.0	0.0	0.0	1.0	0.0	na	0.0	0.8
Urban lower	0.0	0.0	0.0	0.0	0.0	0.0	0.0	0.0
Rural	0.0	0.0	0.7	na	na	0.0	0.0	0.8
Disadvantages relating to, affecting society; concern about overpopulation								
Urban middle	0.0	0.0	0.0	0.0	1.1	na	0.0	0.0
Urban lower	0.8	0.0	0.0	1.3	2.3	0.0	0.8	0.0
Rural	0.0	0.0	0.7	na	na	2.4	0.0	0.0
Other disadvantages								
Urban middle	3.3	1.4	0.0	5.1	5.3	na	1.4	1.7
Urban lower	2.3	0.0	0.0	0.0	5.7	2.6	0.8	7.5
Rural	1.6	0.0	1.5	na	na	1.2	0.0	1.7

na—not applicable because subsample did not include persons in this socioeconomic group.

Table D4 Most important disadvantages of having children
(Percentage of respondents who assigned first ranking to each disadvantage, by socioeconomic group and country)

Disadvantage and SES group	Korea	Taiwan	Japan	U.S. (Hawaii)			Philippines	Thailand
				Japanese	Caucasian	Filipino		
Educational costs								
Urban middle	3.3	0.0	0.7	1.0	2.1	na	6.2	2.5
Urban lower	8.3	0.0	0.0	2.7	3.6	1.7	9.4	2.5
Rural	23.8	2.1	1.4	na	na	1.2	10.5	8.3
General, other costs								
Urban middle	13.3	16.0	6.6	7.2	13.7	na	22.5	24.2
Urban lower	26.5	33.8	6.7	20.3	16.7	28.2	24.8	42.5
Rural	11.9	46.4	7.7	na	na	80.7	29.0	30.0
Responsibility of parenthood								
Urban middle	1.7	5.6	2.9	4.1	4.2	na	3.9	5.0
Urban lower	0.8	3.8	1.5	0.0	3.6	3.4	3.4	2.5
Rural	0.0	5.0	1.4	na	na	0.0	0.9	0.0
Discipline, moral behavior								
Urban middle	3.3	2.8	0.7	5.2	6.3	na	19.4	3.3
Urban lower	2.3	6.0	0.7	6.8	6.0	8.5	22.2	3.3
Rural	3.2	2.9	4.9	na	na	0.0	18.4	10.8
Health problems of children								
Urban middle	7.5	11.1	10.3	2.1	5.3	na	13.1	2.5
Urban lower	8.3	9.8	13.4	0.0	6.0	1.7	10.3	1.7
Rural	12.7	11.4	14.8	na	na	3.6	15.8	1.7
Concern over children's future success, happiness								
Urban middle	5.0	0.0	0.7	0.0	1.1	na	2.3	3.3
Urban lower	1.5	1.5	3.0	0.0	1.2	0.9	0.9	0.8
Rural	1.6	1.4	1.4	na	na	1.2	1.8	0.0

234

Table D4 *(continued)*

Disadvantage and SES group	Korea	Taiwan	Japan	U.S. (Hawaii) Japanese	Caucasian	Filipino	Philippines	Thailand
Concern about satisfying children's present wants								
Urban middle	1.7	0.0	0.0	0.0	0.0	na	0.0	0.0
Urban lower	0.8	0.7	0.7	0.0	0.0	1.7	0.0	0.0
Rural	4.8	0.0	0.7	na	na	0.0	0.0	0.0
Noise, disorder, nuisance								
Urban middle	7.5	16.7	1.5	1.0	0.0	na	2.3	1.7
Urban lower	9.1	19.6	5.2	1.4	1.2	2.6	3.4	0.8
Rural	7.1	9.3	3.5	na	na	1.2	5.3	1.7
General rearing problems								
Urban middle	0.8	5.6	0.7	3.1	6.3	na	10.1	17.5
Urban lower	4.5	0.8	4.5	6.8	10.7	8.5	6.8	14.2
Rural	4.0	2.1	4.2	na	na	3.6	6.1	1.7
General emotional strain								
Urban middle	1.7	7.6	6.6	10.3	2.1	na	3.1	9.2
Urban lower	7.6	3.0	6.0	4.1	2.4	4.3	3.4	5.8
Rural	4.8	1.4	4.2	na	na	1.2	2.6	3.3
Health hazard of pregnancy; maternal health								
Urban middle	0.8	0.0	0.0	0.0	0.0	na	0.8	0.0
Urban lower	0.0	0.0	0.0	0.0	0.0	1.7	0.9	0.0
Rural	0.8	0.0	0.0	na	na	0.0	0.9	2.5
Physical work, tiredness caused by children								
Urban middle	2.5	4.9	1.5	1.0	2.1	na	2.3	6.7
Urban lower	2.3	4.5	3.0	2.7	0.0	5.1	0.0	4.2
Rural	2.4	8.6	1.4	na	na	2.4	2.6	22.5

Restrictions on time								
Urban middle	8.3	11.3	14.0	7.2	3.2	na	0.8	0.0
Urban lower	1.5	2.3	19.4	5.4	1.2	0.9	0.9	0.8
Rural	0.8	2.1	7.7	na	na	0.0	0.0	0.8
Restrictions on travel								
Urban middle	5.0	0.0	0.7	1.0	1.1	na	0.0	0.0
Urban lower	2.3	0.0	0.0	1.4	0.0	0.0	0.0	0.0
Rural	1.6	0.0	0.0	na	na	0.0	0.0	3.3
Restrictions on social life, recreation								
Urban middle	1.7	0.7	5.9	5.2	2.1	na	0.0	0.0
Urban lower	0.0	0.7	5.2	1.4	3.6	0.0	4.3	2.5
Rural	0.0	0.7	1.4	na	na	0.0	0.0	0.0
Restrictions on job, career								
Urban middle	3.3	2.1	5.1	2.1	6.3	na	7.0	4.2
Urban lower	3.8	2.2	5.2	5.4	0.0	0.0	3.4	4.2
Rural	4.0	4.3	5.6	na	na	0.0	4.4	3.3
Restrictions on personal wants								
Urban middle	0.8	0.0	3.7	0.0	1.1	na	1.6	0.0
Urban lower	0.0	0.0	3.7	0.0	3.6	1.7	3.4	0.0
Rural	0.0	0.0	2.8	na	na	0.0	0.0	0.0
Restrictions on privacy								
Urban middle	1.7	2.8	0.7	1.0	1.1	na	0.0	0.8
Urban lower	0.0	0.0	0.0	0.0	1.2	0.0	0.0	0.8
Rural	0.0	0.0	0.0	na	na	0.0	0.0	0.0
General lack of flexibility, freedom								
Urban middle	2.5	7.0	8.8	18.6	24.2	na	3.1	0.8
Urban lower	3.0	8.3	7.5	25.7	11.9	17.1	0.9	2.5
Rural	0.8	2.1	0.7	na	na	1.2	1.8	0.8

Table D4 *(continued)*

Disadvantage and SES group	Korea	Taiwan	Japan	U.S. (Hawaii)			Philippines	Thailand
				Japanese	Caucasian	Filipino		
Less time, interaction between spouses								
Urban middle	8.3	0.0	2.2	1.0	2.1	na	0.8	0.0
Urban lower	0.0	0.0	0.0	1.4	1.2	0.0	0.9	0.0
Rural	0.0	0.0	0.7	na	na	0.0	0.0	0.0
Disagreements over children								
Urban middle	0.0	0.0	0.7	1.0	2.1	na	0.0	0.0
Urban lower	0.0	0.0	0.0	2.7	1.2	0.0	0.0	0.0
Rural	0.0	0.0	0.0	na	na	0.0	0.0	0.0
General marital problems								
Urban middle	1.7	0.0	2.9	0.0	1.1	na	0.0	0.0
Urban lower	0.8	0.0	0.0	0.0	2.4	0.0	0.0	0.0
Rural	0.8	0.0	0.0	na	na	0.0	0.0	0.0
Disadvantages relating to, affecting kin group								
Urban middle	0.0	0.0	0.0	0.0	0.0	na	0.0	0.8
Urban lower	0.0	0.0	0.0	0.0	1.2	0.0	0.0	0.0
Rural	0.0	0.0	0.7	na	na	0.0	0.0	0.0
Disadvantages relating to, affecting society; concern about overpopulation								
Urban middle	0.0	0.0	0.0	0.0	0.0	na	0.0	0.0
Urban lower	0.0	0.0	0.0	0.0	0.0	0.0	0.0	0.0
Rural	0.0	0.0	0.7	na	na	0.0	0.0	0.0
Other disadvantages								
Urban middle	0.8	0.0	0.0	0.0	2.1	na	0.8	0.8
Urban lower	0.8	0.0	0.0	0.0	2.4	0.0	0.9	1.7
Rural	0.8	0.0	0.0	na	na	1.2	0.0	0.0

na—not applicable because subsample did not include persons in this socioeconomic group.

Table D5 Interscale correlations for nine VOC attitude scales
(By country)

Attitude scale and country	VOC 1	VOC 2	VOC 3	VOC 4	VOC 5	VOC 6	VOC 7	VOC 8	VOC 9
VOC 1 Continuity, tradition, security									
Korea	1.00	.14	.44	.36	.10	.58	.31	.22	.17
Taiwan	1.00	.52	.49	.43	.43	.47	.15	.17	.05
Japan	1.00	.35	.45	.44	.34	.27	.21	.06	.16
U.S. (Hawaii)	1.00	.59	.66	.27	.60	.10	.20	.24	-.31
Philippines	1.00	.41	.44	.42	.38	.31	.13	.06	.33
Thailand	1.00	.48	.54	.38	.39	.42	.30	.15	.18
VOC 2 Parenthood satisfactions									
Korea		1.00	.32	.17	.22	.20	-.02	.16	.25
Taiwan		1.00	.44	.44	.45	.34	.11	.16	.11
Japan		1.00	.47	.28	.35	.28	.23	-.02	.20
U.S. (Hawaii)		1.00	.58	.24	.59	.05	.08	.15	-.26
Philippines		1.00	.43	.30	.38	.14	.01	-.08	.22
Thailand		1.00	.47	.50	.37	.28	.15	.17	.09
VOC 3 Role motivations									
Korea			1.00	.49	.41	.55	.10	.32	.22
Taiwan			1.00	.51	.43	.46	.04	.21	.10
Japan			1.00	.39	.45	.36	.28	.10	.14
U.S. (Hawaii)			1.00	.23	.57	.14	.10	.20	-.40
Philippines			1.00	.44	.36	.27	.11	.02	.28
Thailand			1.00	.44	.30	.35	.25	.20	.24
VOC 4 Happiness and affection									
Korea				1.00	.30	.46	.08	.21	.13
Taiwan				1.00	.37	.42	.07	.18	.10
Japan				1.00	.22	.36	.15	.00	.08
U.S. (Hawaii)				1.00	.32	.43	.40	-.08	.11
Philippines				1.00	.26	.40	.17	.08	.25
Thailand				1.00	.30	.32	.17	.22	.11

Table D5 (continued)

Attitude scale and country	VOC 1	VOC 2	VOC 3	VOC 4	VOC 5	VOC 6	VOC 7	VOC 8	VOC 9
VOC 5 Goals and incentives									
Korea					1.00	.21	-.10	.09	.17
Taiwan					1.00	.35	.03	.13	.11
Japan					1.00	.13	.17	.02	.08
U.S. (Hawaii)					1.00	.06	.12	.11	-.26
Philippines					1.00	.09	-.01	-.02	.24
Thailand					1.00	.14	.05	.14	.07
VOC 6 Social status									
Korea						1.00	.25	.21	.15
Taiwan						1.00	.14	.29	.11
Japan						1.00	.19	.14	.09
U.S. (Hawaii)						1.00	.34	.09	.24
Philippines						1.00	.37	.31	.29
Thailand						1.00	.45	.24	.24
VOC 7 External controls									
Korea							1.00	.22	.18
Taiwan							1.00	.12	-.00
Japan							1.00	.15	.19
U.S. (Hawaii)							1.00	.04	.12
Philippines							1.00	.26	.15
Thailand							1.00	.18	.32
VOC 8 Costs of children									
Korea								1.00	.23
Taiwan								1.00	.26
Japan								1.00	.28
U.S. (Hawaii)								1.00	.12
Philippines								1.00	.21
Thailand								1.00	.43
VOC 9 Decision-mindedness in childbearing									

Table D6 Item-total correlations for nine VOC attitude scales
(By country)

Attitude scale and item	Korea	Taiwan	Japan	U.S. (Hawaii)	Philippines	Thailand
VOC 1 Continuity, tradition, security						
Help parents in old age	.79	.71	.65	.82	.66	.69
Family traditions live on	.65	.71	.76	.83	.68	.76
Loyalty to parents	.72	.57	.66	.69	.60	.38
Continue family name	.75	.65	.78	.85	.72	.67
Immortality	.71	.55	.63	.66	.64	.62
Mean	.72	.64	.70	.77	.66	.63
VOC 2 Parenthood satisfactions						
Feeling of being needed	.73	.80	.77	.79	.79	.81
Being a good parent brings complete satisfaction with achievement	.76	.68	.72	.74	.81	.79
A chance to teach children	.54	.69	.72	.76	.68	.64
Mean	.68	.72	.74	.76	.76	.75
VOC 3 Role motivations						
Natural for a man to want children	.47	.54	.65	.67	.57	.64
Girl becomes a woman after having children	.80	.68	.72	.80	.68	.55
Less likely to behave immorally	.43	.65	.47	.64	.61	.57
Natural for a woman to want children	.67	.53	.59	.65	.51	.55
Boy becomes a man after having children	.73	.75	.73	.82	.76	.69
Mean	.62	.63	.63	.72	.63	.60
VOC 4 Happiness and affection						
To express love and affection	.62	.64	.47	.78	.65	.49
To make family a happy and comfortable place	.74	.59	.79	.84	.65	.72
Without children cannot be truly happy	.73	.75	.82	.77	.78	.75
Mean	.70	.66	.69	.79	.69	.65

Table D6 *(continued)*

Attitude scale and item	Korea	Taiwan	Japan	U.S. (Hawaii)	Philippines	Thailand
VOC 5 Goals and incentives						
Incentive to succeed	.57	.65	.59	.75	.75	.68
Stronger bond between spouses	.79	.61	.73	.78	.59	.72
One of life's highest purposes	.73	.80	.82	.84	.72	.76
Mean	.70	.69	.71	.79	.68	.72
VOC 6 Social status						
To be accepted in community	.87	.87	.79	.85	.81	.88
Respect of community	.86	.86	.84	.90	.85	.86
Mean	.86	.86	.82	.88	.83	.87
VOC 7 External controls						
Pressures from family and friends	.80	.79	.71	.76	.77	.80
Not right to interfere with nature	.75	.76	.69	.84	.80	.83
Mean	.78	.78	.70	.80	.78	.82
VOC 8 Costs of children						
Limitations on personal freedom	.69	.69	.72	.65	.71	.73
Disagreements between spouses	.64	.57	.53	.67	.70	.72
Heavy financial burden	.57	.62	.62	.68	.63	.67
Sacrifice other enjoyable things	.73	.68	.76	.70	.51	.53
Mean	.66	.64	.66	.67	.64	.66
VOC 9 Decision-mindedness in childbearing						
Consider inconveniences of children	.72	.68	.58	.77	.66	.62
Consider ability to afford children	.70	.59	.68	.73	.63	.57
Consider alternative uses for money	.55	.62	.53	.74	.65	.68
Consider interference with wife's work	.68	.60	.66	.72	.67	.74
Mean	.66	.62	.61	.74	.65	.65

Table D7 **Zero-order correlations between selected VOC measures and family-size and birth control indices**
(By country)

VOC measure and country	Family-size index		Birth control index	
	Ideal number of children	Number of living children	Situational birth control attitude	Current use of birth control
Economic burden/education				
Korea	.19	.18	-.12	-.11
Taiwan	.17	.25	-.09	-.15
Japan	-.03	.05	.13	-.01
U.S. (Hawaii)	.12	.34	-.07	.00
Philippines	.09	.21	-.06	-.01
Thailand	.01	.23	-.05	.00
Financial ease/large family				
Korea	.12	.20	.10	.02
Taiwan	.08	.13	-.07	.16
Japan	.22	.13	-.03	.05
U.S. (Hawaii)	.36	.29	-.07	-.03
Philippines	.32	.34	-.07	.05
Thailand	.39	.20	-.13	-.11
Expected economic help				
Korea	.34	.31	-.13	-.24
Taiwan	.30	.17	-.18	-.24
Japan	.02	.14	-.07	-.15
U.S. (Hawaii)	.25	.21	-.46	-.30
Philippines	.20	.02	-.05	-.04
Thailand	.06	.25	-.26	-.30
Continuity, tradition, security (VOC 1)				
Korea	.29	.26	-.15	-.22
Taiwan	.30	.20	-.05	-.20
Japan	-.04	.09	-.08	-.18
U.S. (Hawaii)	.27	.23	-.43	-.24
Philippines	.11	.00	-.05	-.01
Thailand	.10	.14	-.18	-.13
Parenthood satisfactions (VOC 2)				
Korea	-.08	.00	-.07	.15
Taiwan	.12	.11	-.06	-.07
Japan	.02	.05	-.09	-.08
U.S. (Hawaii)	.29	.19	-.31	-.11
Philippines	.08	-.05	.11	.00
Thailand	.09	.05	-.09	.02
Role motivations (VOC 3)				
Korea	.11	.15	-.12	.03
Taiwan	.20	.07	-.07	-.03
Japan	.01	.13	-.08	-.14
U.S. (Hawaii)	.23	.20	-.40	-.24
Philippines	.09	.01	.11	-.03
Thailand	.08	.06	-.02	-.11

Table D7 *(continued)*

VOC measure and country	Family-size index		Birth control index	
	Ideal number of children	Number of living children	Situational birth control attitude	Current use of birth control
Happiness and affection (VOC 4)				
Korea	.07	.11	-.06	-.02
Taiwan	.18	.07	-.04	-.13
Japan	.06	.14	-.08	-.08
U.S. (Hawaii)	.09	.04	-.07	-.11
Philippines	.11	.08	.09	.00
Thailand	.08	.12	-.10	-.05
Goals and incentives (VOC 5)				
Korea	-.06	-.07	.05	.12
Taiwan	.19	.12	-.08	-.09
Japan	.01	.10	.00	.00
U.S. (Hawaii)	.27	.16	-.26	-.11
Philippines	.03	-.01	.03	-.01
Thailand	.06	-.06	-.01	.05
Social status (VOC 6)				
Korea	.18	.19	-.13	-.19
Taiwan	.16	.14	-.12	-.14
Japan	.03	.08	-.13	-.12
U.S. (Hawaii)	.00	-.06	.04	.03
Philippines	.07	.07	.04	-.04
Thailand	.15	.23	-.19	-.16
External controls (VOC 7)				
Korea	.22	.11	-.09	-.19
Taiwan	.09	.14	-.13	-.04
Japan	.00	.01	-.07	-.08
U.S. (Hawaii)	.14	.05	-.24	-.12
Philippines	.02	-.03	.00	-.09
Thailand	.13	.17	-.18	-.20
Costs of children (VOC 8)				
Korea	.03	.13	.06	-.01
Taiwan	-.03	.08	.06	-.04
Japan	-.13	-.04	.15	.02
U.S. (Hawaii)	-.05	.10	.03	.06
Philippines	-.04	.04	.16	-.03
Thailand	-.05	.09	.14	.05
Decision-mindedness in childbearing (VOC 9)				
Korea	-.06	-.10	.10	.03
Taiwan	-.17	-.15	.16	-.07
Japan	-.07	-.04	.14	-.02
U.S. (Hawaii)	-.17	-.21	.42	.20
Philippines	.03	-.02	.05	-.02
Thailand	-.04	.08	.12	-.03

Table D7 *(continued)*

VOC measure and country	Family-size index		Birth control index	
	Ideal number of children	Number of living children	Situational birth control attitude	Current use of birth control
Reasons wanting another child				
Korea	.12	.01	-.04	-.14
Taiwan	.04	-.23	-.10	-.25
Japan	.12	-.17	-.07	-.19
U.S. (Hawaii)	.27	-.05	-.42	-.31
Philippines	.11	-.37	.03	-.08
Thailand	.15	-.17	-.11	-.18
Reasons not wanting another child				
Korea	-.01	.21	.14	.17
Taiwan	-.12	.24	.03	.14
Japan	-.15	.03	.06	.08
U.S. (Hawaii)	-.11	.17	.06	.17
Philippines	-.03	.16	.07	.00
Thailand	-.08	.23	-.08	-.09

references

Arnold, Fred, and James T. Fawcett

1975   *Hawaii.* Vol. 3, The Value of Children: A Cross-National Study. Honolulu: East-West Population Institute.

Bardwick, Judith M.

1974   Evolution and parenting. *Journal of Social Issues* 30(4):39–62.

Becker, Gary S.

1960   An economic analysis of fertility. In *Demographic and Economic Change in Developed Countries.* Universities–National Bureau Committee for Economic Research, Special Conference Series, no. 11, pp. 209–240. Princeton: Princeton University Press.

Beckman, Linda J.

1974   Relative costs and benefits of work and children to professional and non-professional women. Paper presented at the annual meeting of the American Psychological Association, New Orleans, September 1974.

Ben-Porath, Yoram

1974   Notes on the micro-economics of fertility. *International Social Science Journal* 26(2):302–314.

Berelson, Bernard

1969   Beyond family planning. *Studies in Family Planning* 38:1–16.

1971   Population policy: personal notes. *Population Studies* 25(2):173–182.

Berelson, Bernard *(continued)*

   1973   The value of children: a taxonomical essay. In *The Population
                Council Annual Report 1972*, pp. 17–27. New York: Population
                Council.

Bourque, Linda B.; April Allison; Leo G. Reedes; and Dianne Inuzuka

   975   The influence of feminist ideology on motivation for parenthood.
                Paper presented at the annual meeting of the Population Associ-
                ation of America, Seattle, April 1975.

Bulatao, Rodolfo A.

   1975   *Philippines.* Vol. 2, The Value of Children: A Cross-National Study.
                Honolulu: East-West Population Institute.

Chung, Bom Mo; Jae Ho Cha; and Sung Jin Lee

   1974   *Boy Preference and Family Planning in Korea.* Seoul: Korean
                Institute for Research in the Behavioral Sciences.

Clausen, John A., and Suzanne R. Clausen

   1973   The effects of family size on parents and children. In James T.
                Fawcett (ed.), *Psychological Perspectives on Population*, pp. 185–
                208. New York: Basic Books.

Cramer, James C.

   1975   The opportunity costs of children and expected family size in the
                United States, 1968–1972. Paper presented at the annual meeting
                of the Population Association of America, Seattle, April 1975.

Crawford, Thomas J.

   1974   Theories of attitude change and the "beyond family planning"
                debate: the case for the persuasion approach in population policy.
                Journal of Social Issues 30(4):211–233.

Davis, Kingsley

   1967   Population policy: will current programs succeed? *Science* 158:
                730–739.

Easterlin, Richard A.

   1969   Toward a socioeconomic theory of fertility: a survey of recent
                research on economic factors in American fertility. In S.J.
                Behrman et al. (eds.), *Fertility and Family Planning: A World
                View*, pp. 127–156. Ann Arbor: University of Michigan Press.

   1975   An economic framework for fertility analysis. *Studies in Family
                Planning* 6(3):54–63.

Edwards, Edgar O.

1975   Population-related choices and development strategy. In *Social Science Research on Population and Development*, pp. 5–21. New York: Ford Foundation.

Espenshade, Thomas J.

1972   The price of children and socioeconomic theories of fertility. *Population Studies* 26(2):207–221.

1973   *The Cost of Children in Urban United States.* Berkeley: University of California, Population Monograph Series, no. 14.

Evanson, Steven E.

1974   Parent belief systems, preferred family size, and completed family size. Paper presented at the annual meeting of the Western Psychological Association, San Francisco, April 1974.

Fawcett, James T.

1970   *Psychology and Population: Behavioral Research Issues in Fertility and Family Planning.* New York: Population Council.

Fawcett, James T. (ed.)

1972   *The Satisfactions and Costs of Children: Theories, Concepts, Methods.* Honolulu: East-West Population Institute.

Fawcett, James T.; Sonia Albores; and Fred Arnold

1972   The value of children among ethnic groups in Hawaii: exploratory measurements. In James T. Fawcett (ed.), *The Satisfactions and Costs of Children: Theories, Concepts, Methods*, pp. 234–259. Honolulu: East-West Population Institute.

Fawcett, James T.; Fred Arnold; Rodolfo A. Bulatao; Chalio Buripakdi; Betty Jamie Chung; Toshio Iritani; Sung Jin Lee; and Tsong-Shien Wu

1974   *The Value of Children in Asia and the United States: Comparative Perspectives.* Papers of the East-West Population Institute, no. 32. Honolulu.

Freedman, Deborah S.

1974   *Economic Data for Fertility Analysis.* London: World Fertility Survey, Occasional Paper no. 11.

Hoffman, Lois Wladis

1972   A psychological perspective on the value of children to parents: concepts and measures. In James T. Fawcett (ed.), *The Satisfactions and Costs of Children: Theories, Concepts, Methods*, pp. 27–56. Honolulu: East-West Population Institute.

Hoffman, Lois Wladis, and Martin L. Hoffman

1973   The value of children to parents. In James T. Fawcett (ed.), *Psychological Perspectives on Population*, pp. 19–76. New York: Basic Books.

Hull, Terence H.

1975   Each child brings its own fortune: an inquiry into the value of children in a Javanese village. Unpublished Ph.D. dissertation, Australian National University.

Kangas, Lenni W.

1970   Integrated incentives for fertility control. *Science* 169:1278–1283.

Kirchner, Elizabeth P.

n.d.   *Reasons for Wanting Children: Factors and Correlates.* National Institute of Child Health and Human Development, U.S. Department of Health, Education and Welfare. Final Report, Grant no. 1 R01 HD 06258-01.

Leibenstein, Harvey

1957   *Economic Backwardness and Economic Growth.* New York: John Wiley.

1974   An interpretation of the economic theory of fertility: promising path or blind alley? *Journal of Economic Literature* 12(2):457–479.

MacDonald, Maurice, and Eva Mueller

1957   The measurement of income in fertility surveys in developing countries. *Studies in Family Planning* 6(1):22–28.

McNicoll, Geoffrey

1975   Community-level population policy: an exploration. *Population and Development Review* 1(1):1–21.

Mueller, Eva

1972a   Economic motives for family limitation: a study conducted in Taiwan. *Population Studies* 27(3):383–403.

1972b   Economic cost and value of children: conceptualization and measurement. In James T. Fawcett (ed.), *The Satisfactions and Costs of Children: Theories, Concepts, Methods,* pp. 174–205. Honolulu: East-West Population Institute.

Namboodiri, N. Krishnan

1972   Some observations on the economic framework for fertility analysis. *Population Studies* 26(2):185–206.

Nie, Norman H., et al.

1975   *SPSS: Statistical Package for the Social Sciences.* 2nd ed. New York: McGraw-Hill.

Nortman, Dorothy

1974   *Parental Age as a Factor in Pregnancy Outcome and Child Development.* Reports on Population/Family Planning, no. 16. New York: Population Council.

O'Donnell, Dennis J.

1974   The micro-economics of the family size decision: a simultaneous equation approach. Unpublished Ph.D. dissertation, Pennsylvania State University.

Reed, R.H., and S. McIntosh

1972   Costs of children. In U.S. Commission on Population Growth and the American Future, *Economic Aspects of Population Change.* Washington, D.C.: U.S. Government Printing Office.

Rich, William

1973   *Smaller Families Through Social and Economic Progress.* Washington, D.C.: Overseas Development Council, Monograph no. 7.

Robinson, Warren E., and David L. Horlacher

1971   *Population Growth and Economic Welfare.* Reports on Population/Family Planning, no. 6. New York: Population Council.

Schultz, Theodore W. (ed.)

1973   New economic approaches to fertility. *Journal of Political Economy* 81(2), part 2.

1974   Marriage, family human capital, and fertility. *Journal of Political Economy* 82(2), part 2.

Smith, D.H., and A. Inkeles

1966   The OM scale: a comparative socio-psychological measure of individual modernity. *Sociometry* 29(4):353–377.

Smith, M. Brewster; Jerome S. Bruner; and Robert W. White

1956   *Opinions and Personality.* New York: Wiley.

Spengler, Joseph

1966   Values and fertility analysis. *Demography* 3(1):109–130.

Stycos, J. Mayone

1974   Some dimensions of population and family planning: goals and means. *Journal of Social Issues* 30(4):1–29.

Teitelbaum, Michael S.
    1974   Population and development: is a consensus possible? *Foreign Affairs* 52(4):742–760.

Terhune, Kenneth W.
    1973   Fertility values: why people stop having children. Paper presented at the annual meeting of the American Psychological Association, Montreal, August 1973.

Thompson, Vaida D.
    1974   Family size: implicit policies and assumed psychological outcomes. *Journal of Social Issues* 30(4):93–124.

Turchi, Boone A.
    1973   The demand for children: an economic analysis of fertility in the United States. Unpublished Ph.D. dissertation, University of Michigan.
    1975   Microeconomic theories of fertility: a critique. Paper presented at the annual meeting of the Population Association of America, Seattle, April 1975. (Also in press in *Social Forces,* 1975.)

Turner, Jean
    1974   Economic context and the meaning of children to parents in Chile. Paper presented at the International Conference of the Association for Cross-Cultural Psychology, Kingston, Ontario, August 1974.

White, Benjamin
    1975   Production and reproduction in a Javanese village. Ph.D. dissertation, Columbia University (in preparation).

Wray, Joe D.
    1971   *Population Pressure on Families: Family Size and Child Spacing.* Reports on Population/Family Planning, no. 9. New York: Population Council.

Wyatt, Frederick
    1967   Clinical notes on the motives of reproduction. *Journal of Social Issues* 23(4):29–56.